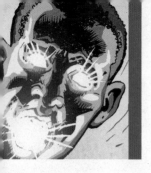

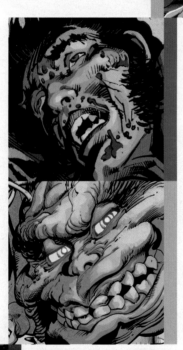

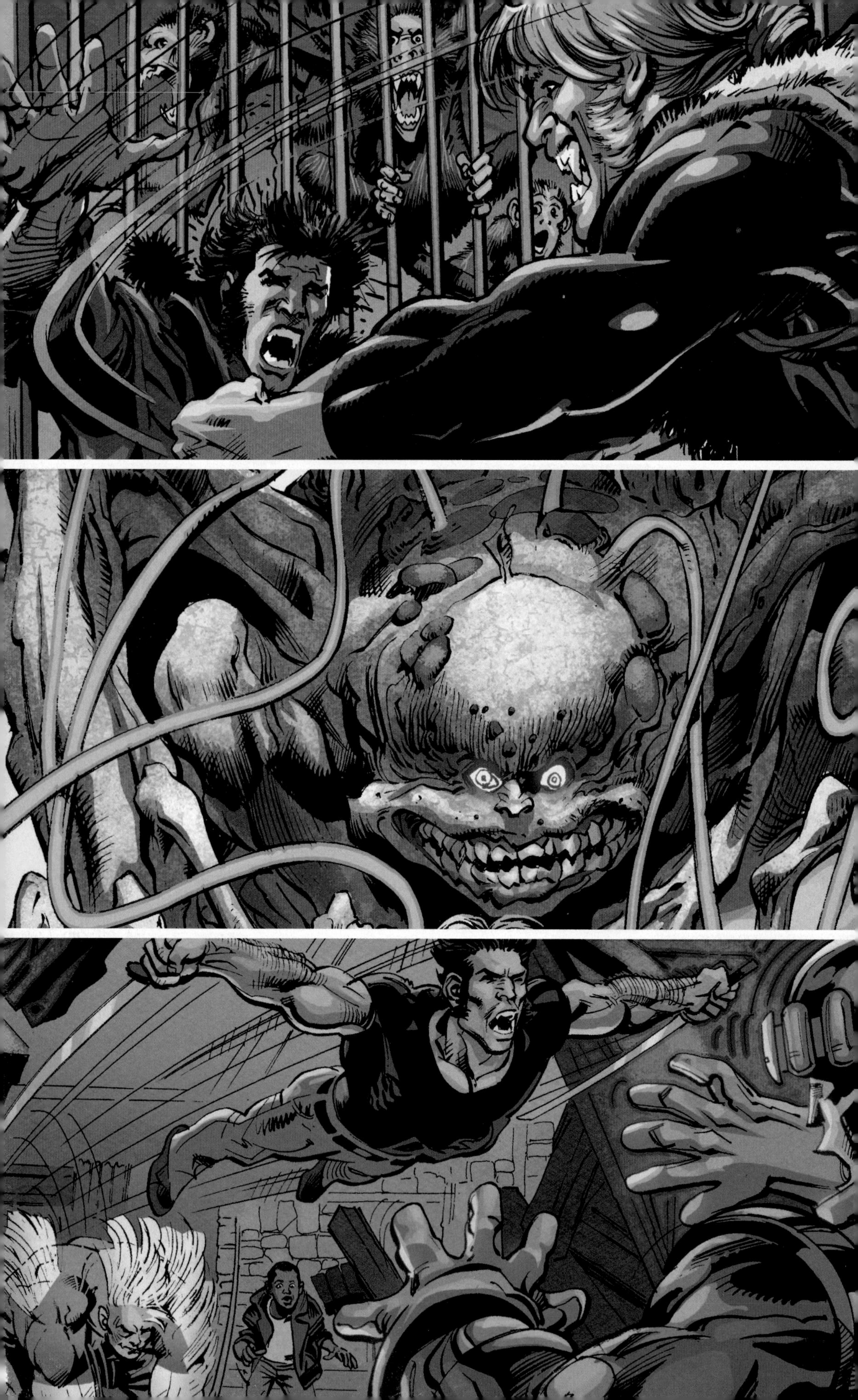

THE FIRST X-MEN

WRITERS
NEAL ADAMS
& CHRISTOS GAGE
PENCILER
NEAL ADAMS
INKERS
ANDREW CURRIE (#1-4) & NEAL ADAMS (#5)
COLORIST
MATTHEW WILSON
LETTERER
VC'S CLAYTON COWLES
ASSISTANT EDITOR
JORDAN D. WHITE
EDITOR
NICK LOWE

COLLECTION EDITOR & DESIGN
CORY LEVINE
ASSISTANT EDITORS
ALEX STARBUCK & NELSON RIBEIRO
EDITORS, SPECIAL PROJECTS
JENNIFER GRÜNWALD & MARK D. BEAZLEY
SENIOR EDITOR, SPECIAL PROJECTS
JEFF YOUNGQUIST
SVP OF PRINT & DIGITAL PUBLISHING SALES
DAVID GABRIEL

EDITOR IN CHIEF
AXEL ALONSO
CHIEF CREATIVE OFFICER
JOE QUESADA
PUBLISHER
DAN BUCKLEY
EXECUTIVE PRODUCER
ALAN FINE

FIRST X-MEN. Contains material originally published in magazine form as FIRST X-MEN #1-5. First printing 2013. ISBN# 978-0-7851-6496-8. Published by MARVEL WORLDWIDE, INC., a subsidiary of MARVEL ENTERTAINMENT, LLC. OFFICE OF PUBLICATION: 135 West 50th Street, New York, NY 10020. Copyright © 2012 and 2013 Marvel Characters, Inc. All rights reserved. All characters featured in this issue and the distinctive names and likenesses thereof, and all related indicia are trademarks of Marvel Characters, Inc. No similarity between any of the names, characters, persons, and/or institutions in this magazine with those of any living or dead person or institution is intended, and any such similarity which may exist is purely coincidental. **Printed in the U.S.A.** ALAN FINE, EVP - Office of the President, Marvel Worldwide, Inc. and EVP & CMO Marvel Characters B.V.; DAN BUCKLEY, Publisher & President - Print, Animation & Digital Divisions; JOE QUESADA, Chief Creative Officer; TOM BREVOORT, SVP of Publishing; DAVID BOGART, SVP of Operations & Procurement, Publishing; C.B. CEBULSKI, SVP of Creator & Content Development; DAVID GABRIEL, SVP of Print & Digital Publishing Sales; JIM O'KEEFE, VP of Operations & Logistics; DAN CARR, Executive Director of Publishing Technology; SUSAN CRESPI, Editorial Operations Manager; ALEX MORALES, Publishing Operations Manager; STAN LEE, Chairman Emeritus. For information regarding advertising in Marvel Comics or on Marvel.com, please contact Niza Disla, Director of Marvel Partnerships, at ndisla@marvel.com. For Marvel subscription inquiries, please call 800-217-9158. **Manufactured between 6/21/2013 and 7/29/2013 by R.R. DONNELLEY, INC., SALEM, VA, USA.**

10 9 8 7 6 5 4 3 2 1

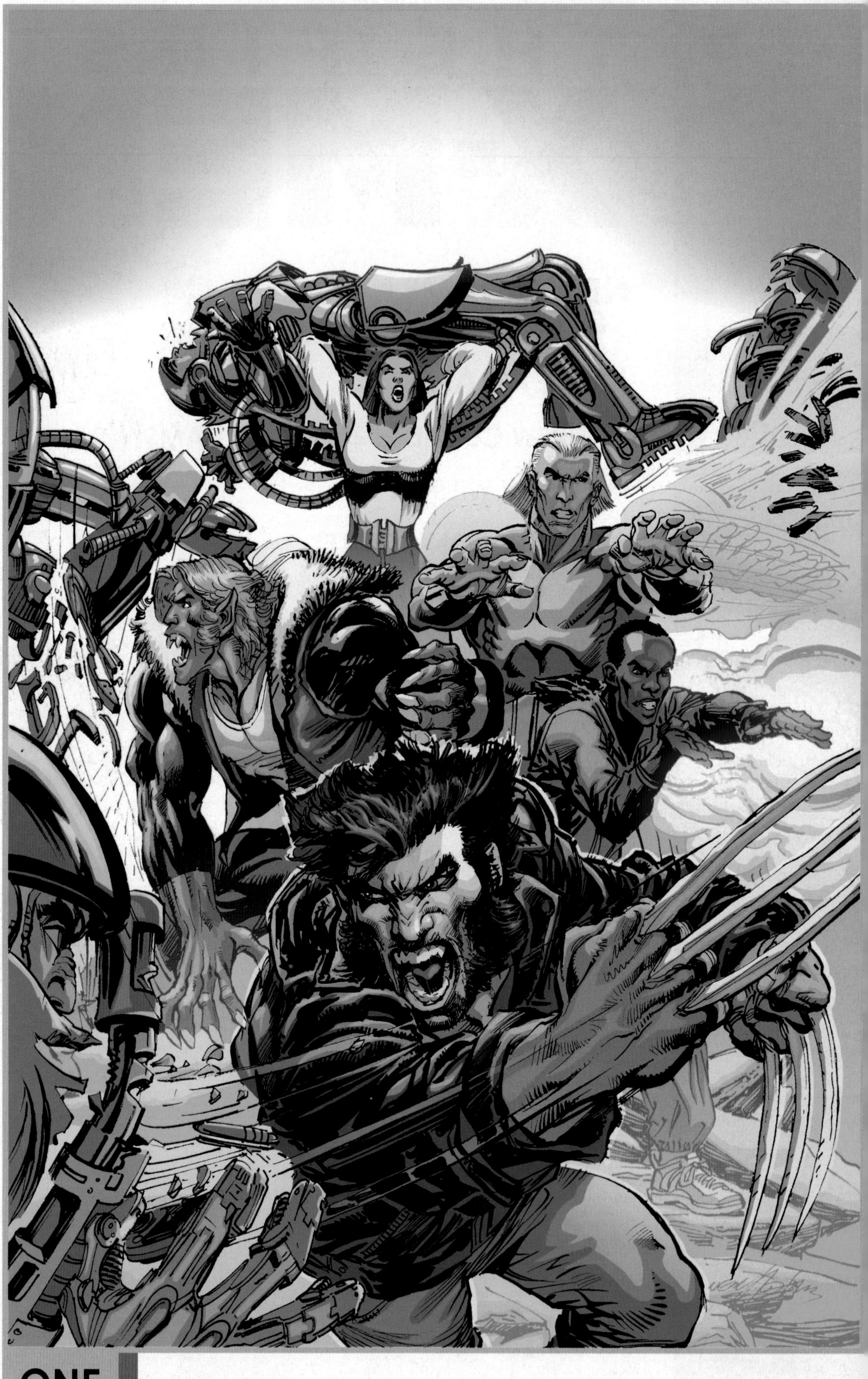

ONE

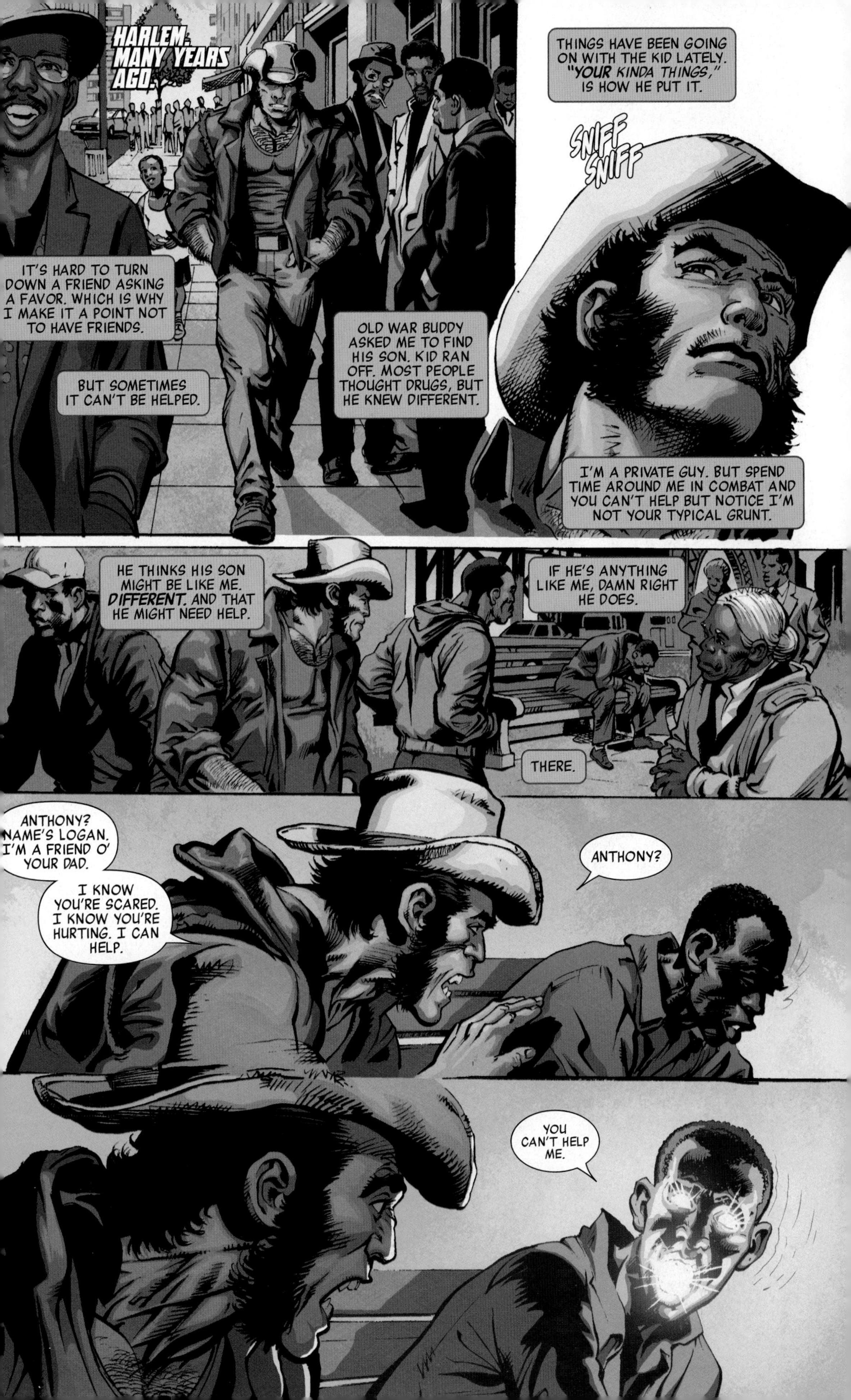
HARLEM. MANY YEARS AGO.
IT'S HARD TO TURN DOWN A FRIEND ASKING A FAVOR. WHICH IS WHY I MAKE IT A POINT NOT TO HAVE FRIENDS.
BUT SOMETIMES IT CAN'T BE HELPED.
OLD WAR BUDDY ASKED ME TO FIND HIS SON. KID RAN OFF. MOST PEOPLE THOUGHT DRUGS, BUT HE KNEW DIFFERENT.
THINGS HAVE BEEN GOING ON WITH THE KID LATELY. "YOUR KINDA THINGS," IS HOW HE PUT IT.
SNIFF SNIFF
I'M A PRIVATE GUY. BUT SPEND TIME AROUND ME IN COMBAT AND YOU CAN'T HELP BUT NOTICE I'M NOT YOUR TYPICAL GRUNT.
HE THINKS HIS SON MIGHT BE LIKE ME. DIFFERENT. AND THAT HE MIGHT NEED HELP.
IF HE'S ANYTHING LIKE ME, DAMN RIGHT HE DOES.
THERE.
ANTHONY? NAME'S LOGAN. I'M A FRIEND O' YOUR DAD.
I KNOW YOU'RE SCARED. I KNOW YOU'RE HURTING. I CAN HELP.
ANTHONY?
YOU CAN'T HELP ME.

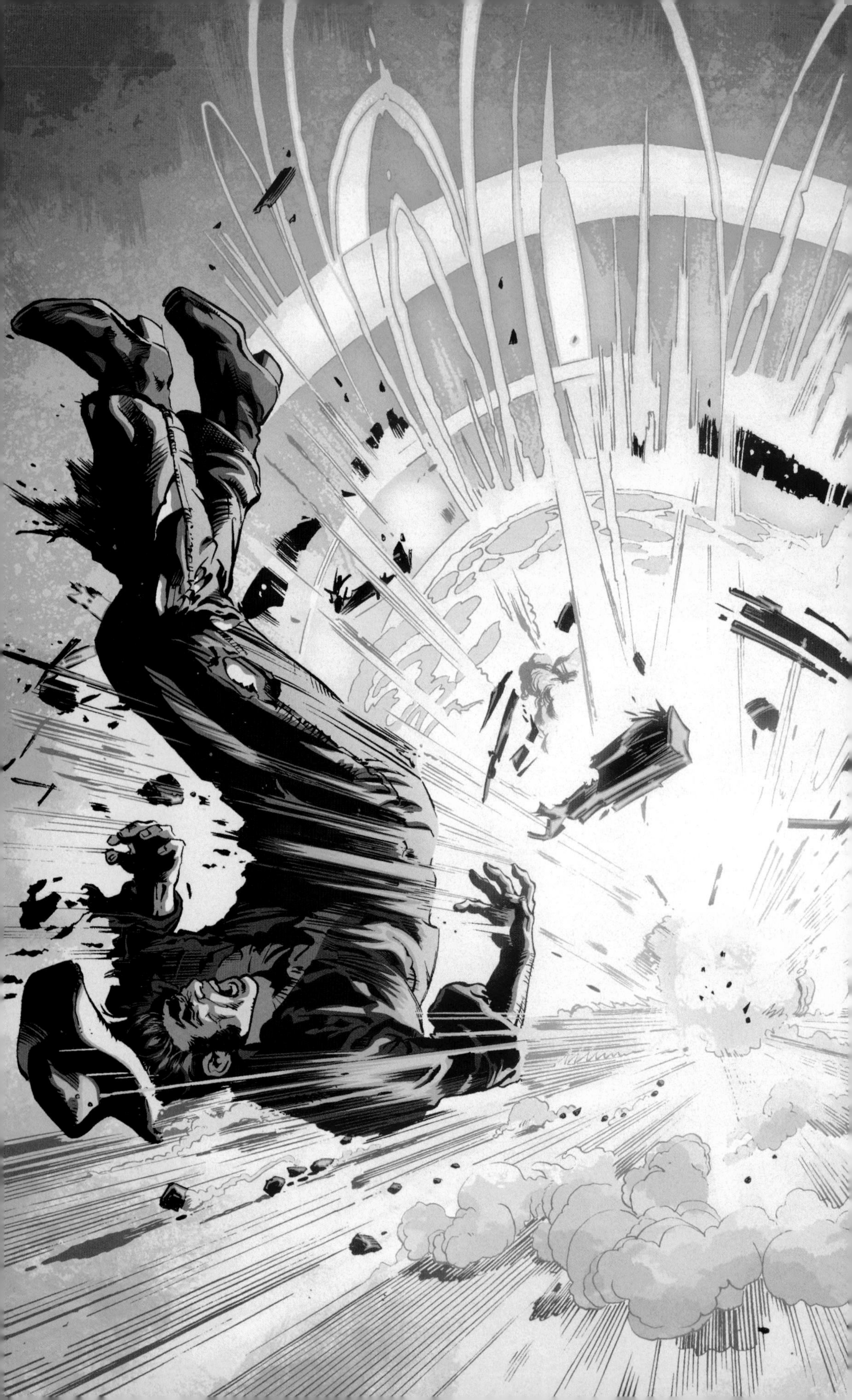

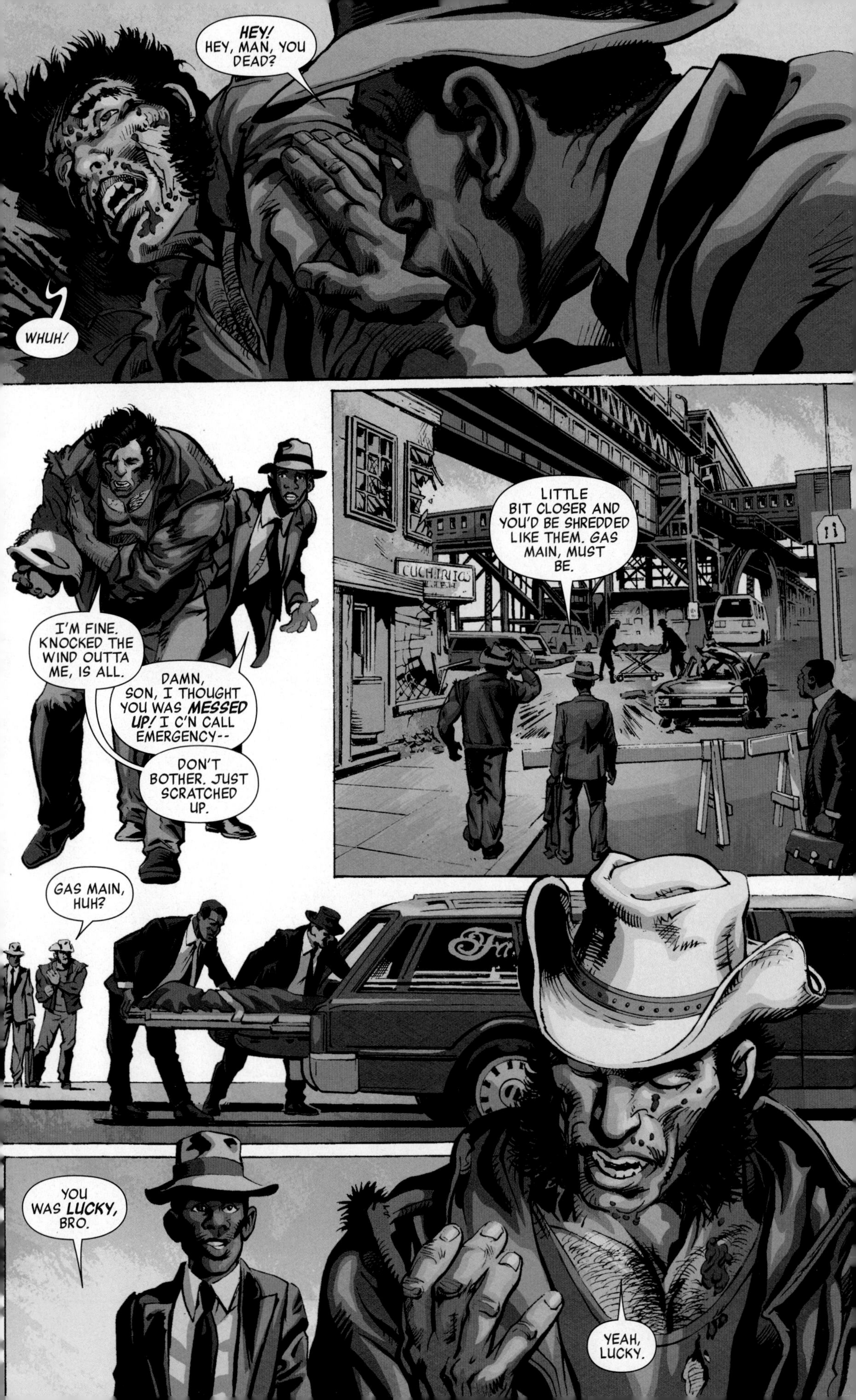
HEY! HEY, MAN, YOU DEAD?
WHUH!
I'M FINE. KNOCKED THE WIND OUTTA ME, IS ALL.
DAMN, SON, I THOUGHT YOU WAS MESSED UP! I C'N CALL EMERGENCY--
DON'T BOTHER. JUST SCRATCHED UP.
LITTLE BIT CLOSER AND YOU'D BE SHREDDED LIKE THEM. GAS MAIN, MUST BE.
GAS MAIN, HUH?
YOU WAS LUCKY, BRO.
YEAH, LUCKY.

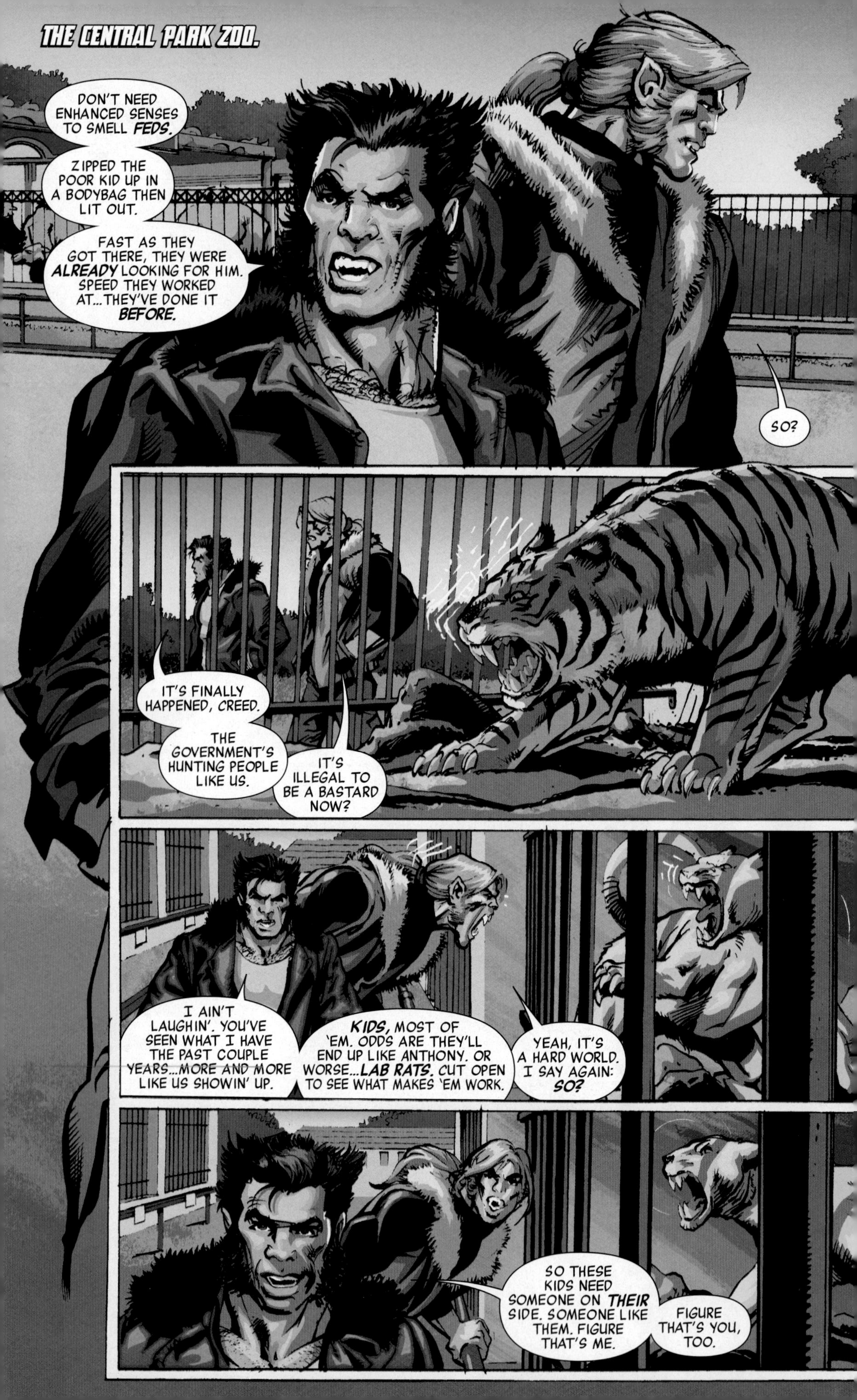
THE CENTRAL PARK ZOO.
DON'T NEED ENHANCED SENSES TO SMELL FEDS.
ZIPPED THE POOR KID UP IN A BODYBAG THEN LIT OUT.
FAST AS THEY GOT THERE, THEY WERE ALREADY LOOKING FOR HIM. SPEED THEY WORKED AT...THEY'VE DONE IT BEFORE.
SO?
IT'S FINALLY HAPPENED, CREED.
THE GOVERNMENT'S HUNTING PEOPLE LIKE US.
IT'S ILLEGAL TO BE A BASTARD NOW?
I AIN'T LAUGHIN'. YOU'VE SEEN WHAT I HAVE THE PAST COUPLE YEARS...MORE AND MORE LIKE US SHOWIN' UP.
KIDS, MOST OF 'EM. ODDS ARE THEY'LL END UP LIKE ANTHONY. OR WORSE...LAB RATS. CUT OPEN TO SEE WHAT MAKES 'EM WORK.
YEAH, IT'S A HARD WORLD. I SAY AGAIN: SO?
SO THESE KIDS NEED SOMEONE ON THEIR SIDE. SOMEONE LIKE THEM. FIGURE THAT'S ME.
FIGURE THAT'S YOU, TOO.

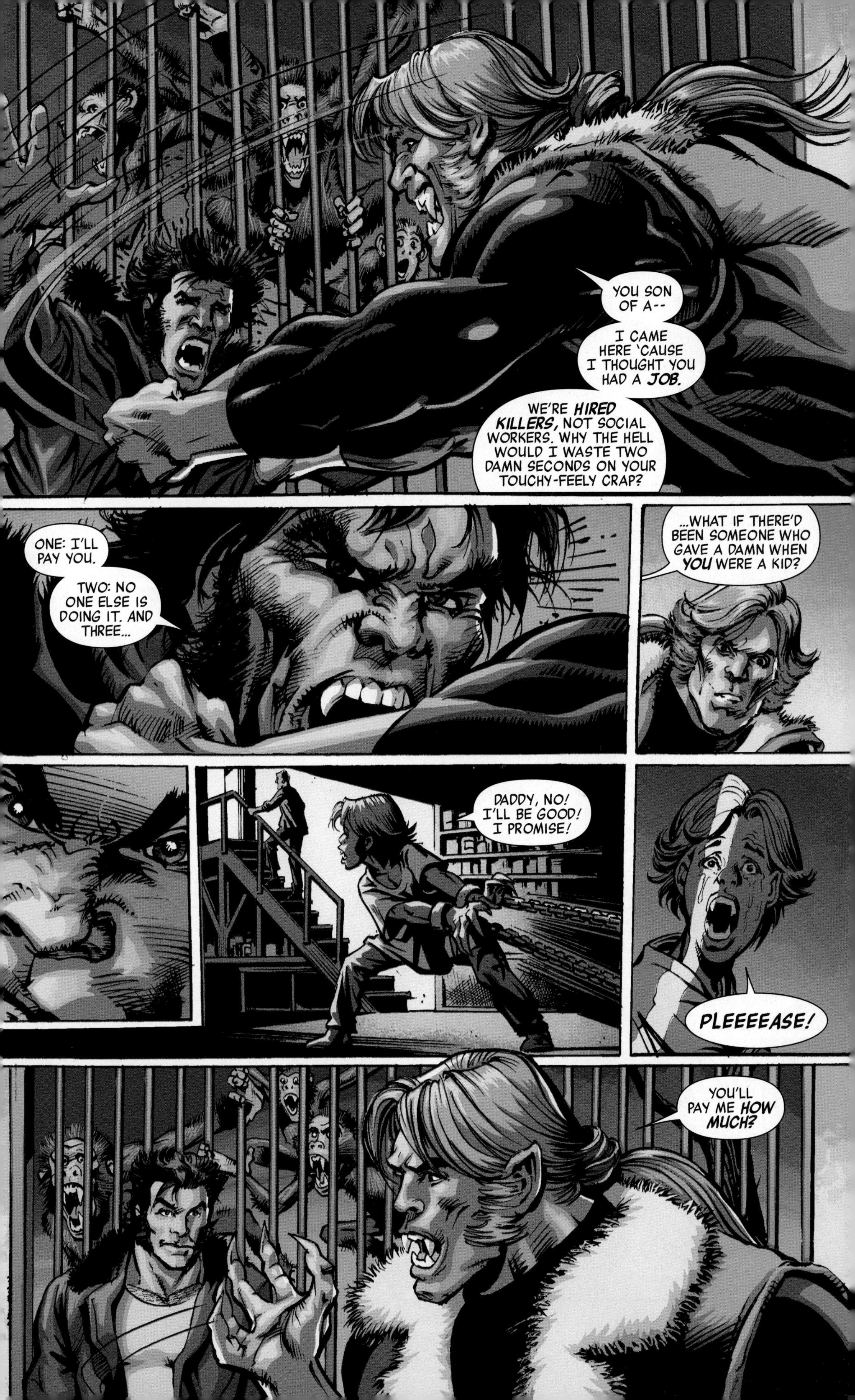

YOU SON OF A--
I CAME HERE 'CAUSE I THOUGHT YOU HAD A JOB.
WE'RE HIRED KILLERS, NOT SOCIAL WORKERS. WHY THE HELL WOULD I WASTE TWO DAMN SECONDS ON YOUR TOUCHY-FEELY CRAP?
ONE: I'LL PAY YOU.
TWO: NO ONE ELSE IS DOING IT. AND THREE...
...WHAT IF THERE'D BEEN SOMEONE WHO GAVE A DAMN WHEN YOU WERE A KID?
DADDY, NO! I'LL BE GOOD! I PROMISE!
PLEEEEASE!
YOU'LL PAY ME HOW MUCH?

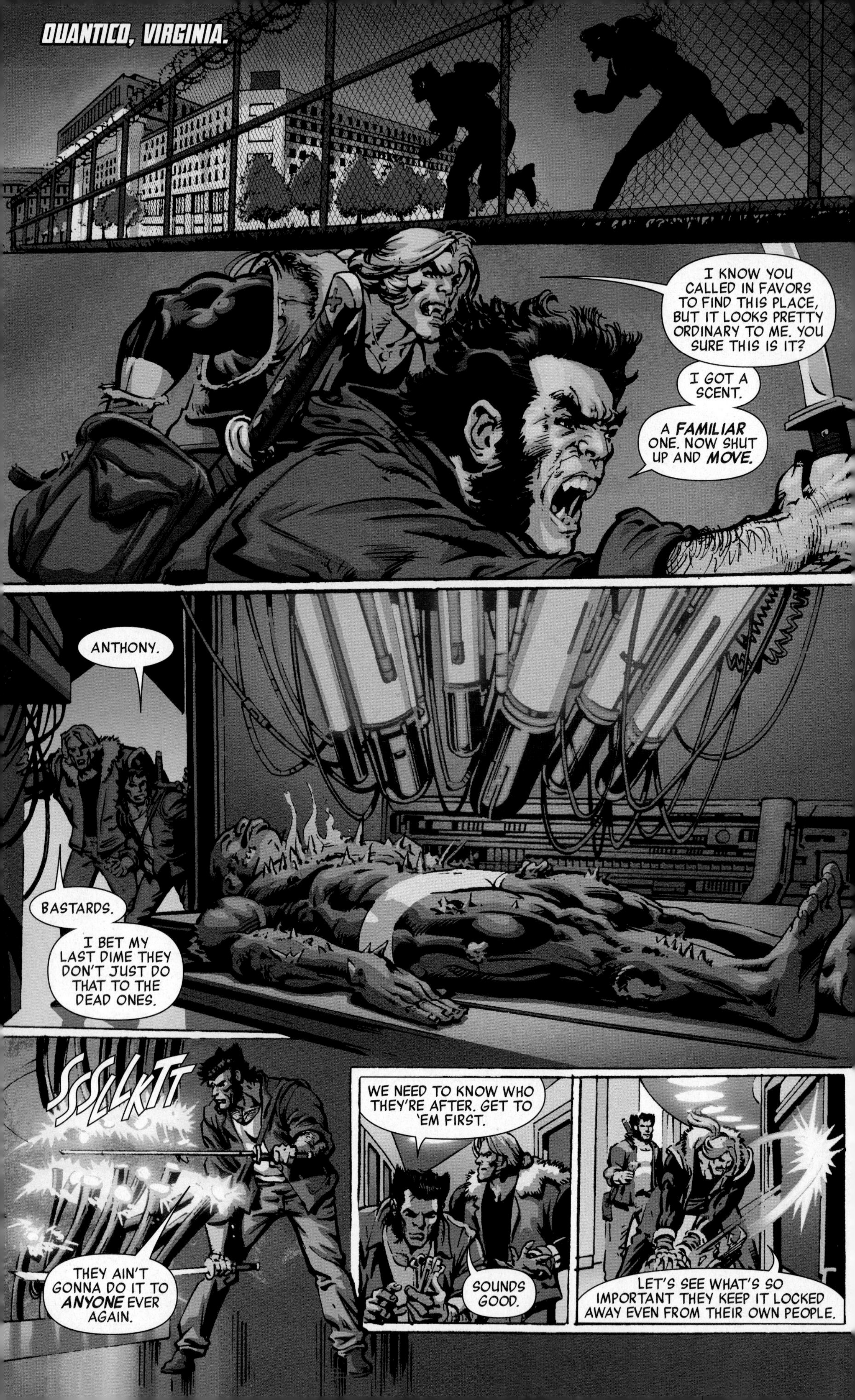
QUANTICO, VIRGINIA.
I KNOW YOU CALLED IN FAVORS TO FIND THIS PLACE, BUT IT LOOKS PRETTY ORDINARY TO ME. YOU SURE THIS IS IT?
I GOT A SCENT.
A **FAMILIAR** ONE. NOW SHUT UP AND **MOVE.**
ANTHONY.
BASTARDS.
I BET MY LAST DIME THEY DON'T JUST DO THAT TO THE DEAD ONES.
SSSLLKTT
THEY AIN'T GONNA DO IT TO **ANYONE** EVER AGAIN.
WE NEED TO KNOW WHO THEY'RE AFTER. GET TO 'EM FIRST.
SOUNDS GOOD.
LET'S SEE WHAT'S SO IMPORTANT THEY KEEP IT LOCKED AWAY EVEN FROM THEIR OWN PEOPLE.

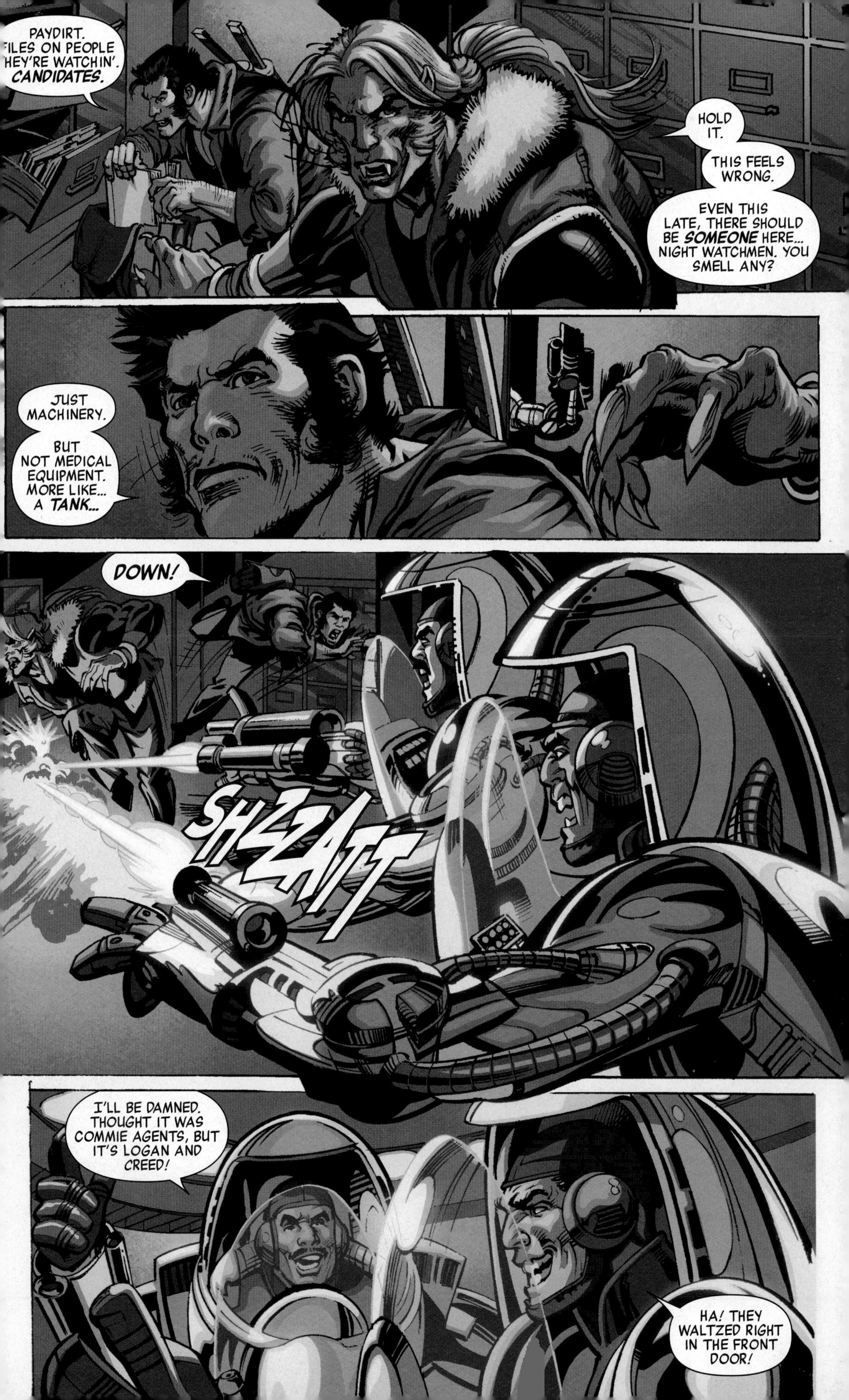

PAYDIRT. FILES ON PEOPLE THEY'RE WATCHIN'. CANDIDATES.
HOLD IT.
THIS FEELS WRONG.
EVEN THIS LATE, THERE SHOULD BE SOMEONE HERE... NIGHT WATCHMEN. YOU SMELL ANY?
JUST MACHINERY.
BUT NOT MEDICAL EQUIPMENT. MORE LIKE... A TANK...
DOWN!
SHZZATT
I'LL BE DAMNED. THOUGHT IT WAS COMMIE AGENTS, BUT IT'S LOGAN AND CREED!
HA! THEY WALTZED RIGHT IN THE FRONT DOOR!

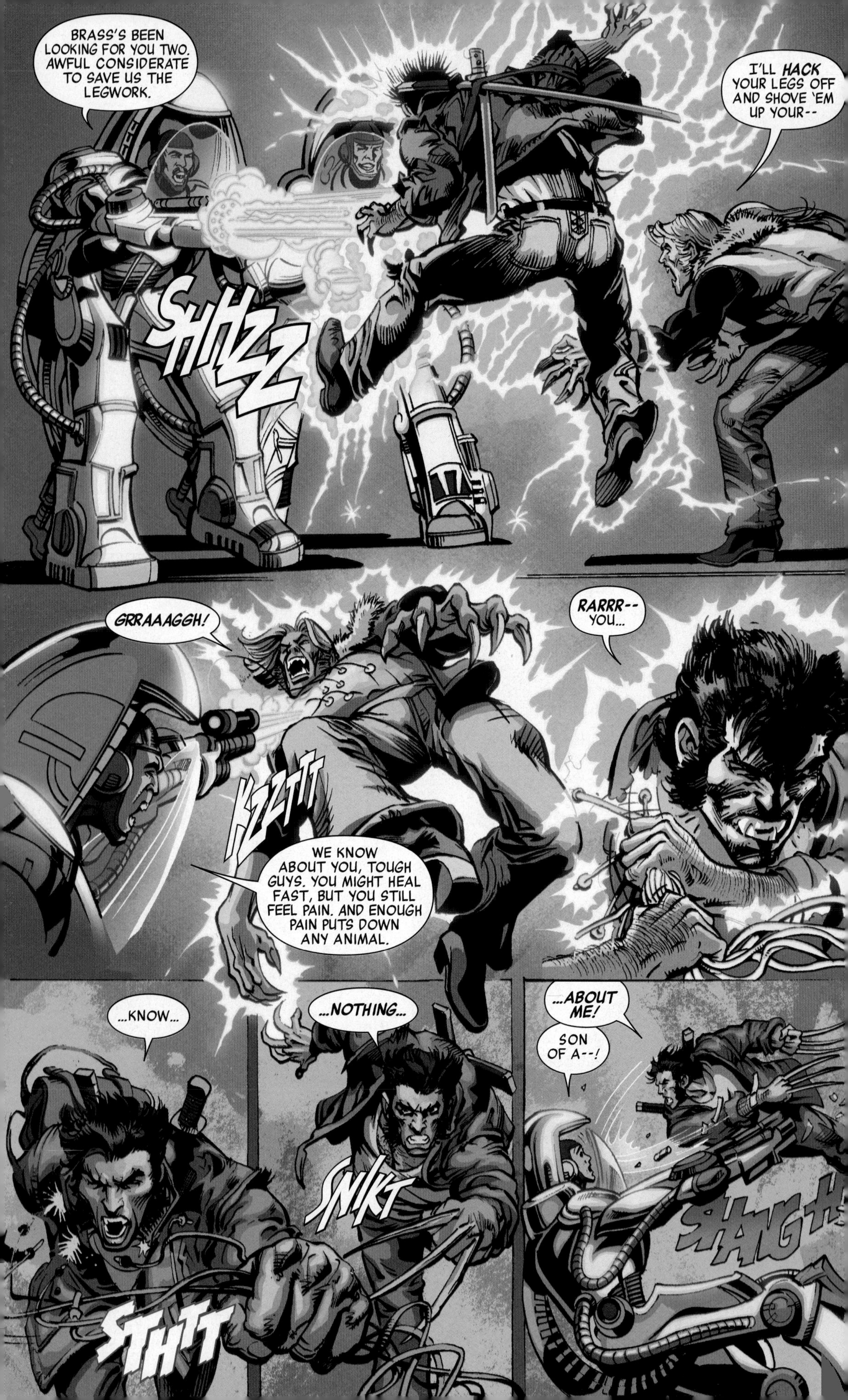
BRASS'S BEEN LOOKING FOR YOU TWO. AWFUL CONSIDERATE TO SAVE US THE LEGWORK.
I'LL **HACK** YOUR LEGS OFF AND SHOVE 'EM UP YOUR--
SHHZZ
GRRAAAGGH!
RARRR-- YOU...
KZZTTT
WE KNOW ABOUT YOU, TOUGH GUYS. YOU MIGHT HEAL FAST, BUT YOU STILL FEEL PAIN. AND ENOUGH PAIN PUTS DOWN ANY ANIMAL.
...KNOW...
STHTT
...NOTHING...
SNIKT
...ABOUT ME!
SON OF A--!
SHANGH!

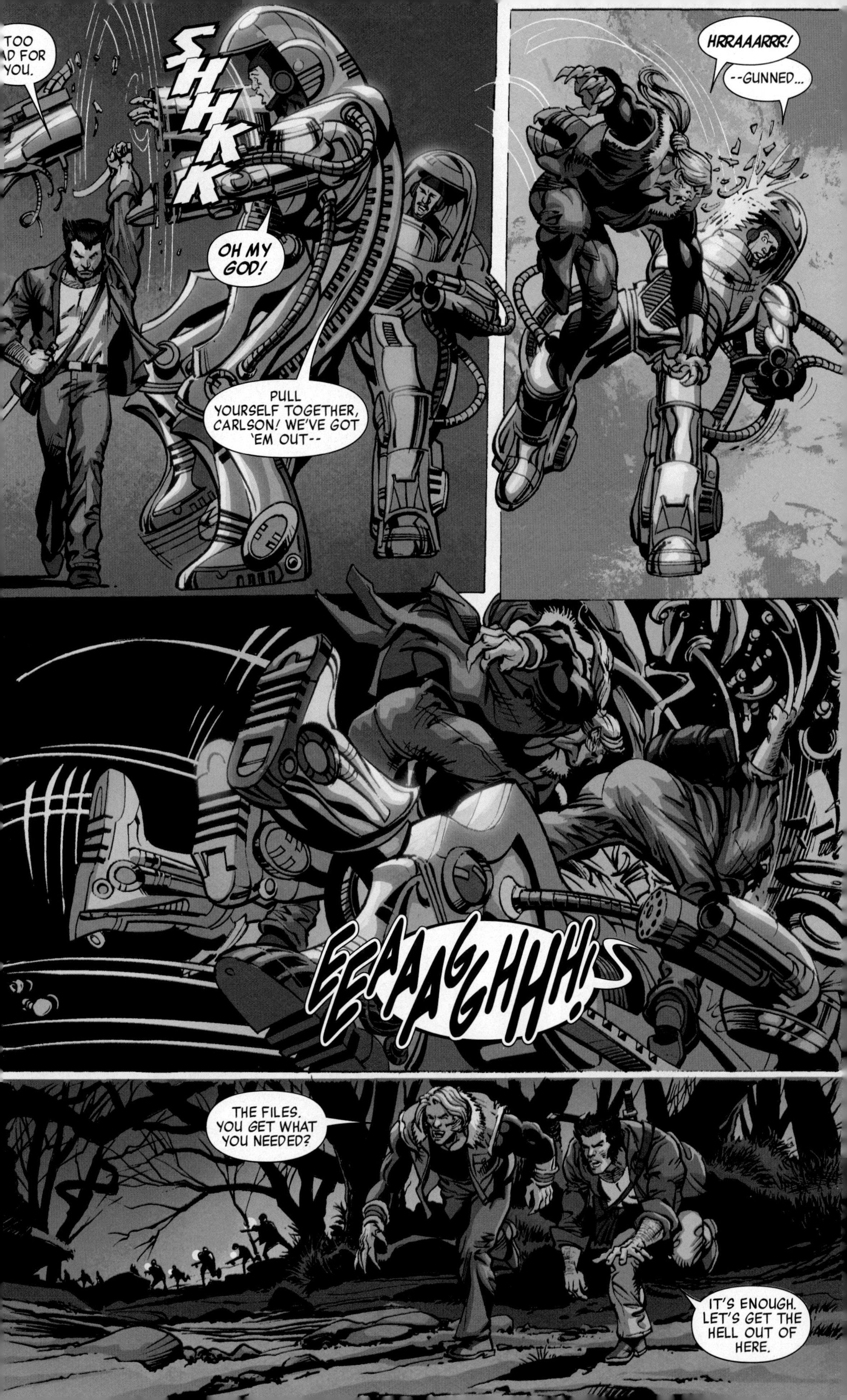
TOO
D FOR
YOU.
SHHKK
OH MY GOD!
PULL YOURSELF TOGETHER, CARLSON! WE'VE GOT 'EM OUT--
HRRAAARRR!
--GUNNED...
EEAAAGHHH!
THE FILES. YOU GET WHAT YOU NEEDED?
IT'S ENOUGH. LET'S GET THE HELL OUT OF HERE.

"NOTHIN' BACK THERE BUT DEATH."

H...HELLO...?

THEY KNEW US, LOGAN. HOW THE HELL DO THEY *KNOW* US?

WE BEEN KICKIN' AROUND AWHILE. I AIN'T SURPRISED.

DON'T MATTER. WE CAN TAKE CARE OF OURSELVES. THESE KIDS *CAN'T*.

WE GOTTA FIGURE OUT WHO THE TOP TARGETS ARE AND--

AH, CRAP.

WHAT?

I JUST FIGURED OUT WHY THEY'RE UNDERSTAFFED. EIGHTEEN-YEAR-OLD KID NAMED HOLLY BRIGHT, IN D.C. A RUNAWAY.

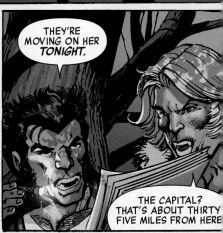

THEY'RE MOVING ON HER *TONIGHT*.

THE CAPITAL? THAT'S ABOUT THIRTY FIVE MILES FROM HERE

WELL, HERE'S OUR RIDE.

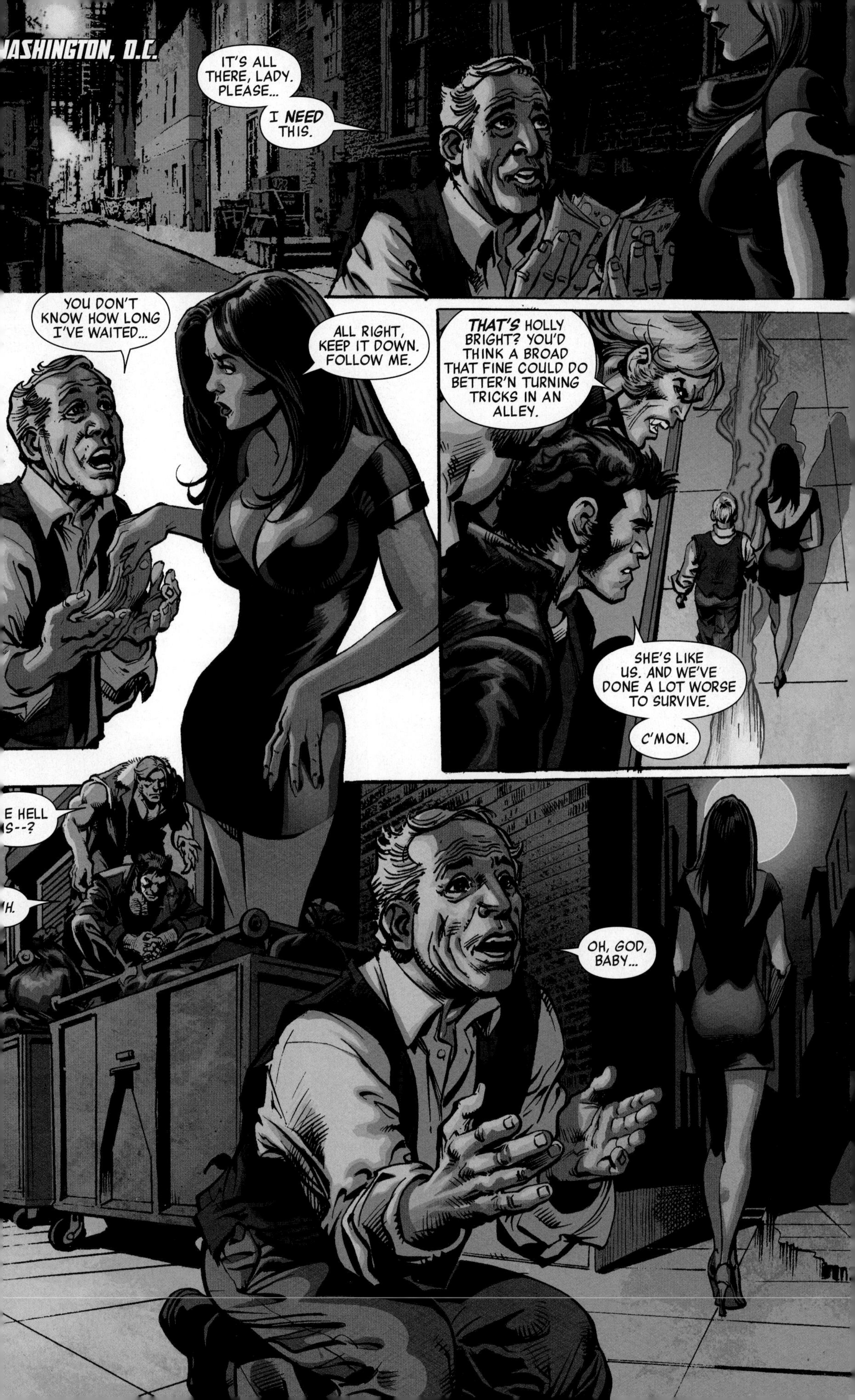
ASHINGTON, D.C.
IT'S ALL THERE, LADY. PLEASE...
I NEED THIS.
YOU DON'T KNOW HOW LONG I'VE WAITED...
ALL RIGHT, KEEP IT DOWN. FOLLOW ME.
THAT'S HOLLY BRIGHT? YOU'D THINK A BROAD THAT FINE COULD DO BETTER'N TURNING TRICKS IN AN ALLEY.
SHE'S LIKE US. AND WE'VE DONE A LOT WORSE TO SURVIVE.
C'MON.
E HELL S--?
H.
OH, GOD, BABY...

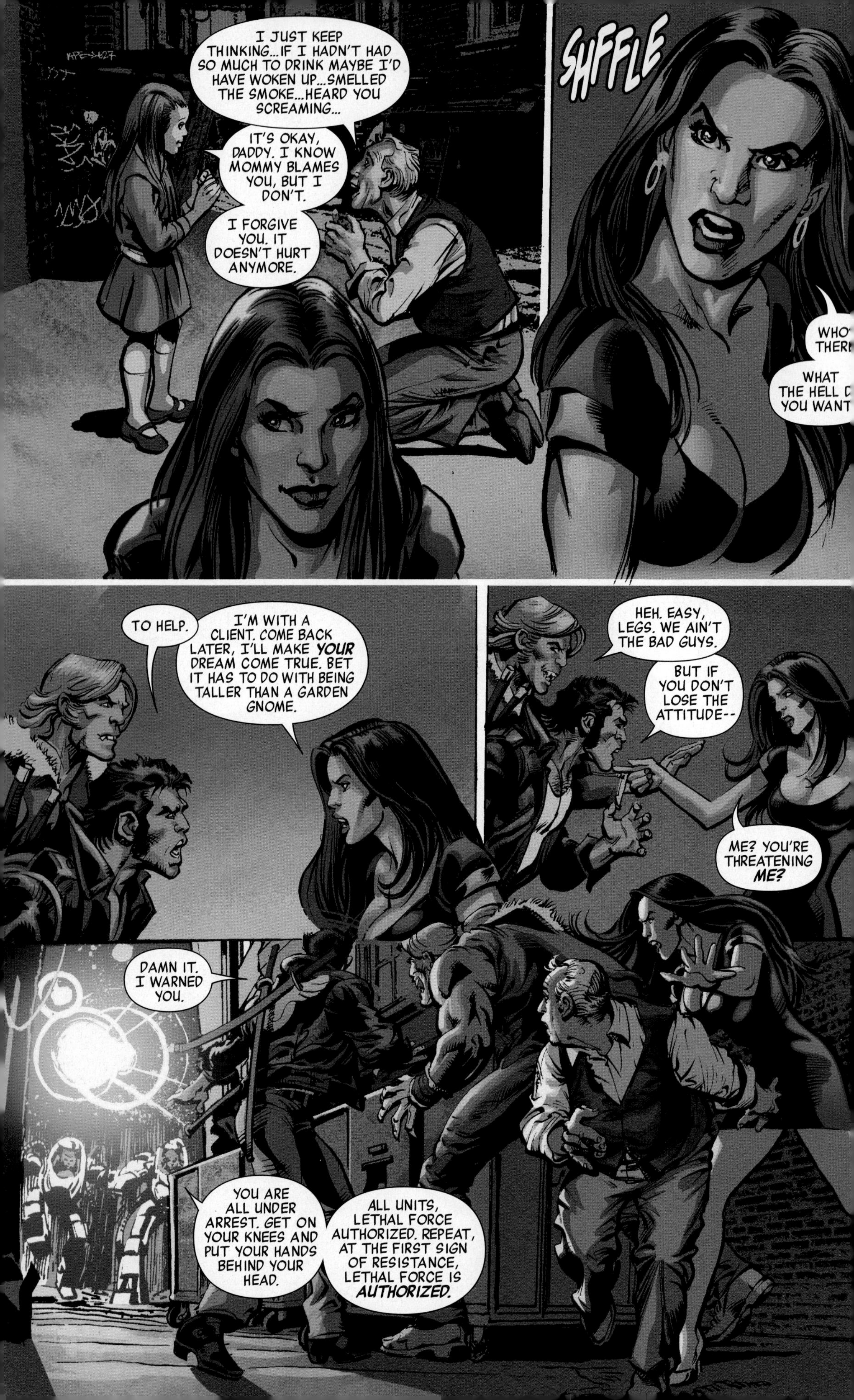

I JUST KEEP THINKING...IF I HADN'T HAD SO MUCH TO DRINK MAYBE I'D HAVE WOKEN UP...SMELLED THE SMOKE...HEARD YOU SCREAMING...
IT'S OKAY, DADDY. I KNOW MOMMY BLAMES YOU, BUT I DON'T.
I FORGIVE YOU. IT DOESN'T HURT ANYMORE.
SHFFLE
WHAT
TO HELP.
I'M WITH A CLIENT. COME BACK LATER, I'LL MAKE YOUR DREAM COME TRUE. BET IT HAS TO DO WITH BEING TALLER THAN A GARDEN GNOME.
HEH. EASY, LEGS. WE AIN'T THE BAD GUYS.
BUT IF YOU DON'T LOSE THE ATTITUDE--
ME? YOU'RE THREATENING ME?
DAMN IT. I WARNED YOU.
YOU ARE ALL UNDER ARREST. GET ON YOUR KNEES AND PUT YOUR HANDS BEHIND YOUR HEAD.
ALL UNITS, LETHAL FORCE AUTHORIZED. REPEAT, AT THE FIRST SIGN OF RESISTANCE, LETHAL FORCE IS AUTHORIZED.

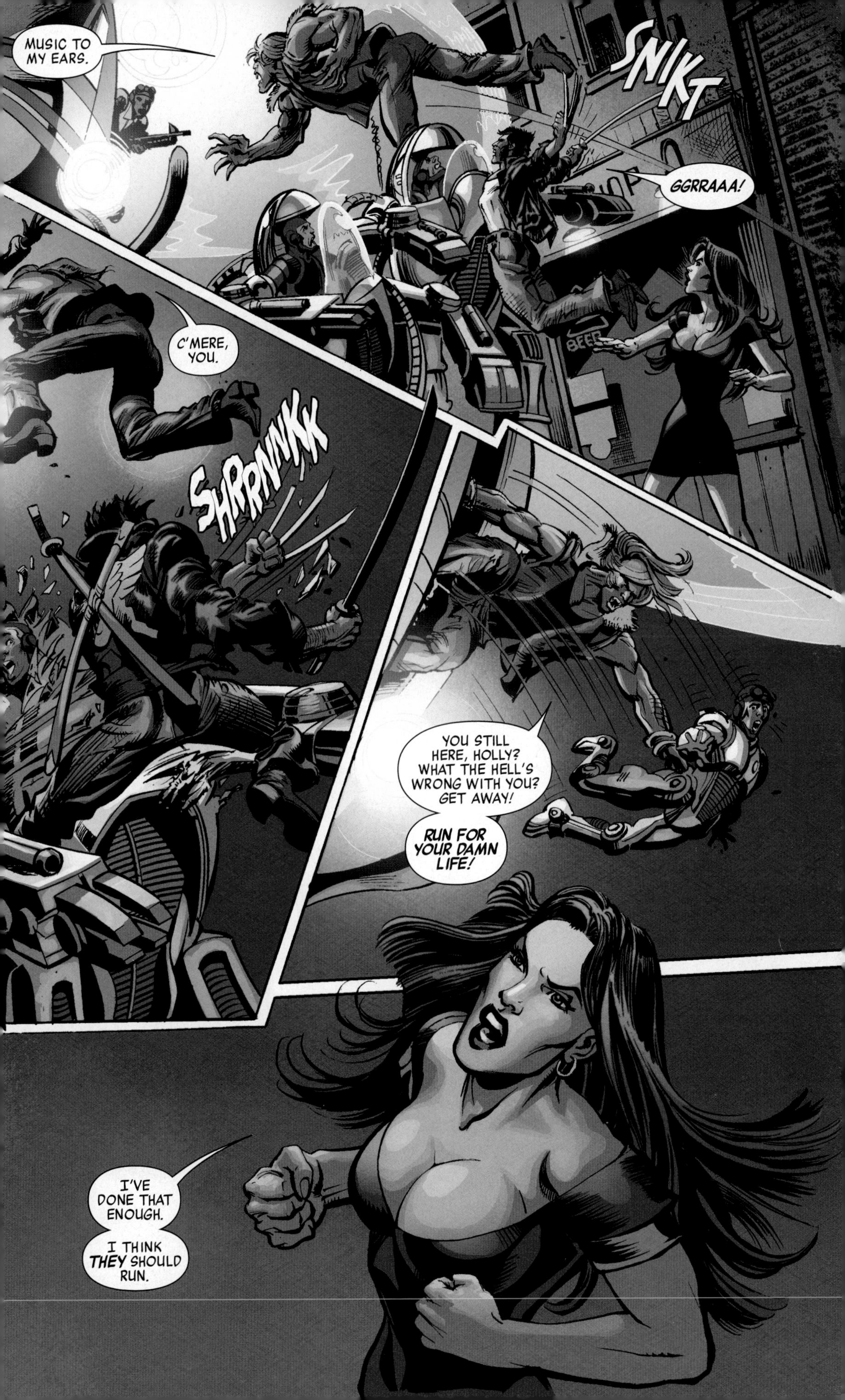
MUSIC TO MY EARS.
SNIKT
GGRRAAA!
C'MERE, YOU.
SHRRNNKK
YOU STILL HERE, HOLLY? WHAT THE HELL'S WRONG WITH YOU? GET AWAY!
RUN FOR YOUR DAMN LIFE!
I'VE DONE THAT ENOUGH.
I THINK THEY SHOULD RUN.

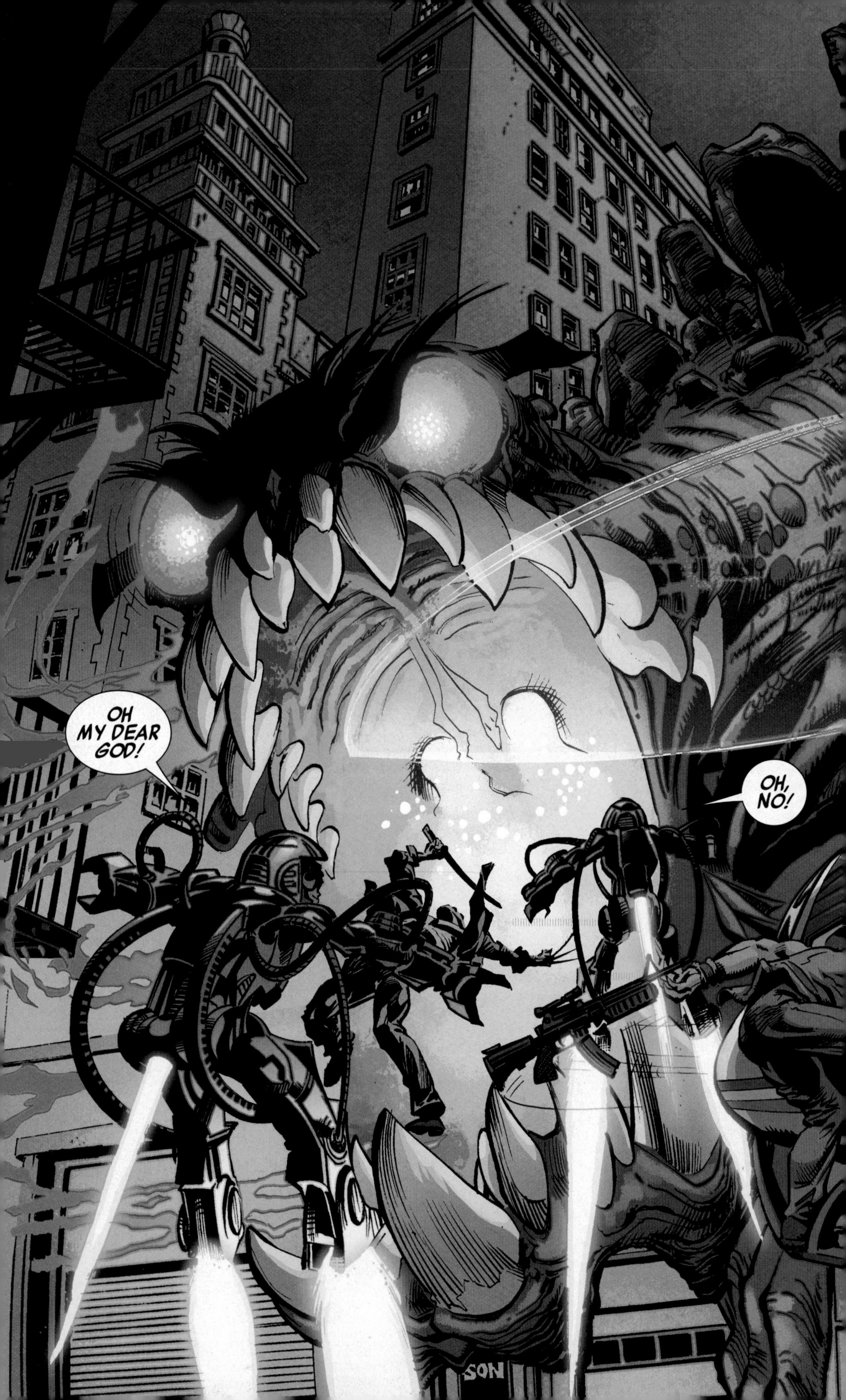
OH MY DEAR GOD!
OH, NO!
SON

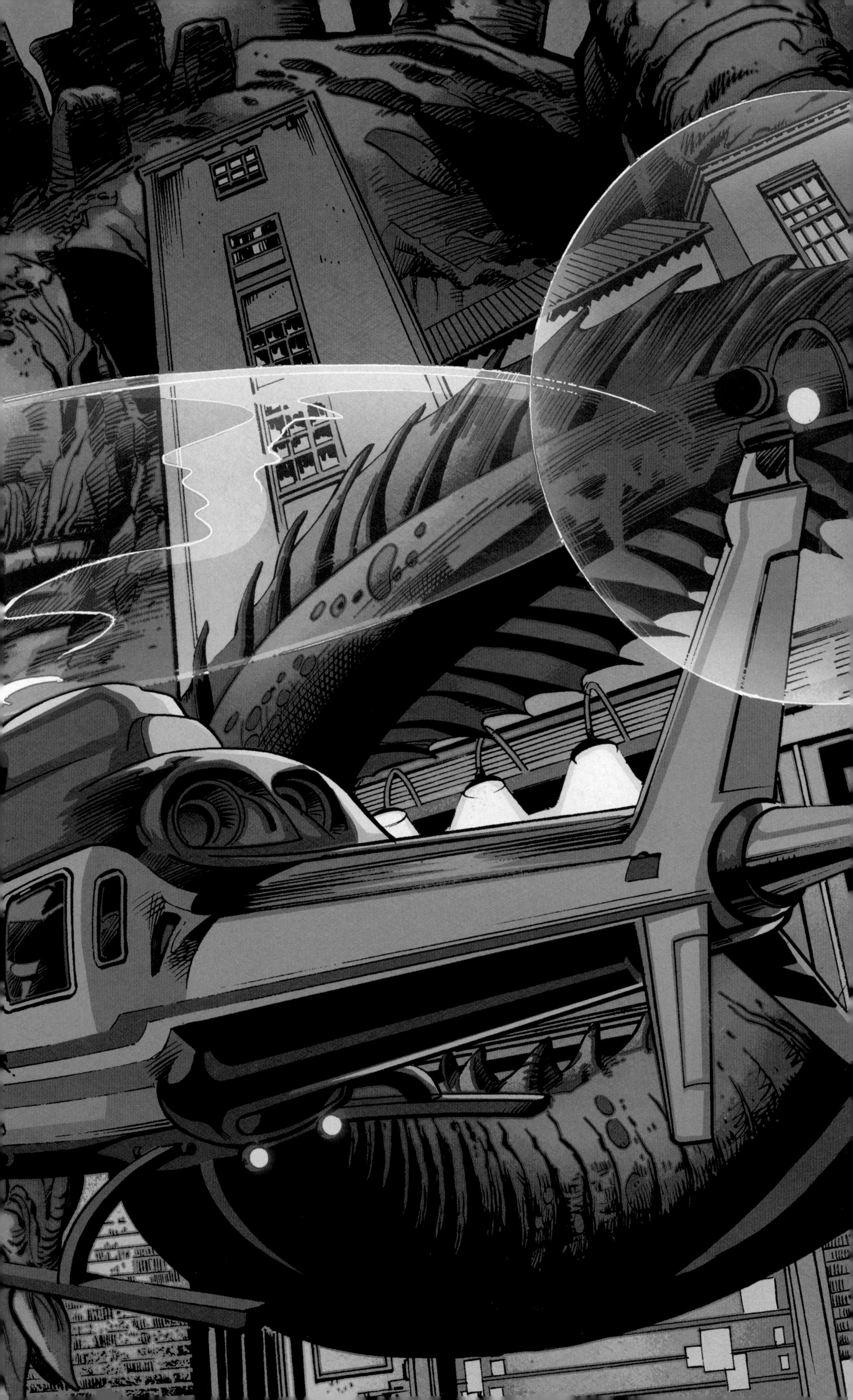

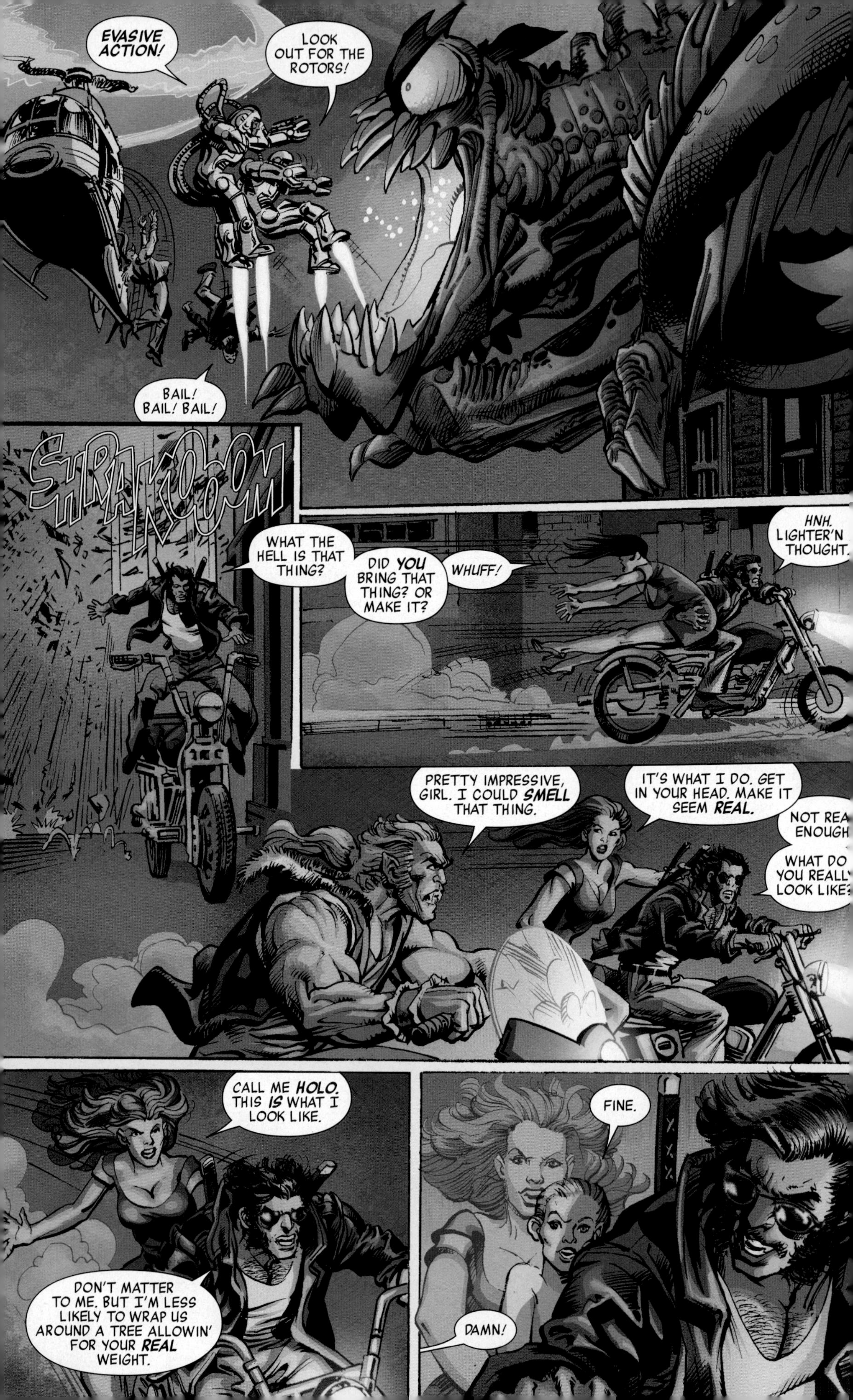
EVASIVE ACTION!
LOOK OUT FOR THE ROTORS!
BAIL! BAIL! BAIL!
SHRAKOOOM
WHAT THE HELL IS THAT THING?
DID YOU BRING THAT THING? OR MAKE IT?
WHUFF!
HNH. LIGHTER'N THOUGHT.
PRETTY IMPRESSIVE, GIRL. I COULD SMELL THAT THING.
IT'S WHAT I DO. GET IN YOUR HEAD. MAKE IT SEEM REAL.
NOT REA ENOUGH
WHAT DO YOU REALLY LOOK LIKE?
CALL ME HOLO. THIS IS WHAT I LOOK LIKE.
DON'T MATTER TO ME. BUT I'M LESS LIKELY TO WRAP US AROUND A TREE ALLOWIN' FOR YOUR REAL WEIGHT.
FINE.
DAMN!

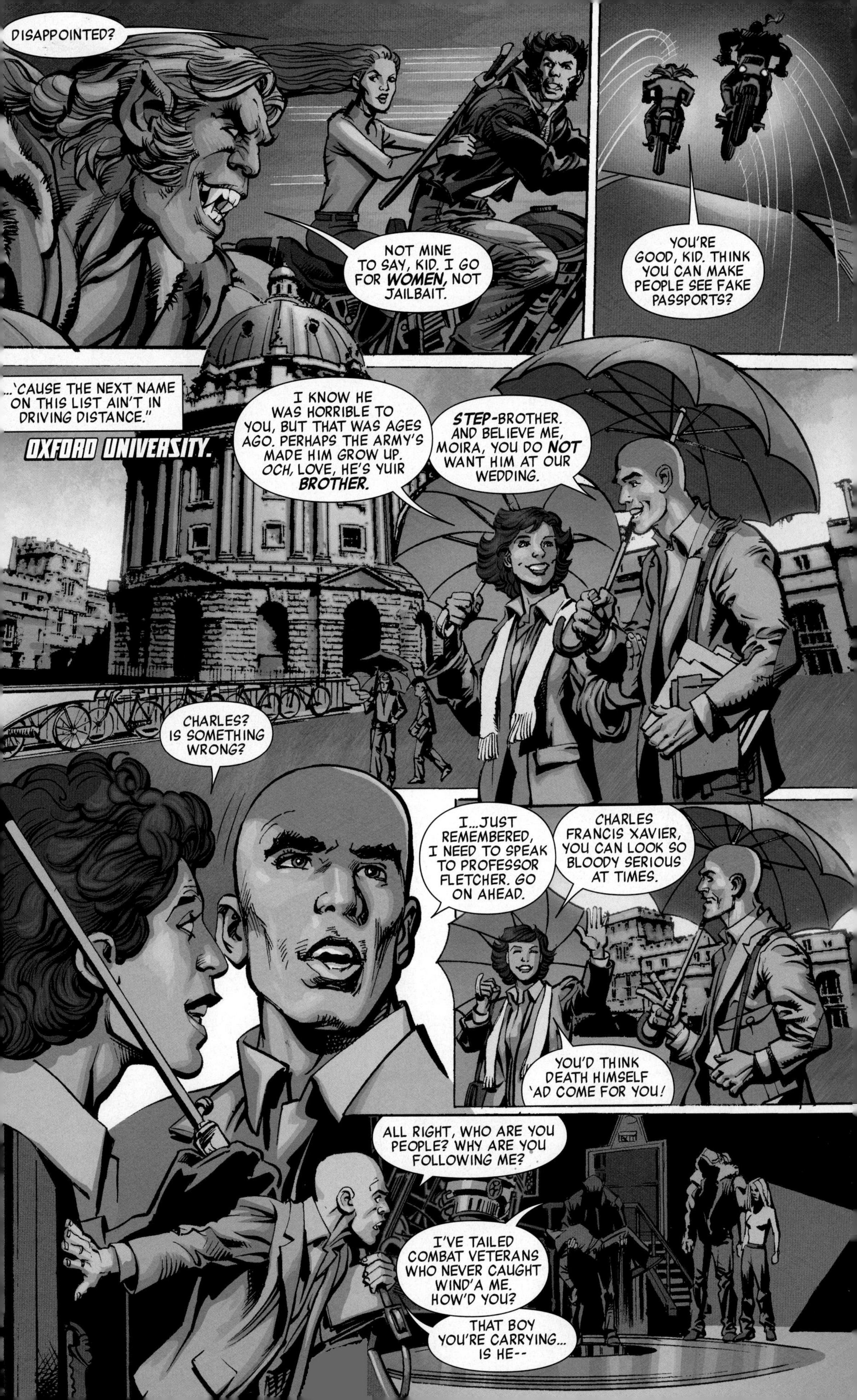
DISAPPOINTED?
NOT MINE TO SAY, KID. I GO FOR WOMEN, NOT JAILBAIT.
YOU'RE GOOD, KID. THINK YOU CAN MAKE PEOPLE SEE FAKE PASSPORTS?
...'CAUSE THE NEXT NAME ON THIS LIST AIN'T IN DRIVING DISTANCE."
OXFORD UNIVERSITY.
I KNOW HE WAS HORRIBLE TO YOU, BUT THAT WAS AGES AGO. PERHAPS THE ARMY'S MADE HIM GROW UP. OCH, LOVE, HE'S YUIR BROTHER.
STEP-BROTHER. AND BELIEVE ME, MOIRA, YOU DO NOT WANT HIM AT OUR WEDDING.
CHARLES? IS SOMETHING WRONG?
I...JUST REMEMBERED, I NEED TO SPEAK TO PROFESSOR FLETCHER. GO ON AHEAD.
CHARLES FRANCIS XAVIER, YOU CAN LOOK SO BLOODY SERIOUS AT TIMES.
YOU'D THINK DEATH HIMSELF 'AD COME FOR YOU!
ALL RIGHT, WHO ARE YOU PEOPLE? WHY ARE YOU FOLLOWING ME?
I'VE TAILED COMBAT VETERANS WHO NEVER CAUGHT WIND'A ME. HOW'D YOU?
THAT BOY YOU'RE CARRYING... IS HE--

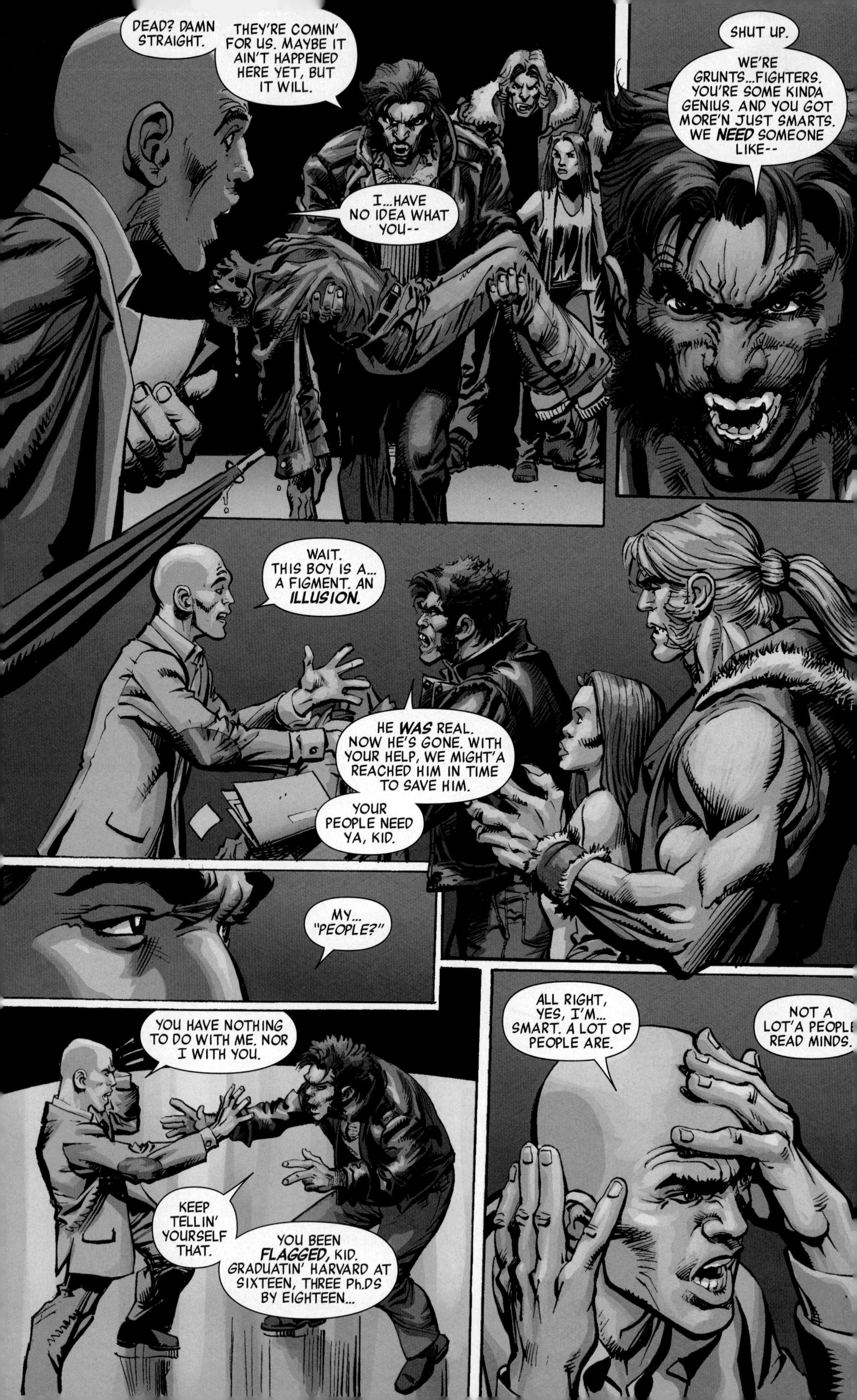
DEAD? DAMN STRAIGHT.
THEY'RE COMIN' FOR US. MAYBE IT AIN'T HAPPENED HERE YET, BUT IT WILL.
I...HAVE NO IDEA WHAT YOU--
SHUT UP.
WE'RE GRUNTS...FIGHTERS. YOU'RE SOME KINDA GENIUS. AND YOU GOT MORE'N JUST SMARTS. WE NEED SOMEONE LIKE--
WAIT. THIS BOY IS A... A FIGMENT. AN ILLUSION.
HE WAS REAL. NOW HE'S GONE. WITH YOUR HELP, WE MIGHT'A REACHED HIM IN TIME TO SAVE HIM.
YOUR PEOPLE NEED YA, KID.
MY... "PEOPLE?"
YOU HAVE NOTHING TO DO WITH ME. NOR I WITH YOU.
KEEP TELLIN' YOURSELF THAT.
YOU BEEN FLAGGED, KID. GRADUATIN' HARVARD AT SIXTEEN, THREE Ph.DS BY EIGHTEEN...
ALL RIGHT, YES, I'M... SMART. A LOT OF PEOPLE ARE.
NOT A LOT'A PEOPLE READ MINDS.

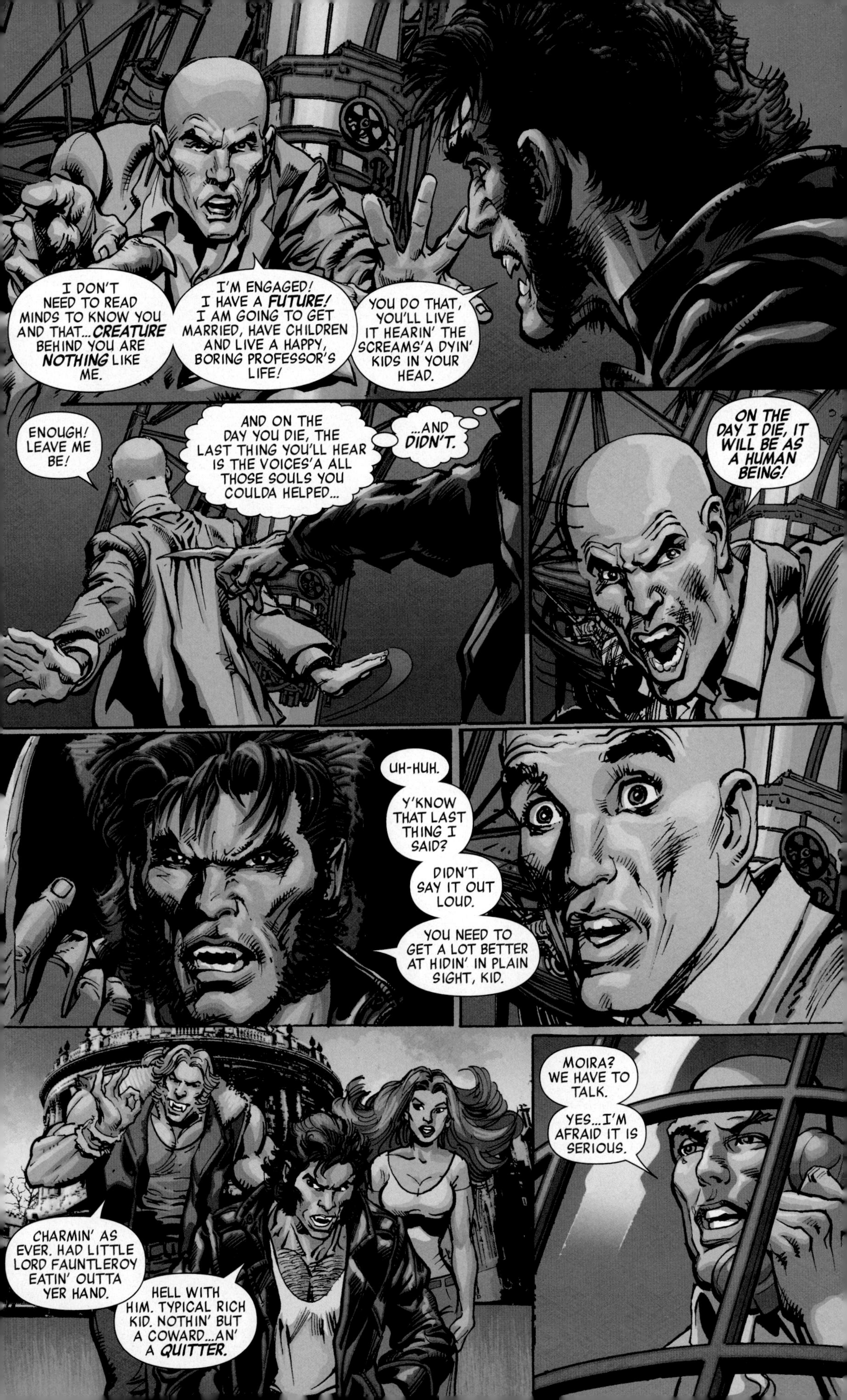
I DON'T NEED TO READ MINDS TO KNOW YOU AND THAT...*CREATURE* BEHIND YOU ARE *NOTHING* LIKE ME.
I'M ENGAGED! I HAVE A *FUTURE!* I AM GOING TO GET MARRIED, HAVE CHILDREN AND LIVE A HAPPY, BORING PROFESSOR'S LIFE!
YOU DO THAT, YOU'LL LIVE IT HEARIN' THE SCREAMS'A DYIN' KIDS IN YOUR HEAD.
ENOUGH! LEAVE ME BE!
AND ON THE DAY YOU DIE, THE LAST THING YOU'LL HEAR IS THE VOICES'A ALL THOSE SOULS YOU COULDA HELPED...
...AND *DIDN'T.*
ON THE DAY I DIE, IT WILL BE AS A HUMAN BEING!
UH-HUH.
Y'KNOW THAT LAST THING I SAID?
DIDN'T SAY IT OUT LOUD.
YOU NEED TO GET A LOT BETTER AT HIDIN' IN PLAIN SIGHT, KID.
CHARMIN' AS EVER. HAD LITTLE LORD FAUNTLEROY EATIN' OUTTA YER HAND.
HELL WITH HIM. TYPICAL RICH KID. NOTHIN' BUT A COWARD...AN' A *QUITTER.*
MOIRA? WE HAVE TO TALK.
YES...I'M AFRAID IT IS SERIOUS.

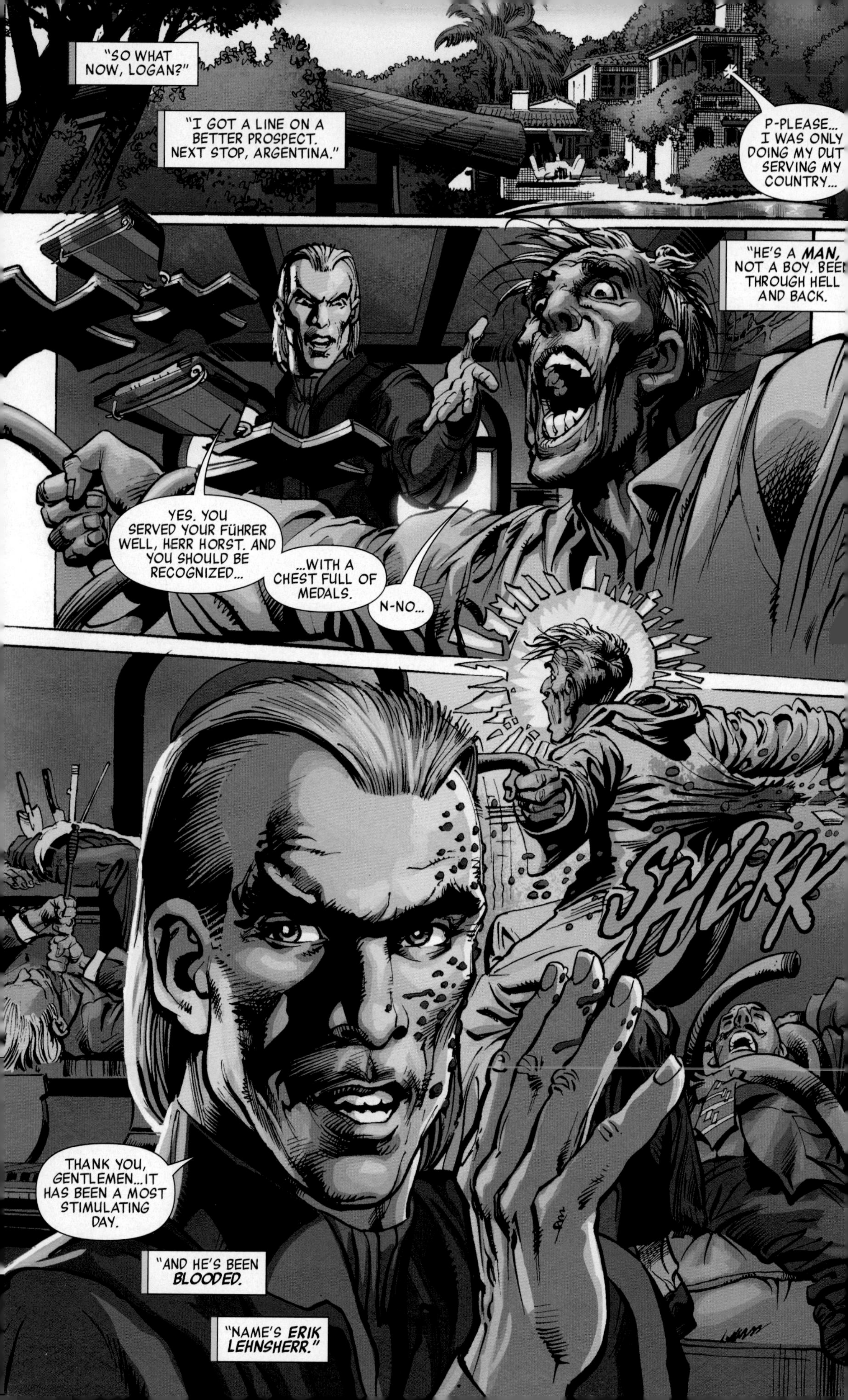
"SO WHAT NOW, LOGAN?"
"I GOT A LINE ON A BETTER PROSPECT. NEXT STOP, ARGENTINA."
P-PLEASE... I WAS ONLY DOING MY DUT SERVING MY COUNTRY...
"HE'S A **MAN,** NOT A BOY. BEE THROUGH HELL AND BACK.
YES. YOU SERVED YOUR FÜHRER WELL, HERR HORST. AND YOU SHOULD BE RECOGNIZED...
...WITH A CHEST FULL OF MEDALS.
N-NO...
SHLKK
THANK YOU, GENTLEMEN...IT HAS BEEN A MOST STIMULATING DAY.
"AND HE'S BEEN ***BLOODED.***
"NAME'S ***ERIK LEHNSHERR.***"

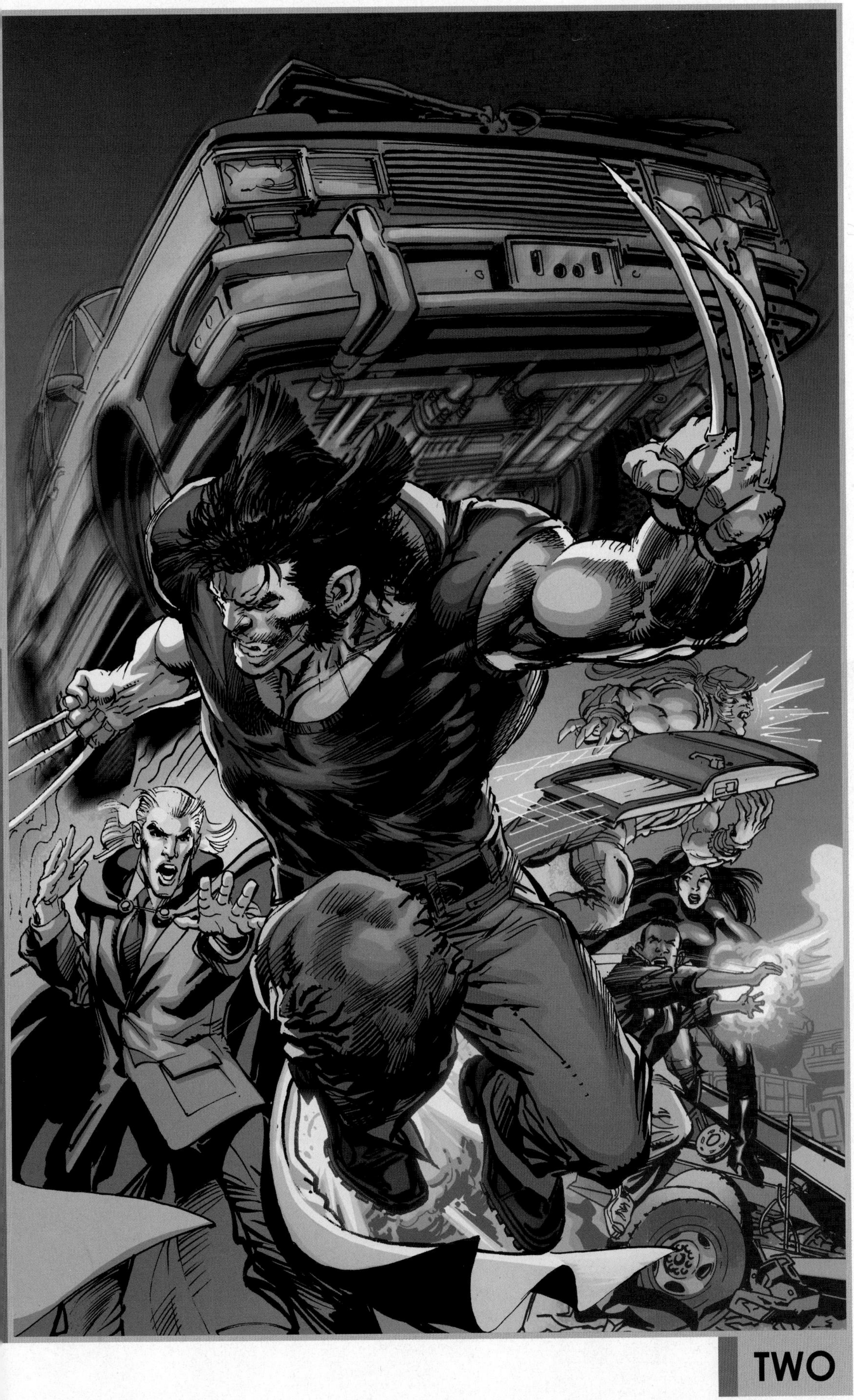

TWO

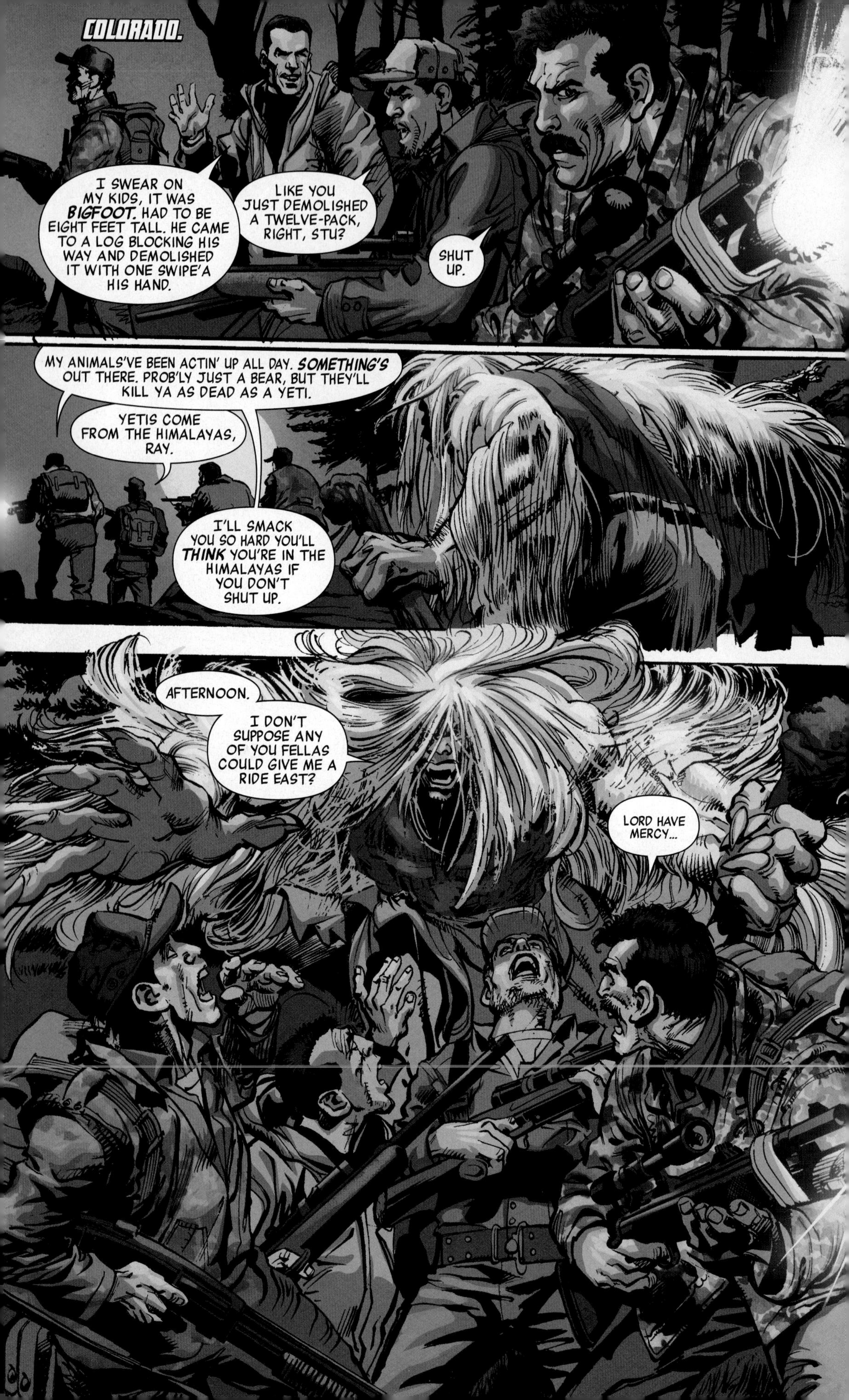
COLORADO.
I SWEAR ON MY KIDS, IT WAS BIGFOOT. HAD TO BE EIGHT FEET TALL. HE CAME TO A LOG BLOCKING HIS WAY AND DEMOLISHED IT WITH ONE SWIPE'A HIS HAND.
LIKE YOU JUST DEMOLISHED A TWELVE-PACK, RIGHT, STU?
SHUT UP.
MY ANIMALS'VE BEEN ACTIN' UP ALL DAY. SOMETHING'S OUT THERE. PROB'LY JUST A BEAR, BUT THEY'LL KILL YA AS DEAD AS A YETI.
YETIS COME FROM THE HIMALAYAS, RAY.
I'LL SMACK YOU SO HARD YOU'LL THINK YOU'RE IN THE HIMALAYAS IF YOU DON'T SHUT UP.
AFTERNOON.
I DON'T SUPPOSE ANY OF YOU FELLAS COULD GIVE ME A RIDE EAST?
LORD HAVE MERCY...

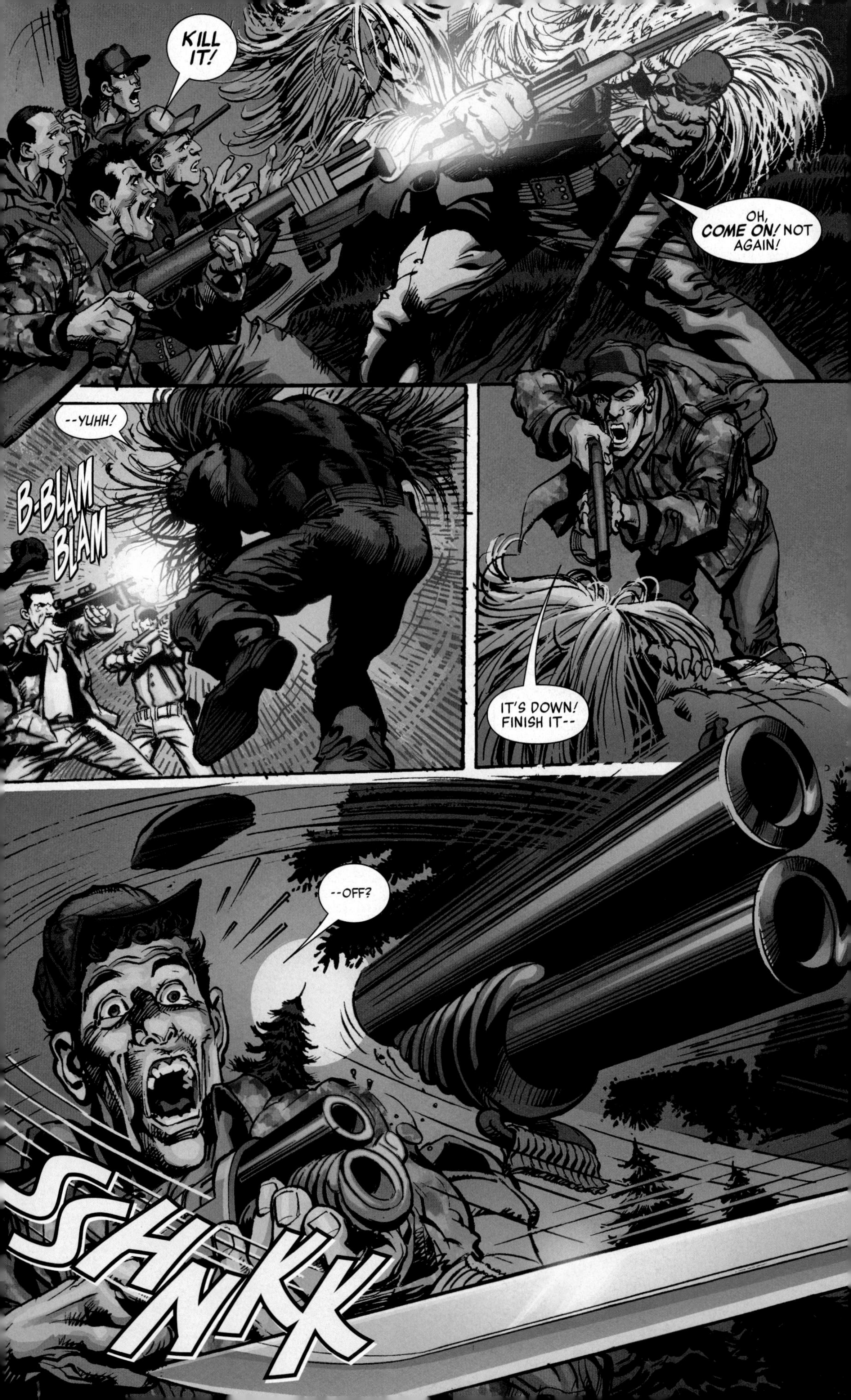
KILL IT!
OH, COME ON! NOT AGAIN!
--YUHH!
B-BLAM BLAM
IT'S DOWN! FINISH IT--
--OFF?
SHNKK

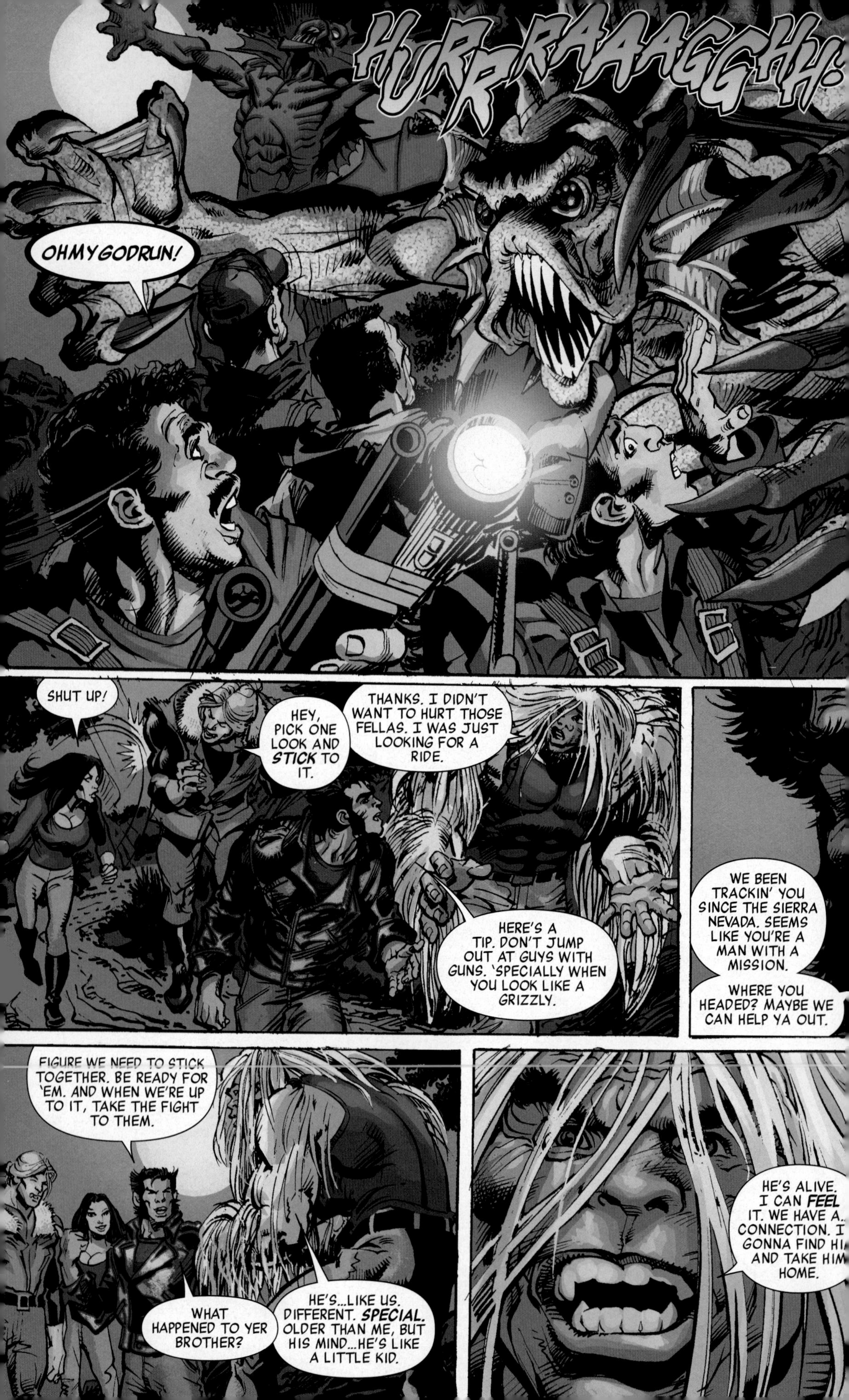
HURRRAAAGGHH!
OHMYGODRUN!
SHUT UP!
HEY, PICK ONE LOOK AND STICK TO IT.
THANKS. I DIDN'T WANT TO HURT THOSE FELLAS. I WAS JUST LOOKING FOR A RIDE.
HERE'S A TIP. DON'T JUMP OUT AT GUYS WITH GUNS. 'SPECIALLY WHEN YOU LOOK LIKE A GRIZZLY.
WE BEEN TRACKIN' YOU SINCE THE SIERRA NEVADA. SEEMS LIKE YOU'RE A MAN WITH A MISSION.
WHERE YOU HEADED? MAYBE WE CAN HELP YA OUT.
FIGURE WE NEED TO STICK TOGETHER. BE READY FOR 'EM. AND WHEN WE'RE UP TO IT, TAKE THE FIGHT TO THEM.
WHAT HAPPENED TO YER BROTHER?
HE'S...LIKE US. DIFFERENT. SPECIAL. OLDER THAN ME, BUT HIS MIND...HE'S LIKE A LITTLE KID.
HE'S ALIVE. I CAN FEEL IT. WE HAVE A CONNECTION. I GONNA FIND HI AND TAKE HIM HOME.

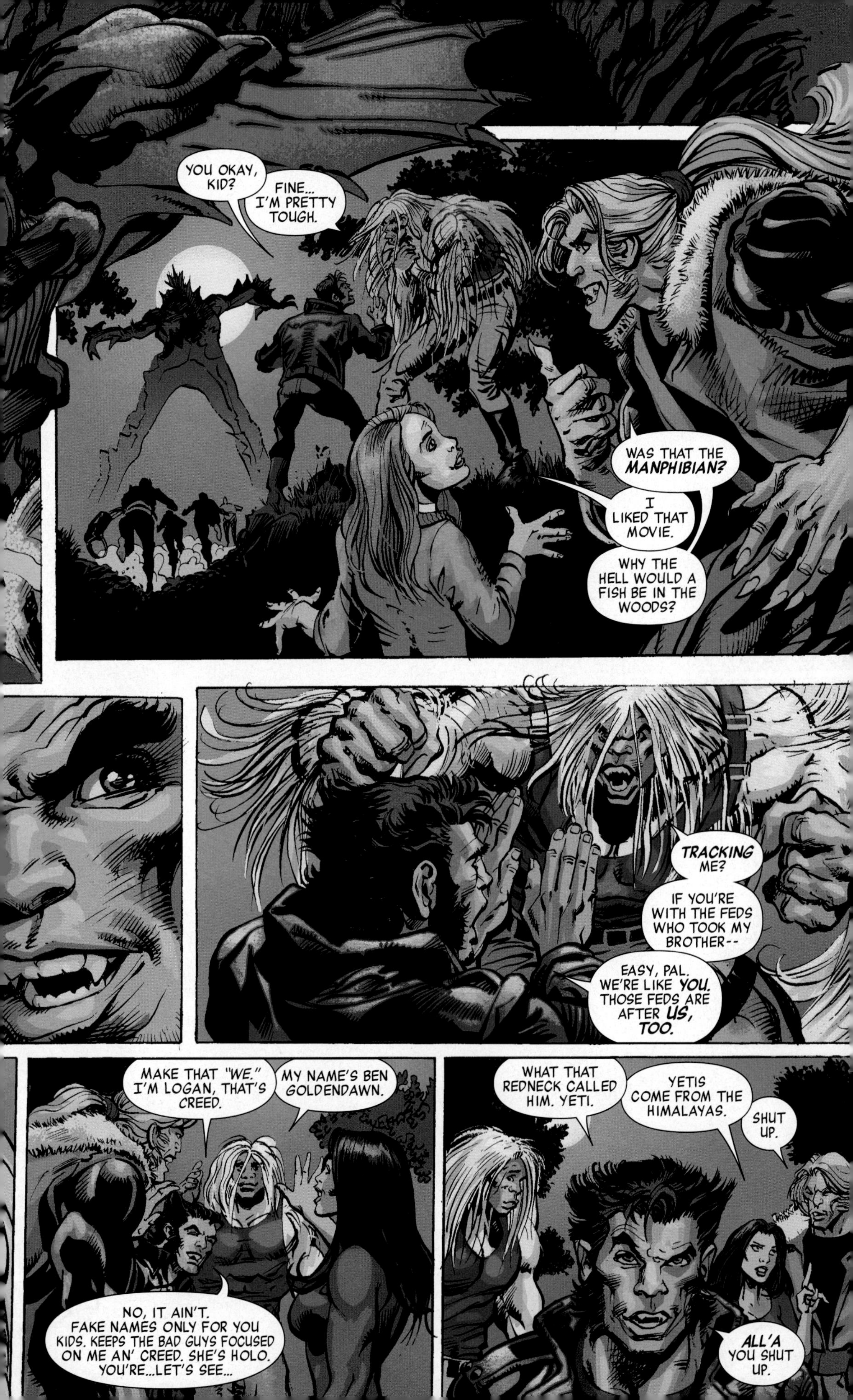
YOU OKAY, KID?
FINE... I'M PRETTY TOUGH.
WAS THAT THE MANPHIBIAN?
I LIKED THAT MOVIE.
WHY THE HELL WOULD A FISH BE IN THE WOODS?
TRACKING ME?
IF YOU'RE WITH THE FEDS WHO TOOK MY BROTHER--
EASY, PAL. WE'RE LIKE YOU. THOSE FEDS ARE AFTER US, TOO.
MAKE THAT "WE." I'M LOGAN, THAT'S CREED.
MY NAME'S BEN GOLDENDAWN.
NO, IT AIN'T. FAKE NAMES ONLY FOR YOU KIDS. KEEPS THE BAD GUYS FOCUSED ON ME AN' CREED. SHE'S HOLO. YOU'RE...LET'S SEE...
WHAT THAT REDNECK CALLED HIM. YETI.
YETIS COME FROM THE HIMALAYAS.
SHUT UP.
ALL'A YOU SHUT UP.

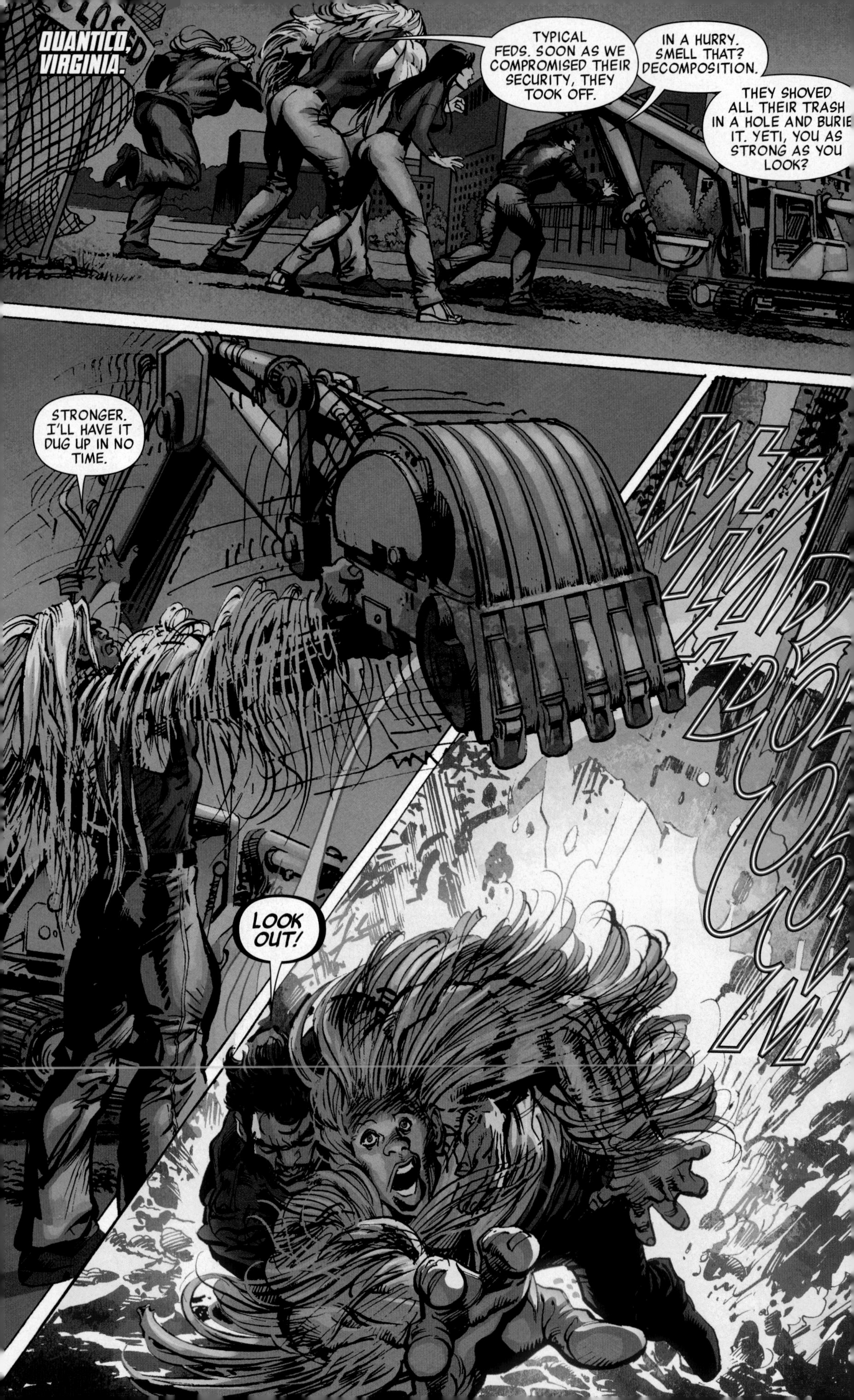
QUANTICO, VIRGINIA.
TYPICAL FEDS. SOON AS WE COMPROMISED THEIR SECURITY, THEY TOOK OFF.
IN A HURRY. SMELL THAT? DECOMPOSITION.
THEY SHOVED ALL THEIR TRASH IN A HOLE AND BURIE IT. YETI, YOU AS STRONG AS YOU LOOK?
STRONGER. I'LL HAVE IT DUG UP IN NO TIME.
LOOK OUT!

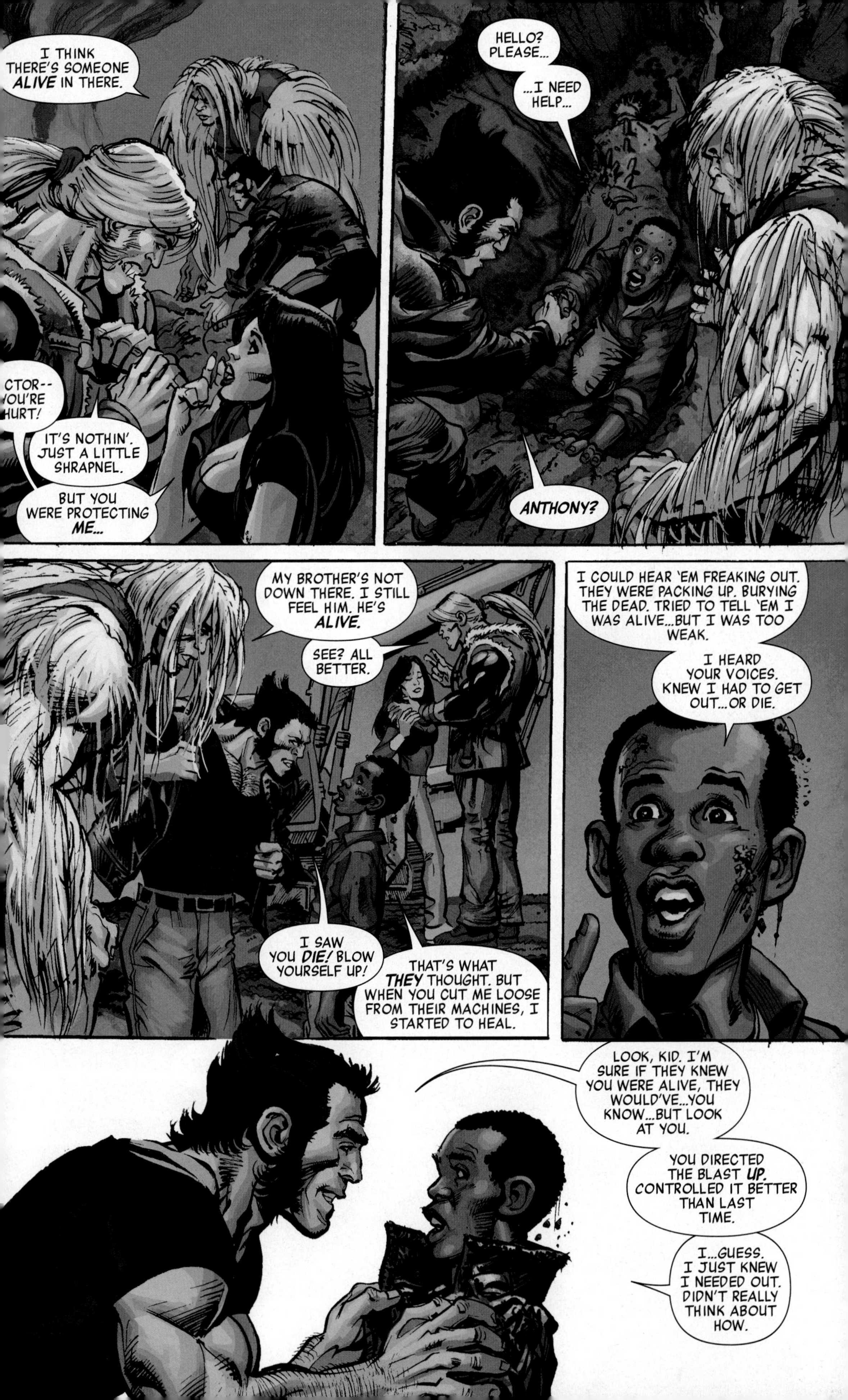
I THINK THERE'S SOMEONE ALIVE IN THERE.
CTOR-- YOU'RE HURT!
IT'S NOTHIN'. JUST A LITTLE SHRAPNEL.
BUT YOU WERE PROTECTING ME...
HELLO? PLEASE...
...I NEED HELP...
ANTHONY?
MY BROTHER'S NOT DOWN THERE. I STILL FEEL HIM. HE'S ALIVE.
SEE? ALL BETTER.
I SAW YOU DIE! BLOW YOURSELF UP!
THAT'S WHAT THEY THOUGHT. BUT WHEN YOU CUT ME LOOSE FROM THEIR MACHINES, I STARTED TO HEAL.
I COULD HEAR 'EM FREAKING OUT. THEY WERE PACKING UP. BURYING THE DEAD. TRIED TO TELL 'EM I WAS ALIVE...BUT I WAS TOO WEAK.
I HEARD YOUR VOICES. KNEW I HAD TO GET OUT...OR DIE.
LOOK, KID. I'M SURE IF THEY KNEW YOU WERE ALIVE, THEY WOULD'VE...YOU KNOW...BUT LOOK AT YOU.
YOU DIRECTED THE BLAST UP. CONTROLLED IT BETTER THAN LAST TIME.
I...GUESS. I JUST KNEW I NEEDED OUT. DIDN'T REALLY THINK ABOUT HOW.

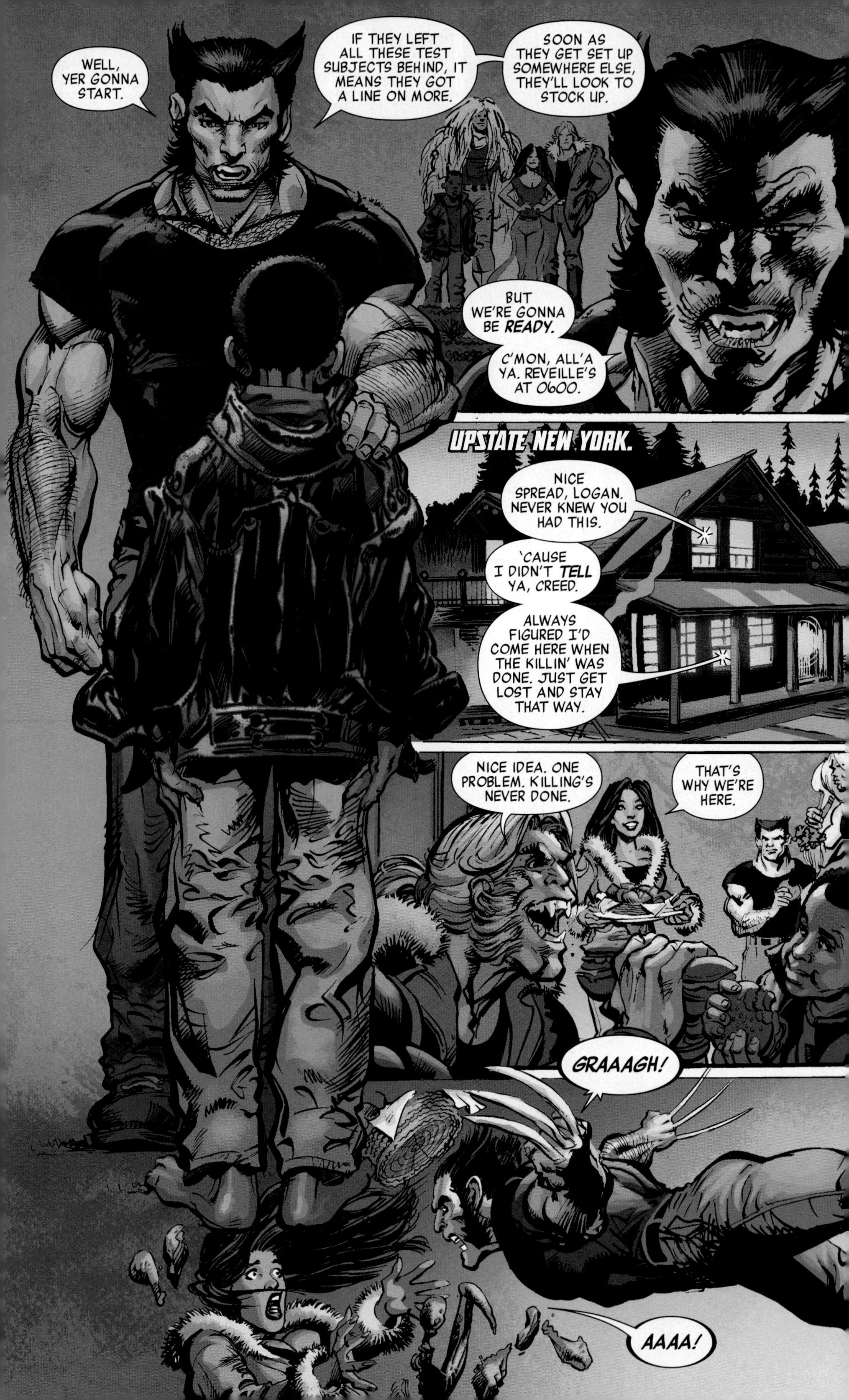
WELL, YER GONNA START.
IF THEY LEFT ALL THESE TEST SUBJECTS BEHIND, IT MEANS THEY GOT A LINE ON MORE.
SOON AS THEY GET SET UP SOMEWHERE ELSE, THEY'LL LOOK TO STOCK UP.
BUT WE'RE GONNA BE READY.
C'MON, ALL'A YA. REVEILLE'S AT 0600.
UPSTATE NEW YORK.
NICE SPREAD, LOGAN. NEVER KNEW YOU HAD THIS.
'CAUSE I DIDN'T TELL YA, CREED.
ALWAYS FIGURED I'D COME HERE WHEN THE KILLIN' WAS DONE. JUST GET LOST AND STAY THAT WAY.
NICE IDEA. ONE PROBLEM. KILLING'S NEVER DONE.
THAT'S WHY WE'RE HERE.
GRAAAGH!
AAAA!

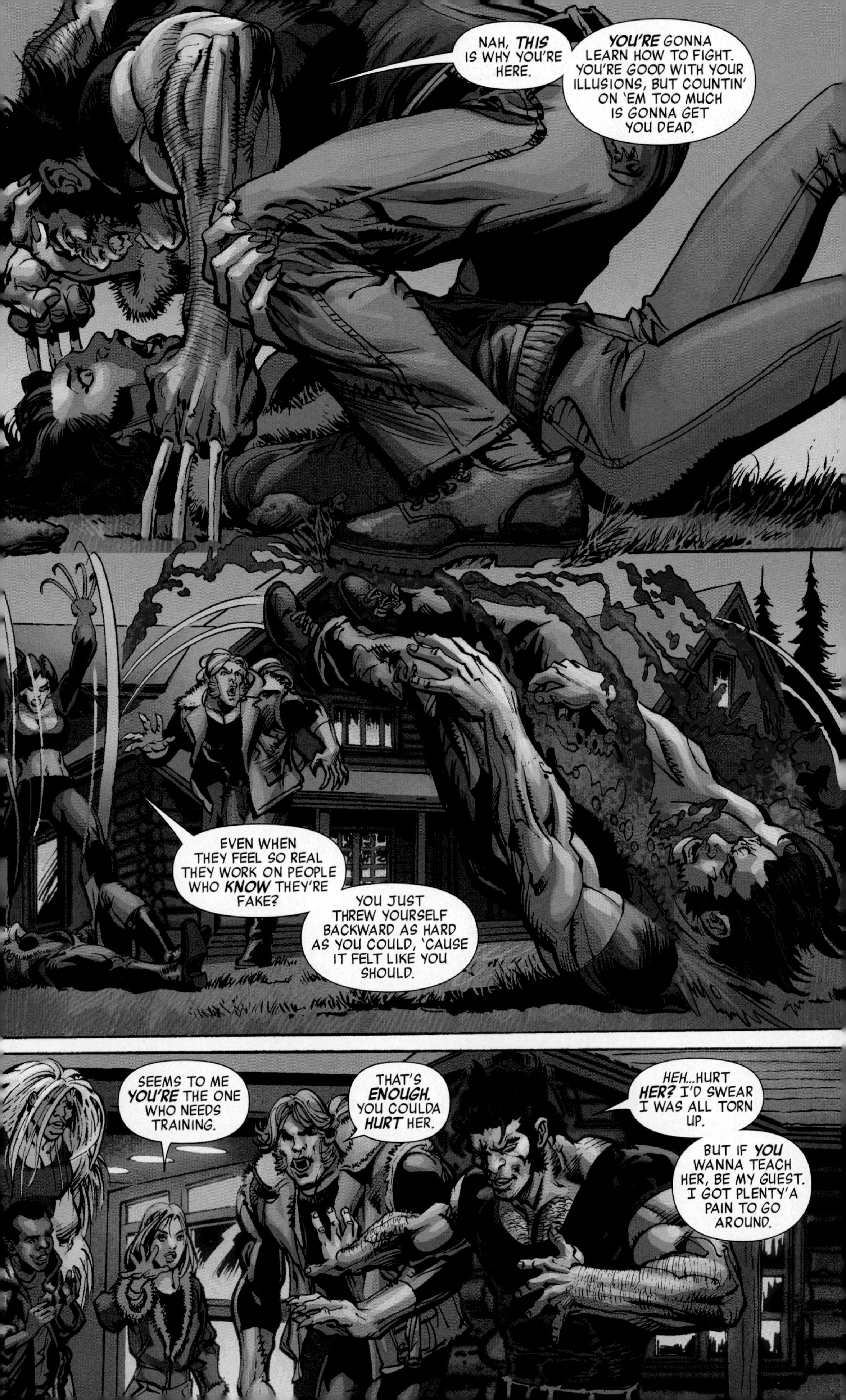
NAH, THIS IS WHY YOU'RE HERE.
YOU'RE GONNA LEARN HOW TO FIGHT. YOU'RE GOOD WITH YOUR ILLUSIONS, BUT COUNTIN' ON 'EM TOO MUCH IS GONNA GET YOU DEAD.
EVEN WHEN THEY FEEL SO REAL THEY WORK ON PEOPLE WHO KNOW THEY'RE FAKE?
YOU JUST THREW YOURSELF BACKWARD AS HARD AS YOU COULD, 'CAUSE IT FELT LIKE YOU SHOULD.
SEEMS TO ME YOU'RE THE ONE WHO NEEDS TRAINING.
THAT'S ENOUGH. YOU COULDA HURT HER.
HEH...HURT HER? I'D SWEAR I WAS ALL TORN UP.
BUT IF YOU WANNA TEACH HER, BE MY GUEST. I GOT PLENTY'A PAIN TO GO AROUND.

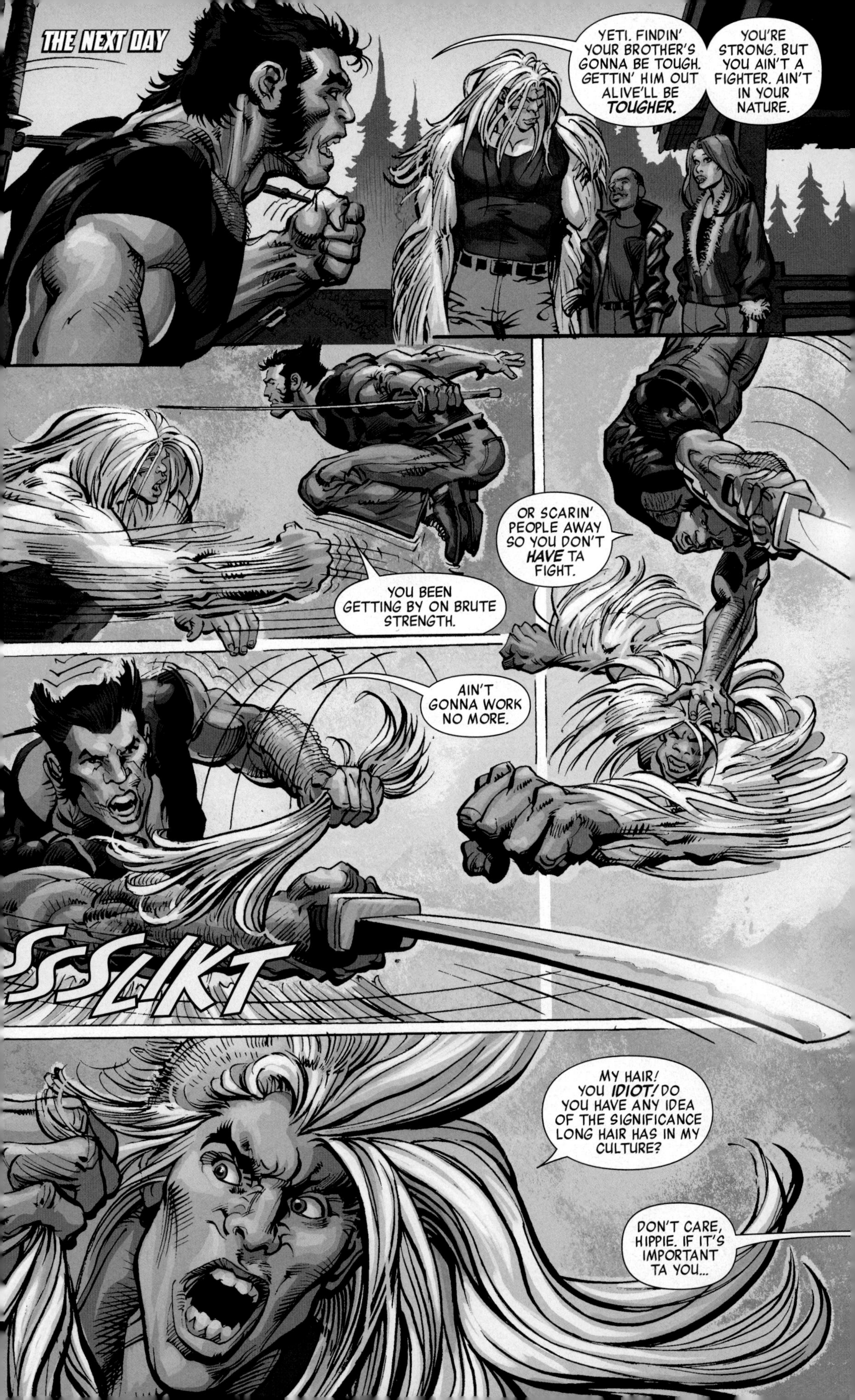
THE NEXT DAY
YETI. FINDIN' YOUR BROTHER'S GONNA BE TOUGH. GETTIN' HIM OUT ALIVE'LL BE TOUGHER.
YOU'RE STRONG. BUT YOU AIN'T A FIGHTER. AIN'T IN YOUR NATURE.
YOU BEEN GETTING BY ON BRUTE STRENGTH.
OR SCARIN' PEOPLE AWAY SO YOU DON'T HAVE TA FIGHT.
AIN'T GONNA WORK NO MORE.
SSSLIKT
MY HAIR! YOU IDIOT! DO YOU HAVE ANY IDEA OF THE SIGNIFICANCE LONG HAIR HAS IN MY CULTURE?
DON'T CARE, HIPPIE. IF IT'S IMPORTANT TA YOU...

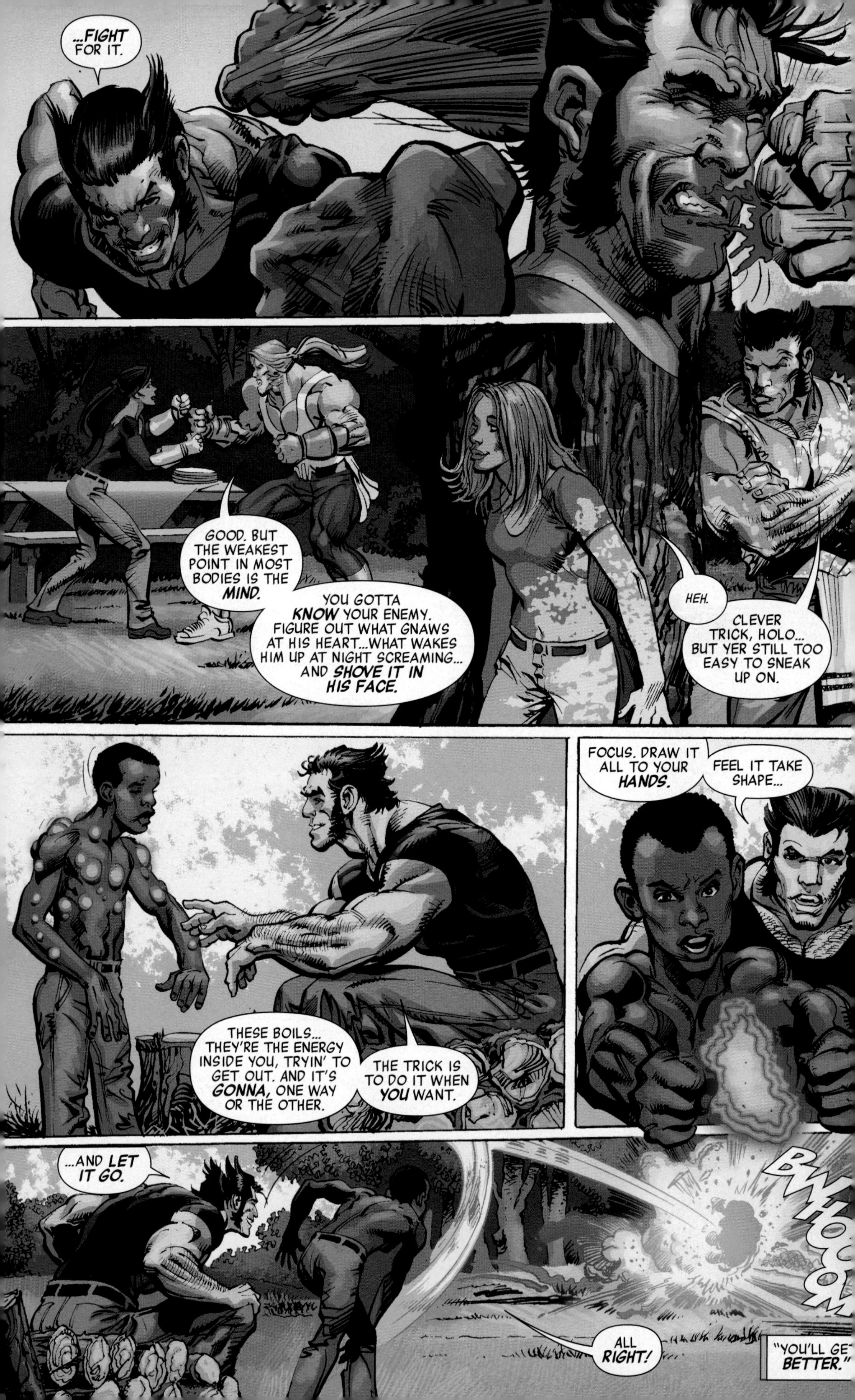
...FIGHT FOR IT.
GOOD. BUT THE WEAKEST POINT IN MOST BODIES IS THE MIND.
YOU GOTTA KNOW YOUR ENEMY. FIGURE OUT WHAT GNAWS AT HIS HEART...WHAT WAKES HIM UP AT NIGHT SCREAMING... AND SHOVE IT IN HIS FACE.
HEH.
CLEVER TRICK, HOLO... BUT YER STILL TOO EASY TO SNEAK UP ON.
THESE BOILS... THEY'RE THE ENERGY INSIDE YOU, TRYIN' TO GET OUT. AND IT'S GONNA, ONE WAY OR THE OTHER.
THE TRICK IS TO DO IT WHEN YOU WANT.
FOCUS. DRAW IT ALL TO YOUR HANDS.
FEEL IT TAKE SHAPE...
...AND LET IT GO.
BWHOOOM
ALL RIGHT!
"YOU'LL GE BETTER."

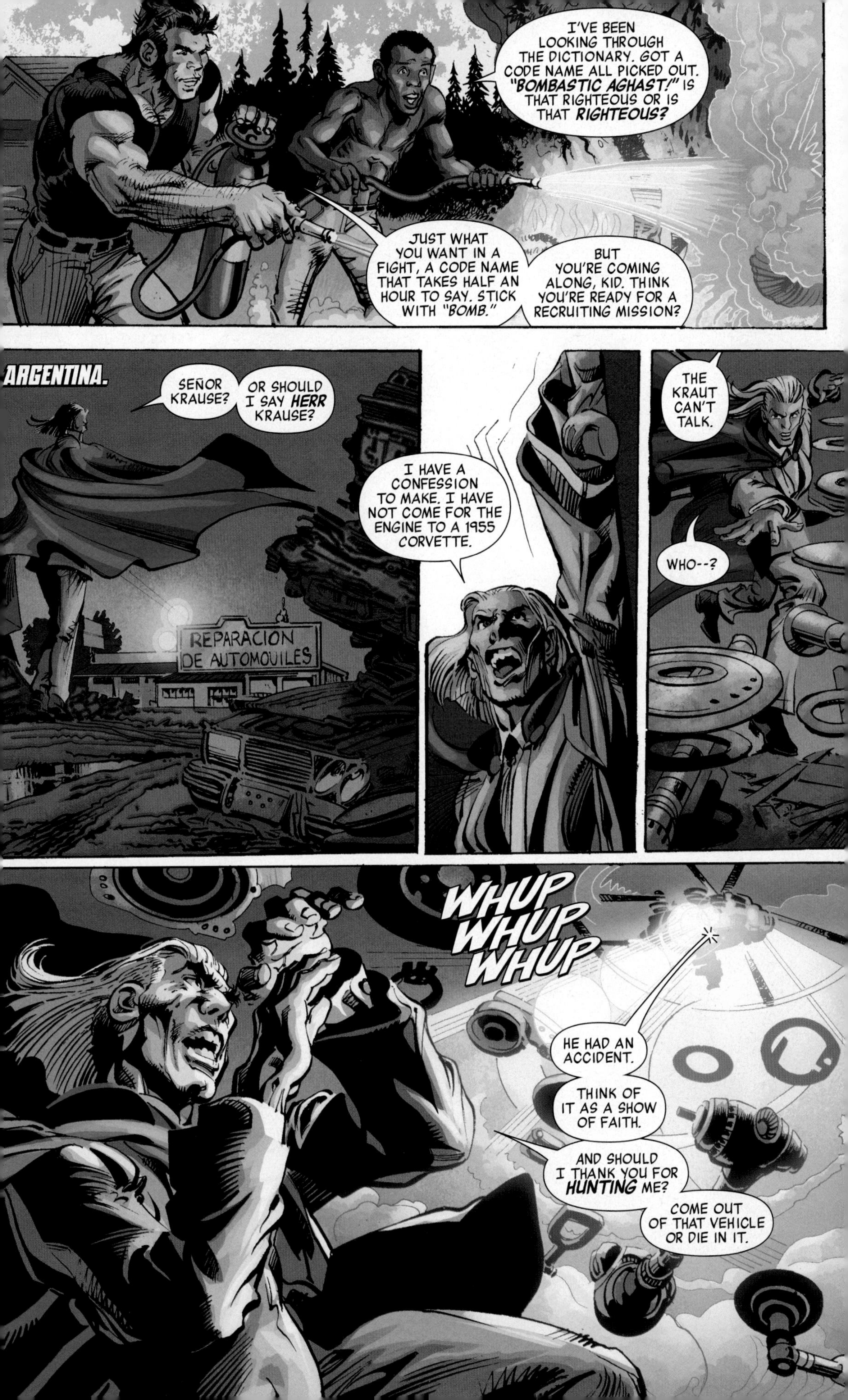
I'VE BEEN LOOKING THROUGH THE DICTIONARY. GOT A CODE NAME ALL PICKED OUT. "BOMBASTIC AGHAST!" IS THAT RIGHTEOUS OR IS THAT RIGHTEOUS?
JUST WHAT YOU WANT IN A FIGHT, A CODE NAME THAT TAKES HALF AN HOUR TO SAY. STICK WITH "BOMB."
BUT YOU'RE COMING ALONG, KID. THINK YOU'RE READY FOR A RECRUITING MISSION?
ARGENTINA.
SEÑOR KRAUSE?
OR SHOULD I SAY HERR KRAUSE?
REPARACION DE AUTOMOUILES
I HAVE A CONFESSION TO MAKE. I HAVE NOT COME FOR THE ENGINE TO A 1955 CORVETTE.
THE KRAUT CAN'T TALK.
WHO--?
WHUP WHUP WHUP
HE HAD AN ACCIDENT.
THINK OF IT AS A SHOW OF FAITH.
AND SHOULD I THANK YOU FOR HUNTING ME?
COME OUT OF THAT VEHICLE OR DIE IN IT.

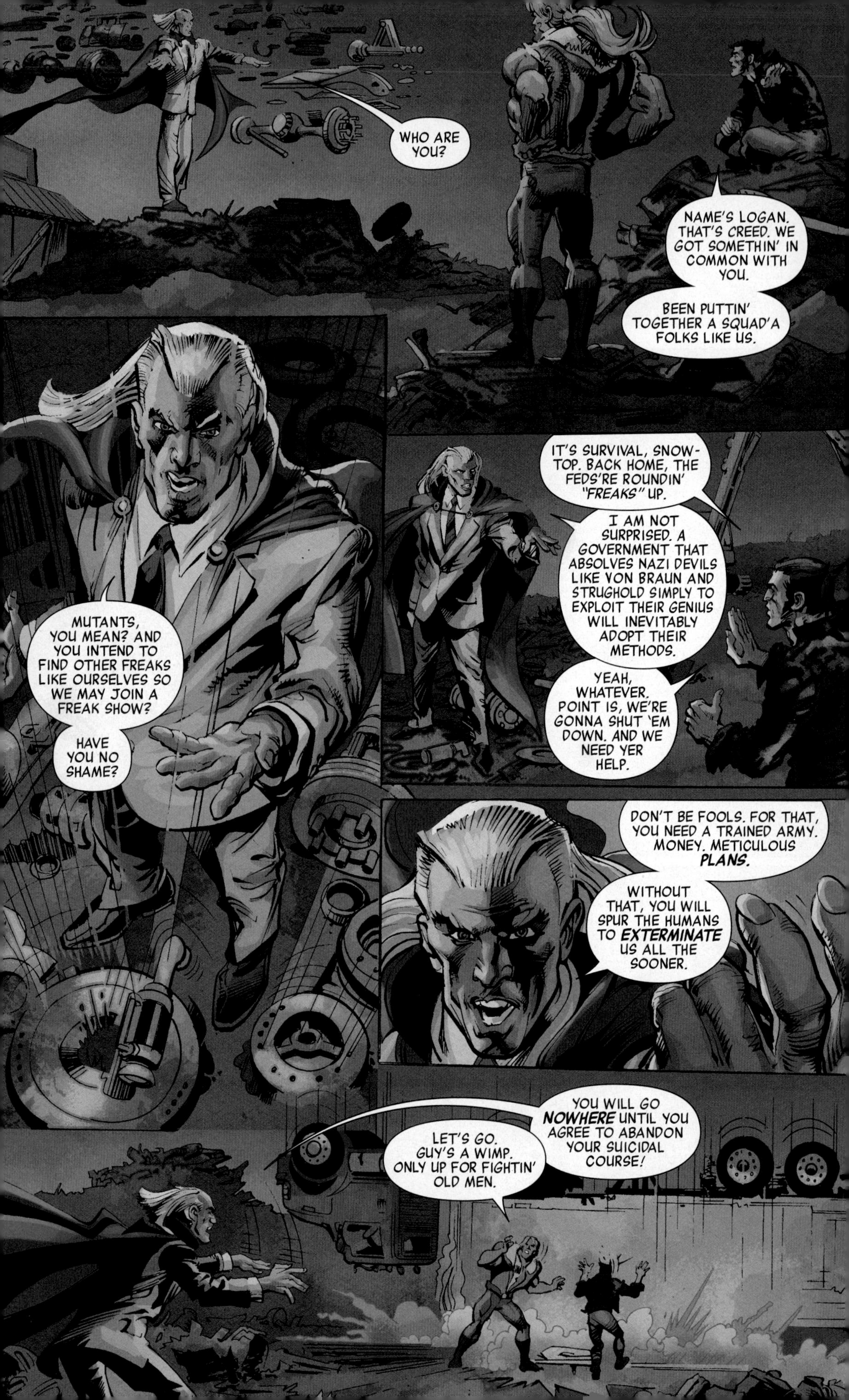
WHO ARE YOU?
NAME'S LOGAN. THAT'S CREED. WE GOT SOMETHIN' IN COMMON WITH YOU.
BEEN PUTTIN' TOGETHER A SQUAD'A FOLKS LIKE US.
MUTANTS, YOU MEAN? AND YOU INTEND TO FIND OTHER FREAKS LIKE OURSELVES SO WE MAY JOIN A FREAK SHOW?
HAVE YOU NO SHAME?
IT'S SURVIVAL, SNOW-TOP. BACK HOME, THE FEDS'RE ROUNDIN' "FREAKS" UP.
I AM NOT SURPRISED. A GOVERNMENT THAT ABSOLVES NAZI DEVILS LIKE VON BRAUN AND STRUGHOLD SIMPLY TO EXPLOIT THEIR GENIUS WILL INEVITABLY ADOPT THEIR METHODS.
YEAH, WHATEVER. POINT IS, WE'RE GONNA SHUT 'EM DOWN. AND WE NEED YER HELP.
DON'T BE FOOLS. FOR THAT, YOU NEED A TRAINED ARMY. MONEY. METICULOUS PLANS.
WITHOUT THAT, YOU WILL SPUR THE HUMANS TO EXTERMINATE US ALL THE SOONER.
LET'S GO. GUY'S A WIMP. ONLY UP FOR FIGHTIN' OLD MEN.
YOU WILL GO NOWHERE UNTIL YOU AGREE TO ABANDON YOUR SUICIDAL COURSE!

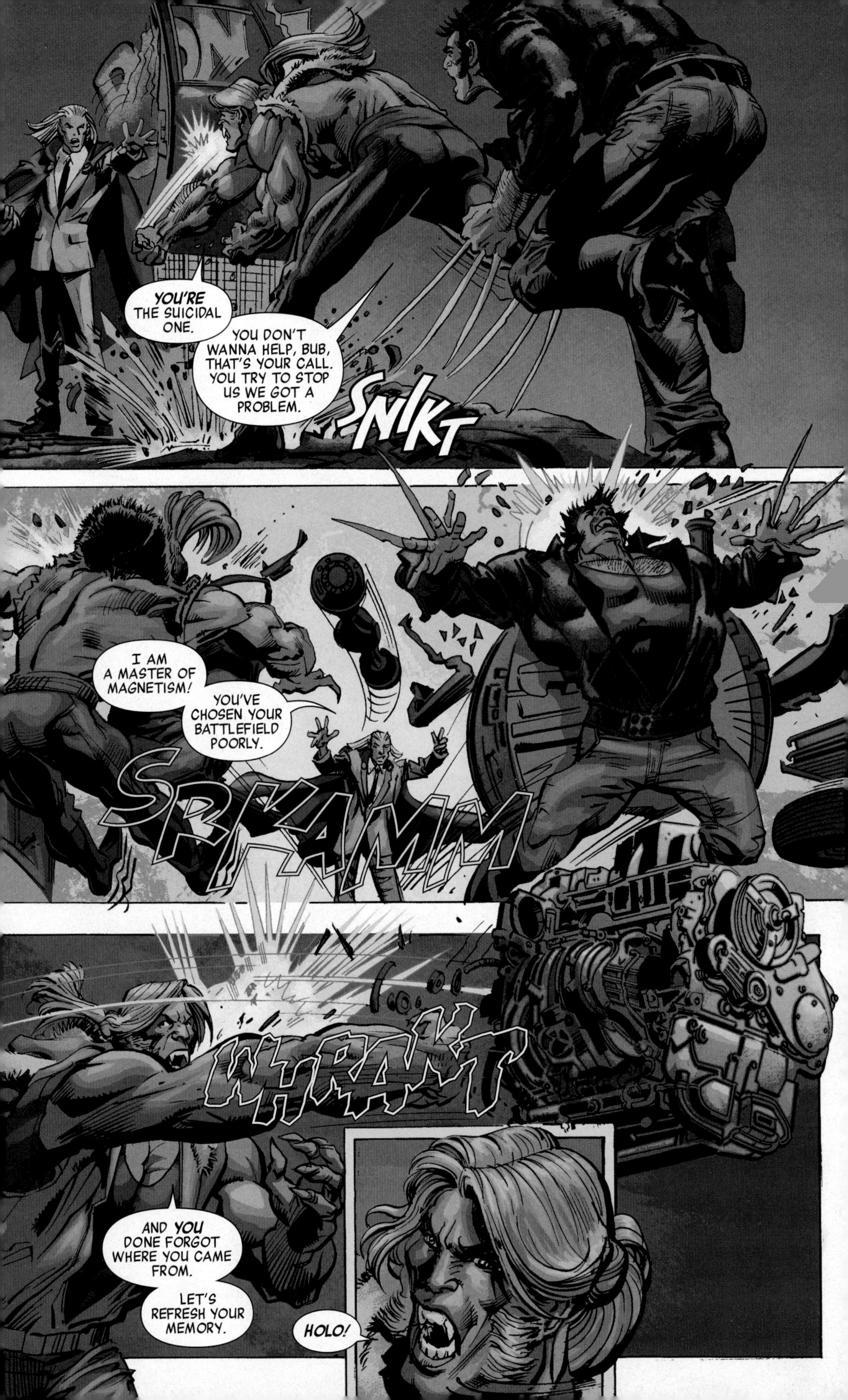
YOU'RE THE SUICIDAL ONE.
YOU DON'T WANNA HELP, BUB, THAT'S YOUR CALL. YOU TRY TO STOP US WE GOT A PROBLEM.
SNIKT
I AM A MASTER OF MAGNETISM!
YOU'VE CHOSEN YOUR BATTLEFIELD POORLY.
SPKAMM
WHRAKT
AND YOU DONE FORGOT WHERE YOU CAME FROM.
LET'S REFRESH YOUR MEMORY.
HOLO!

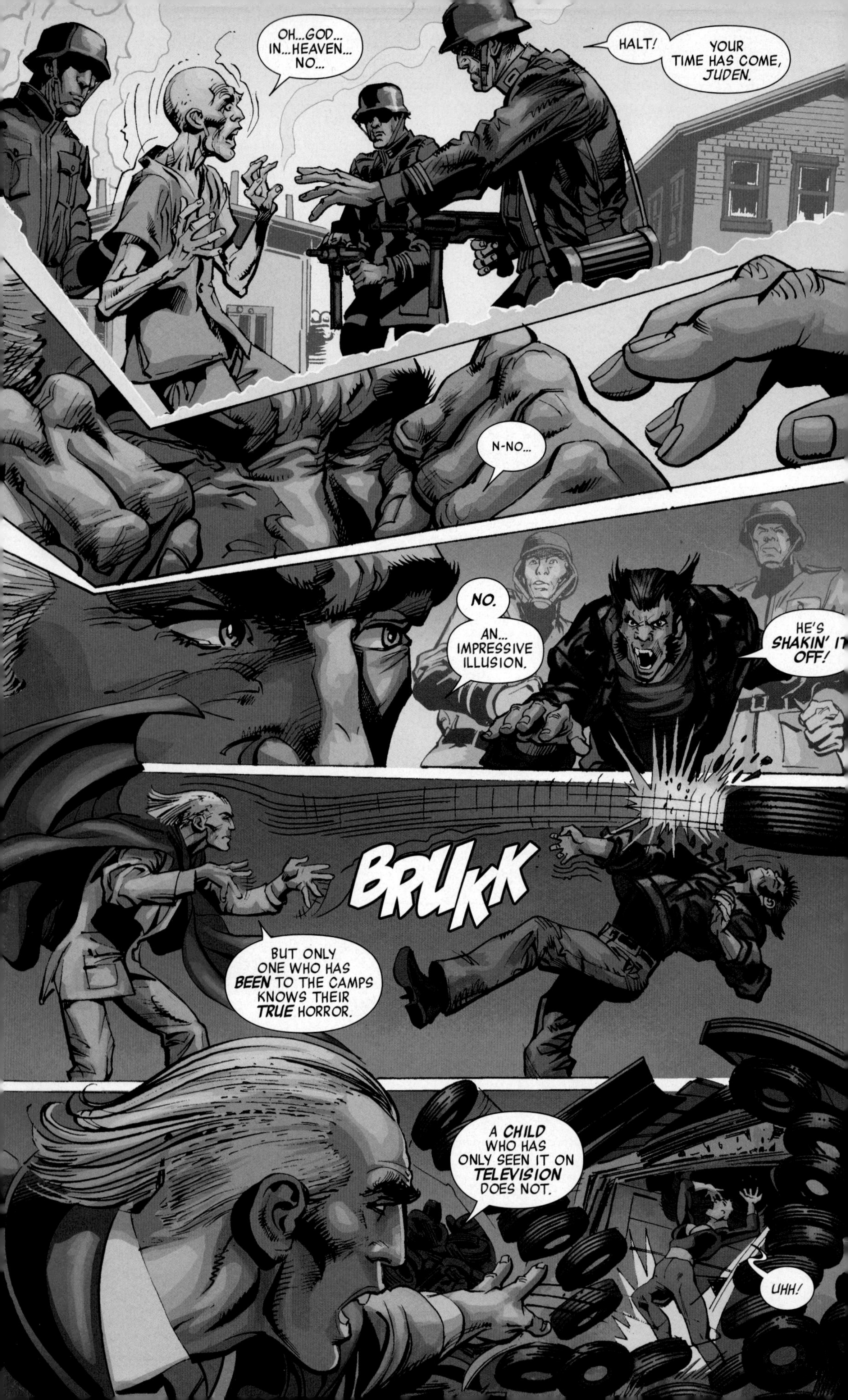
OH...GOD... IN...HEAVEN... NO...
HALT!
YOUR TIME HAS COME, JUDEN.
N-NO...
NO.
AN... IMPRESSIVE ILLUSION.
HE'S SHAKIN' IT OFF!
BRUKK
BUT ONLY ONE WHO HAS BEEN TO THE CAMPS KNOWS THEIR TRUE HORROR.
A CHILD WHO HAS ONLY SEEN IT ON TELEVISION DOES NOT.
UHH!

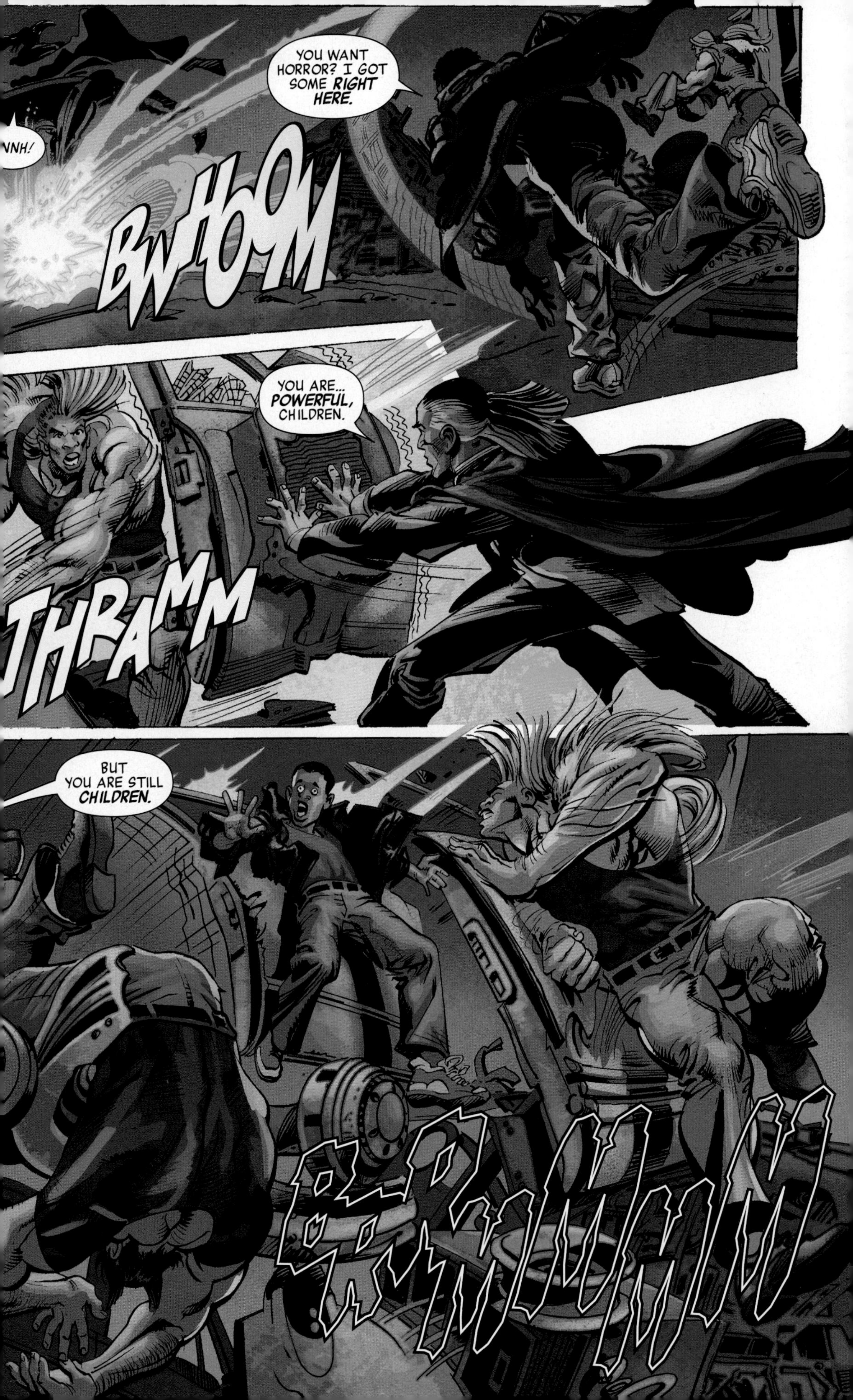
YOU WANT HORROR? I GOT SOME RIGHT HERE.
NNH!
BWHOOM
YOU ARE... POWERFUL, CHILDREN.
THRAMMM
BUT YOU ARE STILL CHILDREN.

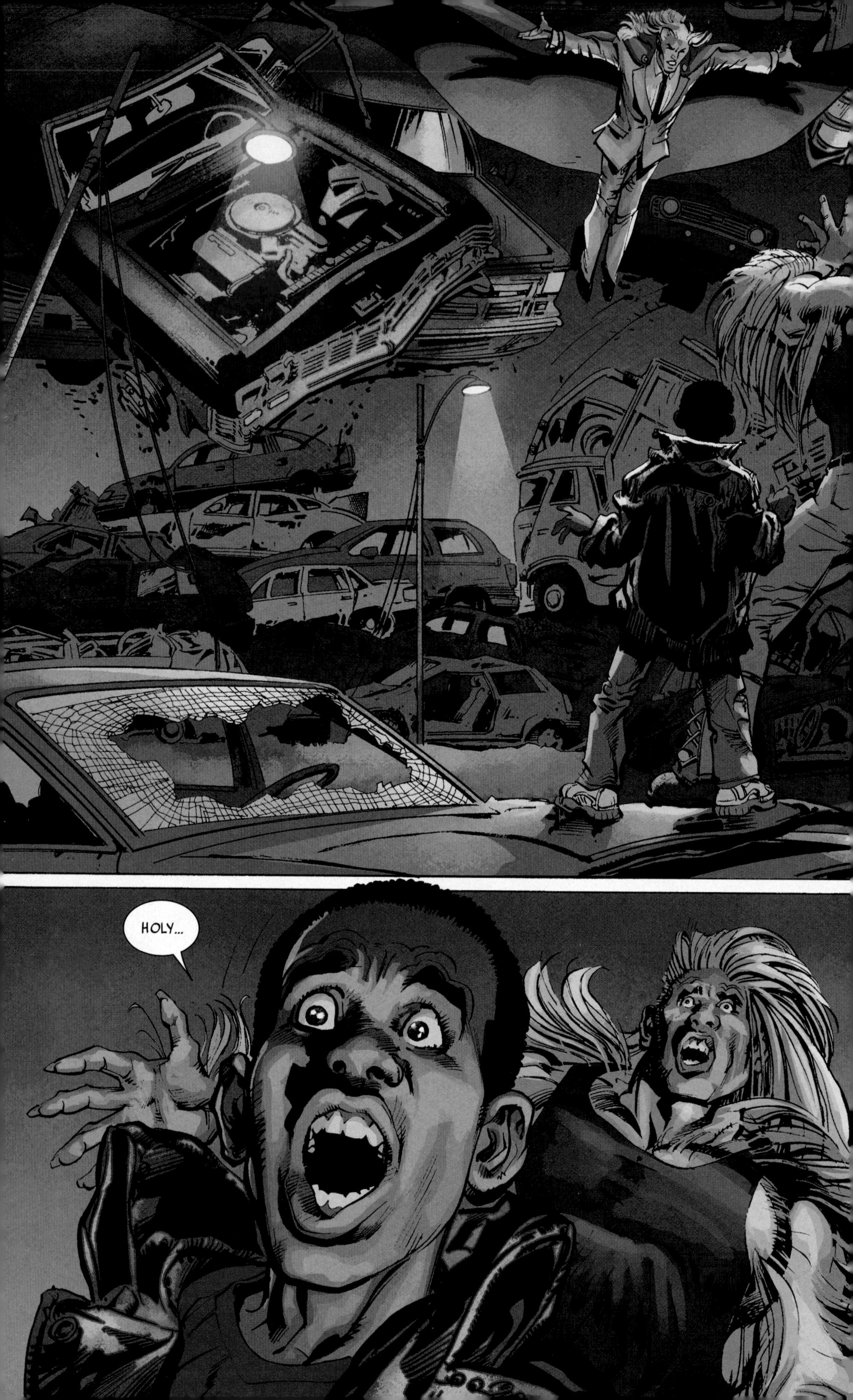
HOLY...

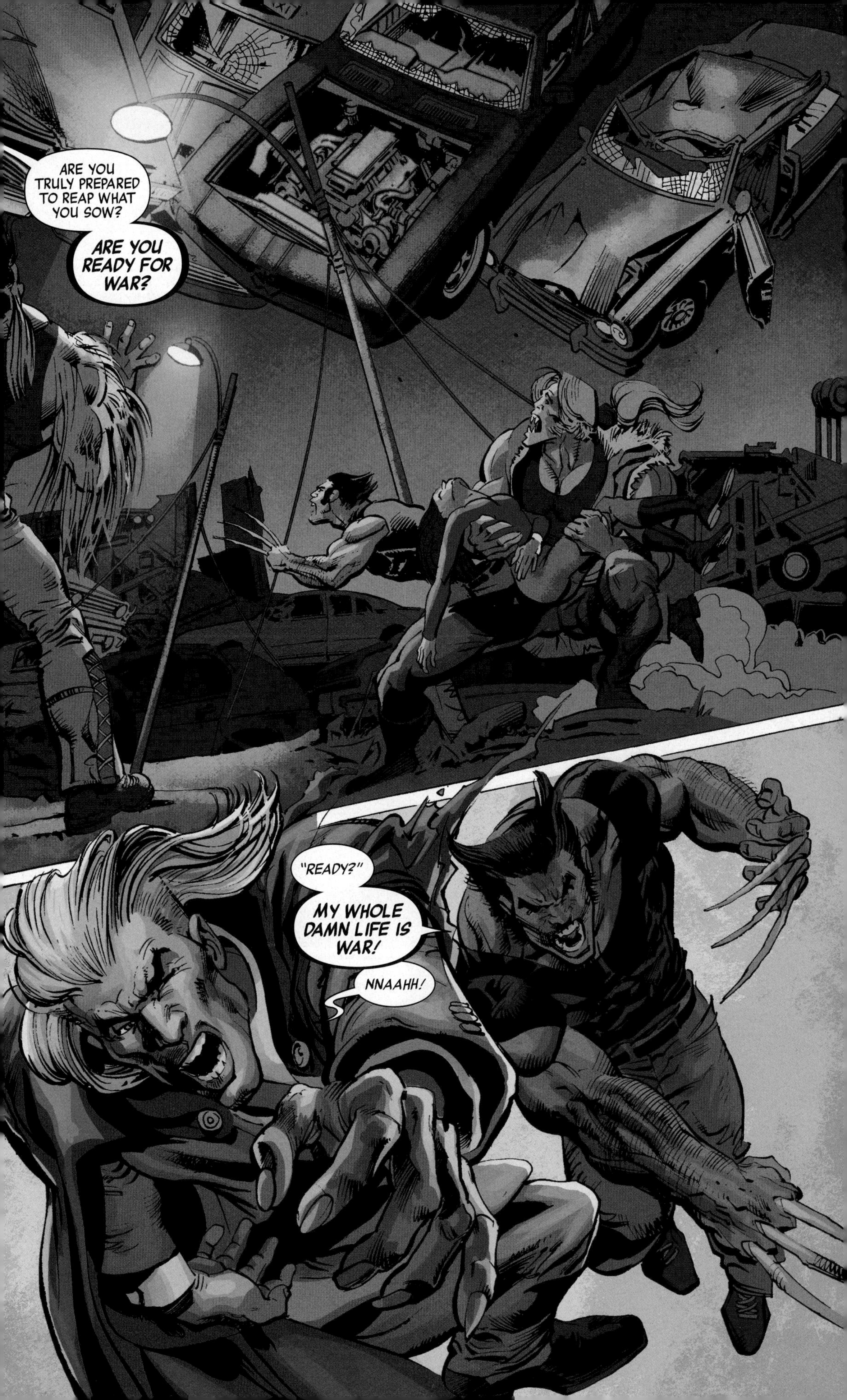
ARE YOU TRULY PREPARED TO REAP WHAT YOU SOW?
ARE YOU READY FOR WAR?
"READY?"
MY WHOLE DAMN LIFE IS WAR!
NNAAHH!

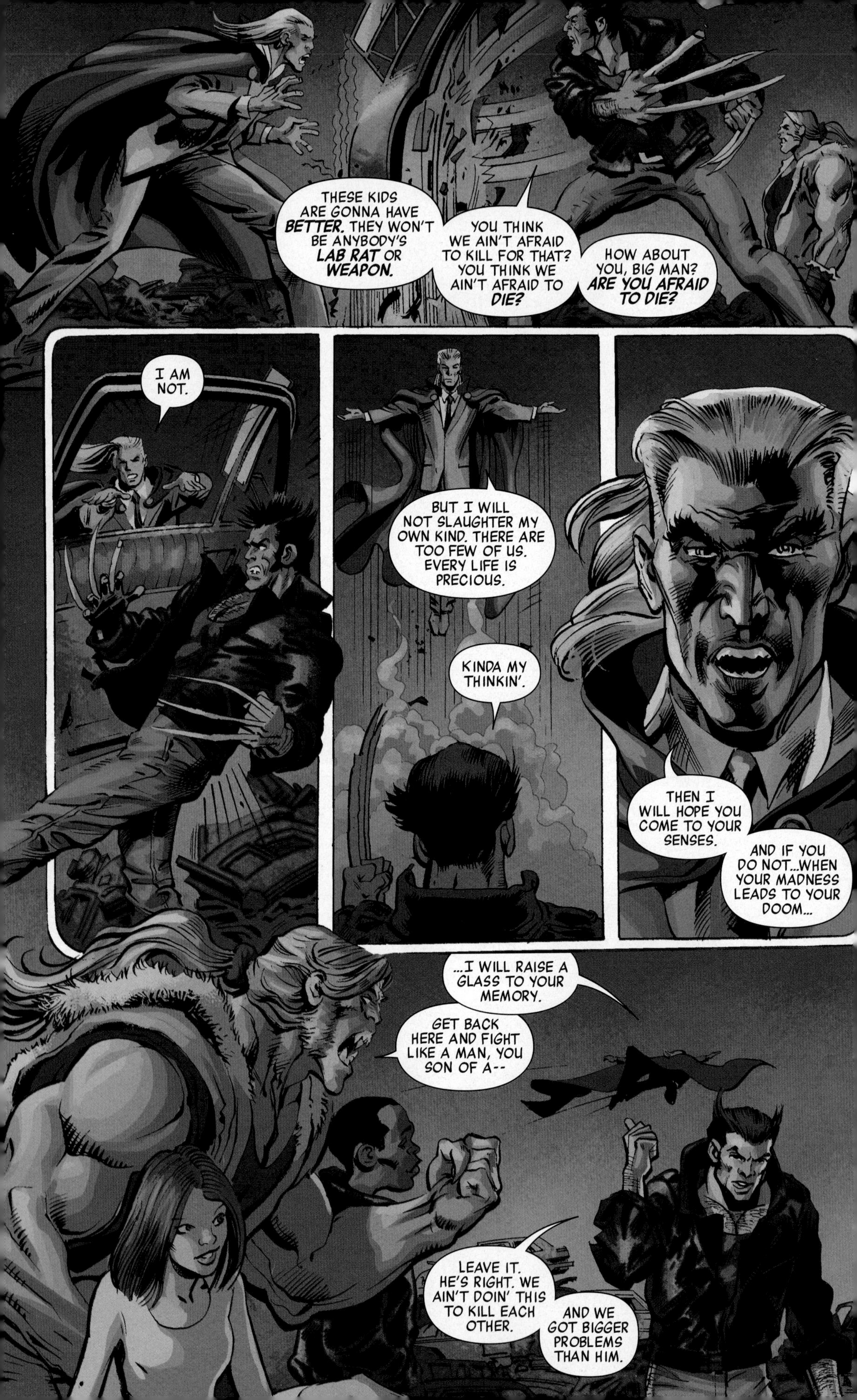

THESE KIDS ARE GONNA HAVE BETTER. THEY WON'T BE ANYBODY'S LAB RAT OR WEAPON.
YOU THINK WE AIN'T AFRAID TO KILL FOR THAT? YOU THINK WE AIN'T AFRAID TO DIE?
HOW ABOUT YOU, BIG MAN? ARE YOU AFRAID TO DIE?
I AM NOT.
BUT I WILL NOT SLAUGHTER MY OWN KIND. THERE ARE TOO FEW OF US. EVERY LIFE IS PRECIOUS.
KINDA MY THINKIN'.
THEN I WILL HOPE YOU COME TO YOUR SENSES.
AND IF YOU DO NOT...WHEN YOUR MADNESS LEADS TO YOUR DOOM...
...I WILL RAISE A GLASS TO YOUR MEMORY.
GET BACK HERE AND FIGHT LIKE A MAN, YOU SON OF A--
LEAVE IT. HE'S RIGHT. WE AIN'T DOIN' THIS TO KILL EACH OTHER.
AND WE GOT BIGGER PROBLEMS THAN HIM.

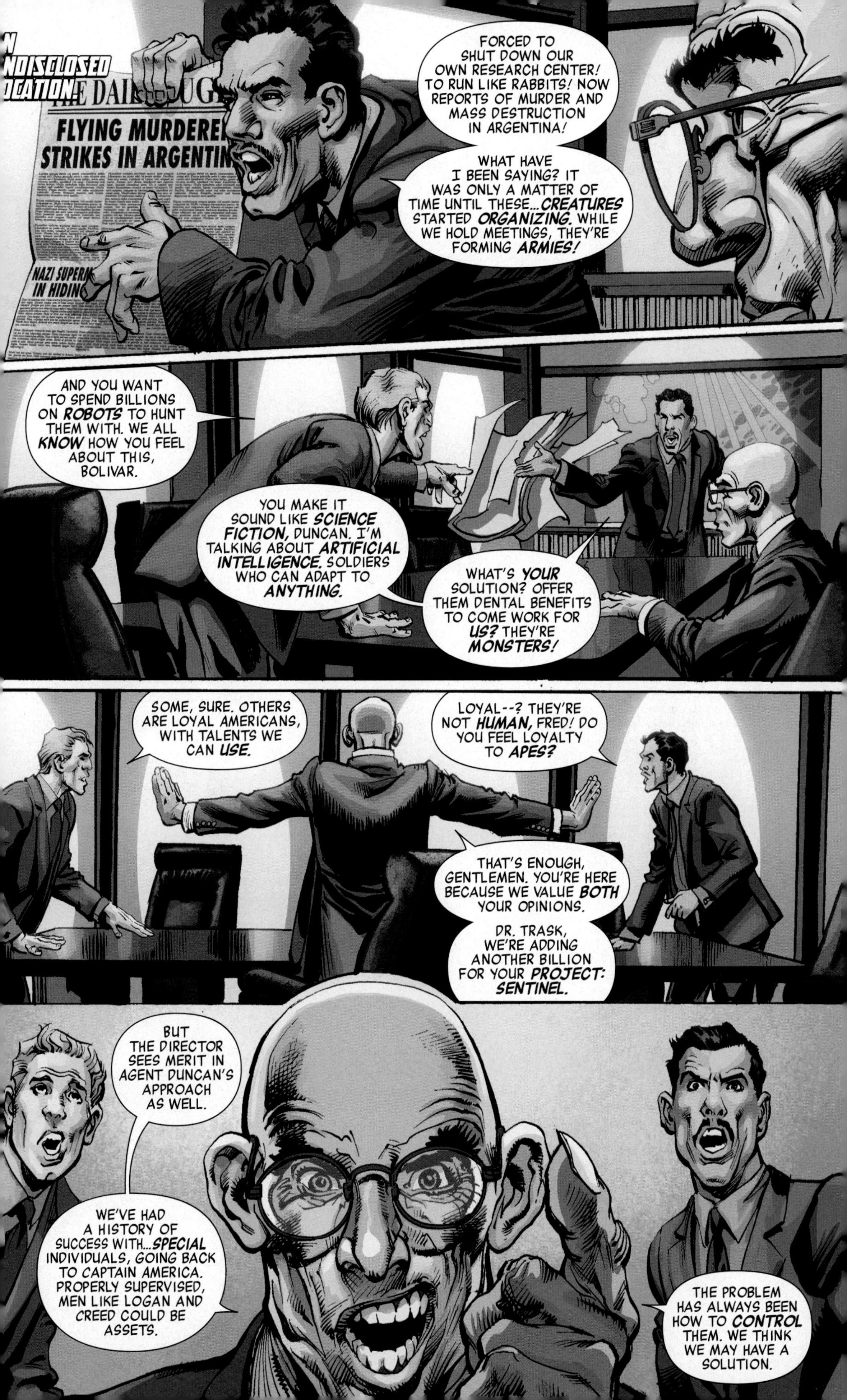
N
NDISCLOSED
OCATION.
FLYING MURDERE
STRIKES IN ARGENTIN
NAZI SUPERM
IN HIDING
FORCED TO SHUT DOWN OUR OWN RESEARCH CENTER! TO RUN LIKE RABBITS! NOW REPORTS OF MURDER AND MASS DESTRUCTION IN ARGENTINA!
WHAT HAVE I BEEN SAYING? IT WAS ONLY A MATTER OF TIME UNTIL THESE... CREATURES STARTED ORGANIZING. WHILE WE HOLD MEETINGS, THEY'RE FORMING ARMIES!
AND YOU WANT TO SPEND BILLIONS ON ROBOTS TO HUNT THEM WITH. WE ALL KNOW HOW YOU FEEL ABOUT THIS, BOLIVAR.
YOU MAKE IT SOUND LIKE SCIENCE FICTION, DUNCAN. I'M TALKING ABOUT ARTIFICIAL INTELLIGENCE. SOLDIERS WHO CAN ADAPT TO ANYTHING.
WHAT'S YOUR SOLUTION? OFFER THEM DENTAL BENEFITS TO COME WORK FOR US? THEY'RE MONSTERS!
SOME, SURE. OTHERS ARE LOYAL AMERICANS, WITH TALENTS WE CAN USE.
LOYAL--? THEY'RE NOT HUMAN, FRED! DO YOU FEEL LOYALTY TO APES?
THAT'S ENOUGH, GENTLEMEN. YOU'RE HERE BECAUSE WE VALUE BOTH YOUR OPINIONS.
DR. TRASK, WE'RE ADDING ANOTHER BILLION FOR YOUR PROJECT: SENTINEL.
BUT THE DIRECTOR SEES MERIT IN AGENT DUNCAN'S APPROACH AS WELL.
WE'VE HAD A HISTORY OF SUCCESS WITH... SPECIAL INDIVIDUALS, GOING BACK TO CAPTAIN AMERICA. PROPERLY SUPERVISED, MEN LIKE LOGAN AND CREED COULD BE ASSETS.
THE PROBLEM HAS ALWAYS BEEN HOW TO CONTROL THEM. WE THINK WE MAY HAVE A SOLUTION.

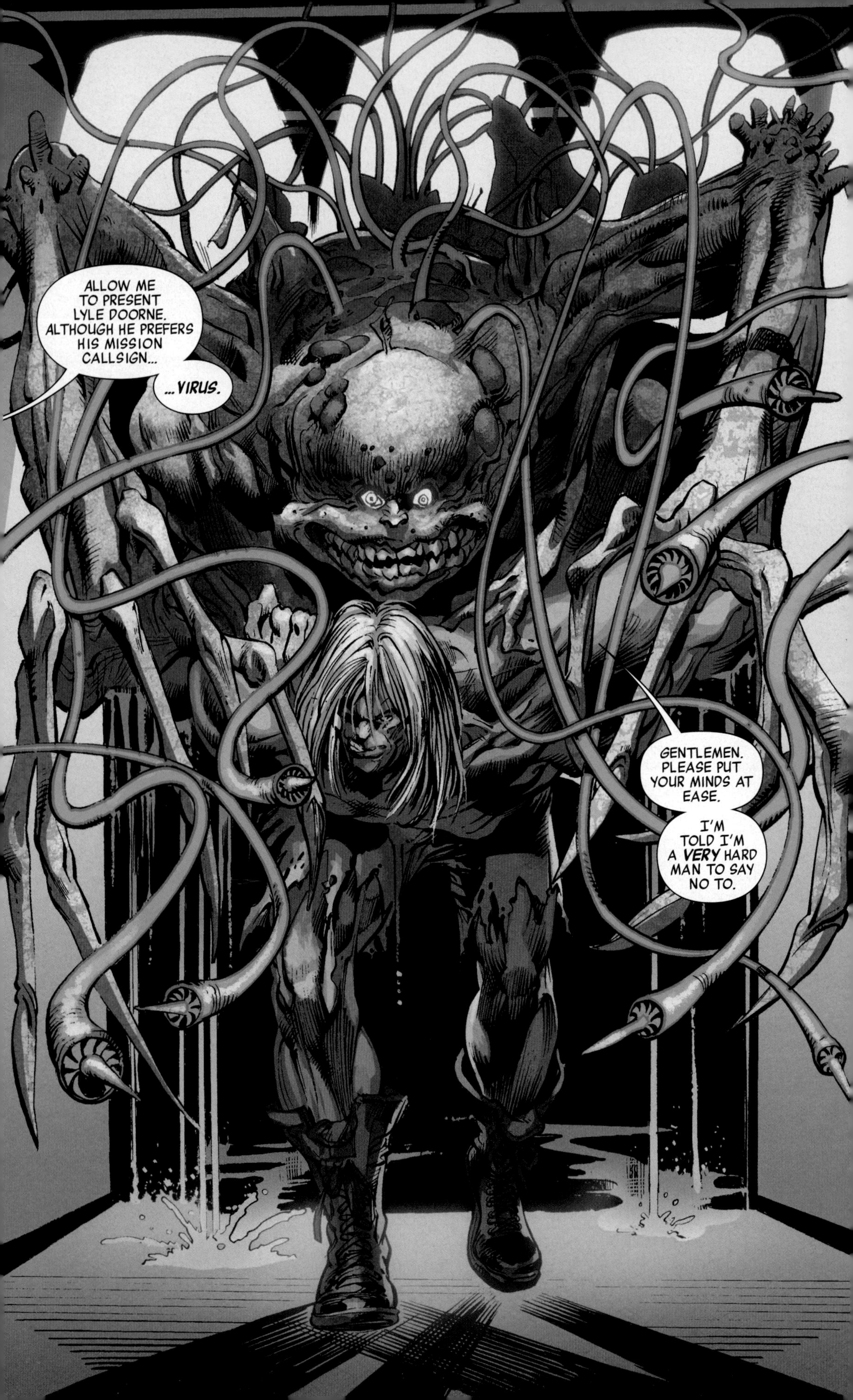

ALLOW ME TO PRESENT LYLE DOORNE. ALTHOUGH HE PREFERS HIS MISSION CALLSIGN...
...VIRUS.
GENTLEMEN. PLEASE PUT YOUR MINDS AT EASE.
I'M TOLD I'M A VERY HARD MAN TO SAY NO TO.

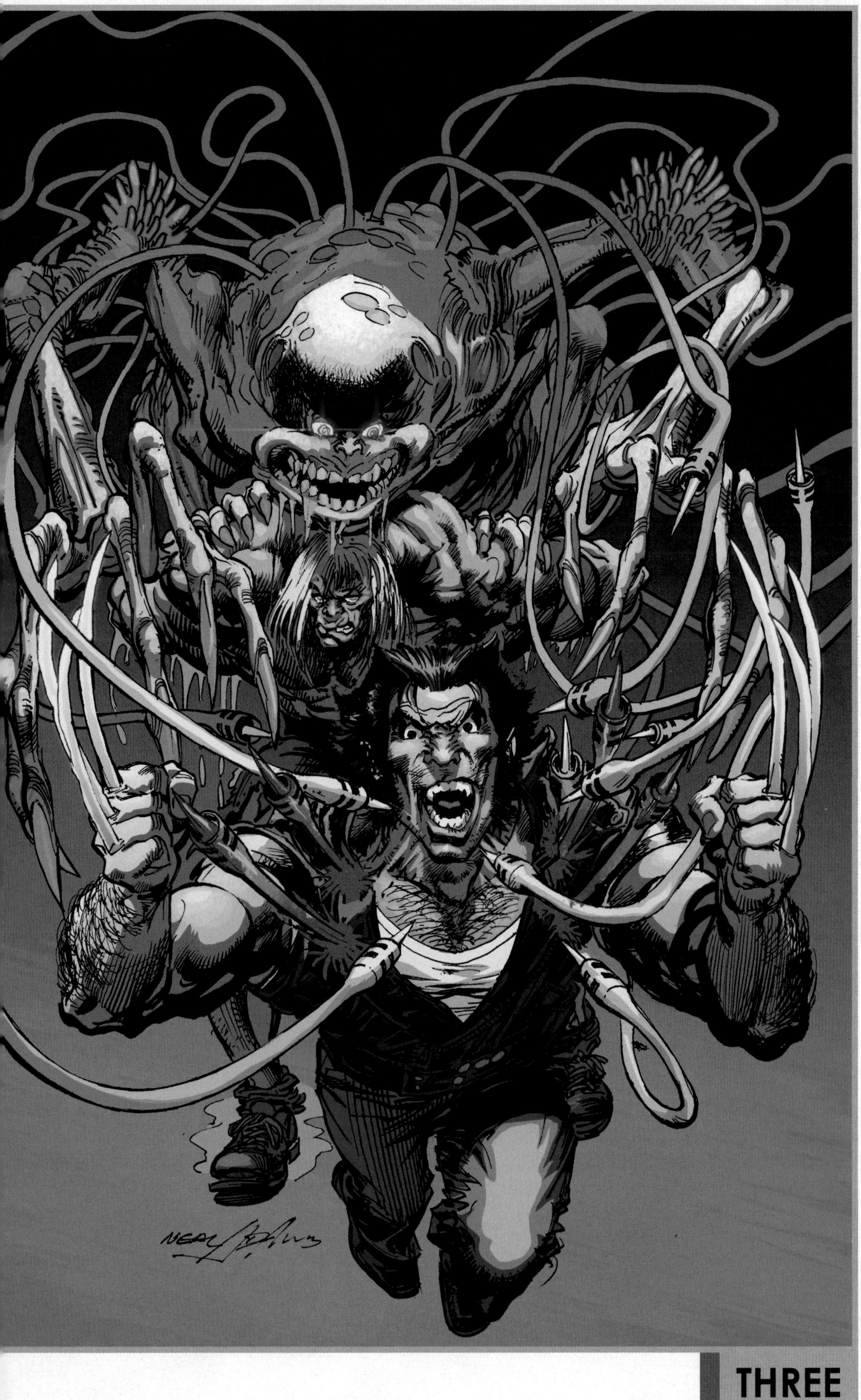

THREE

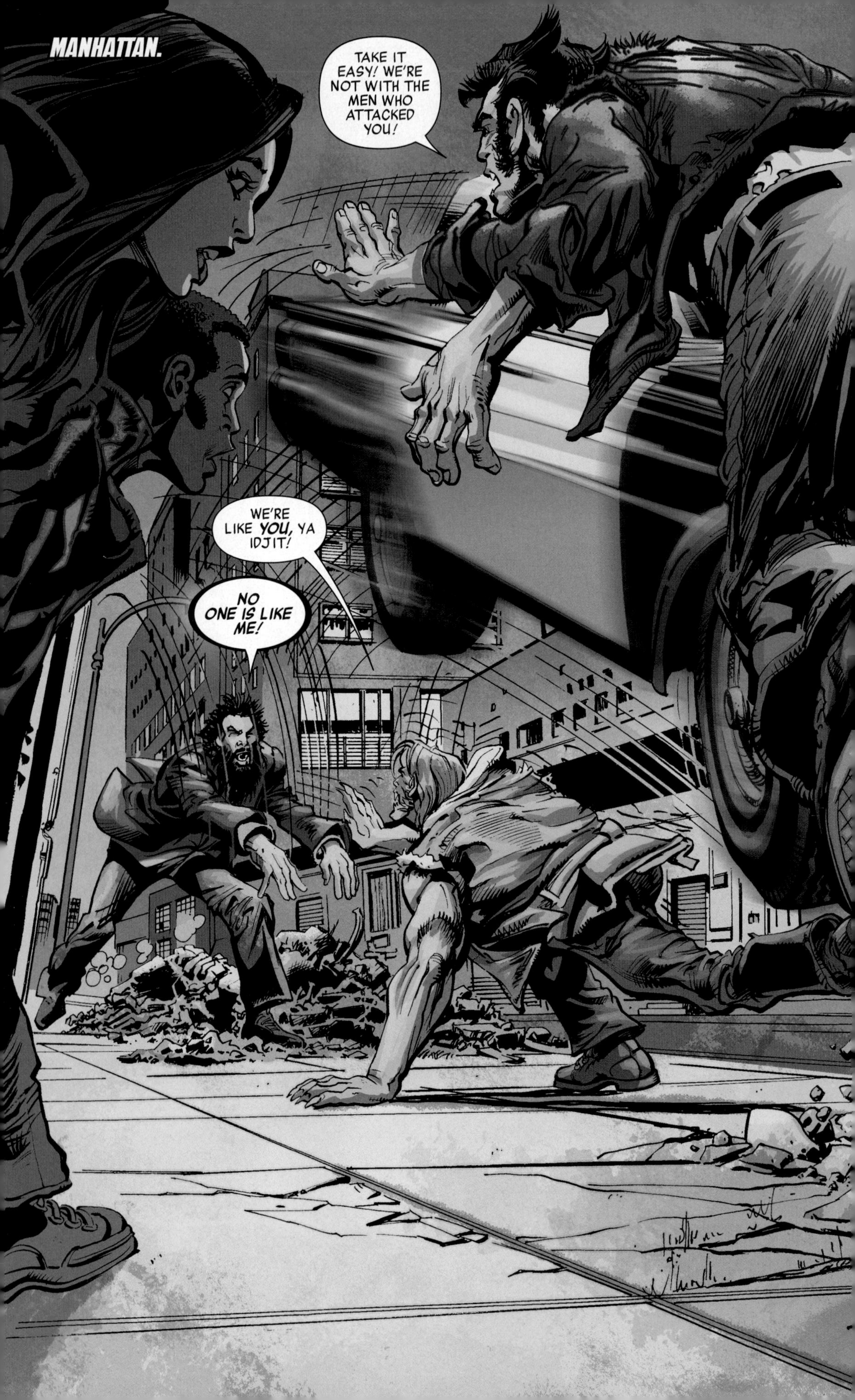
MANHATTAN.
TAKE IT EASY! WE'RE NOT WITH THE MEN WHO ATTACKED YOU!
WE'RE LIKE YOU, YA IDJIT!
NO ONE IS LIKE ME!

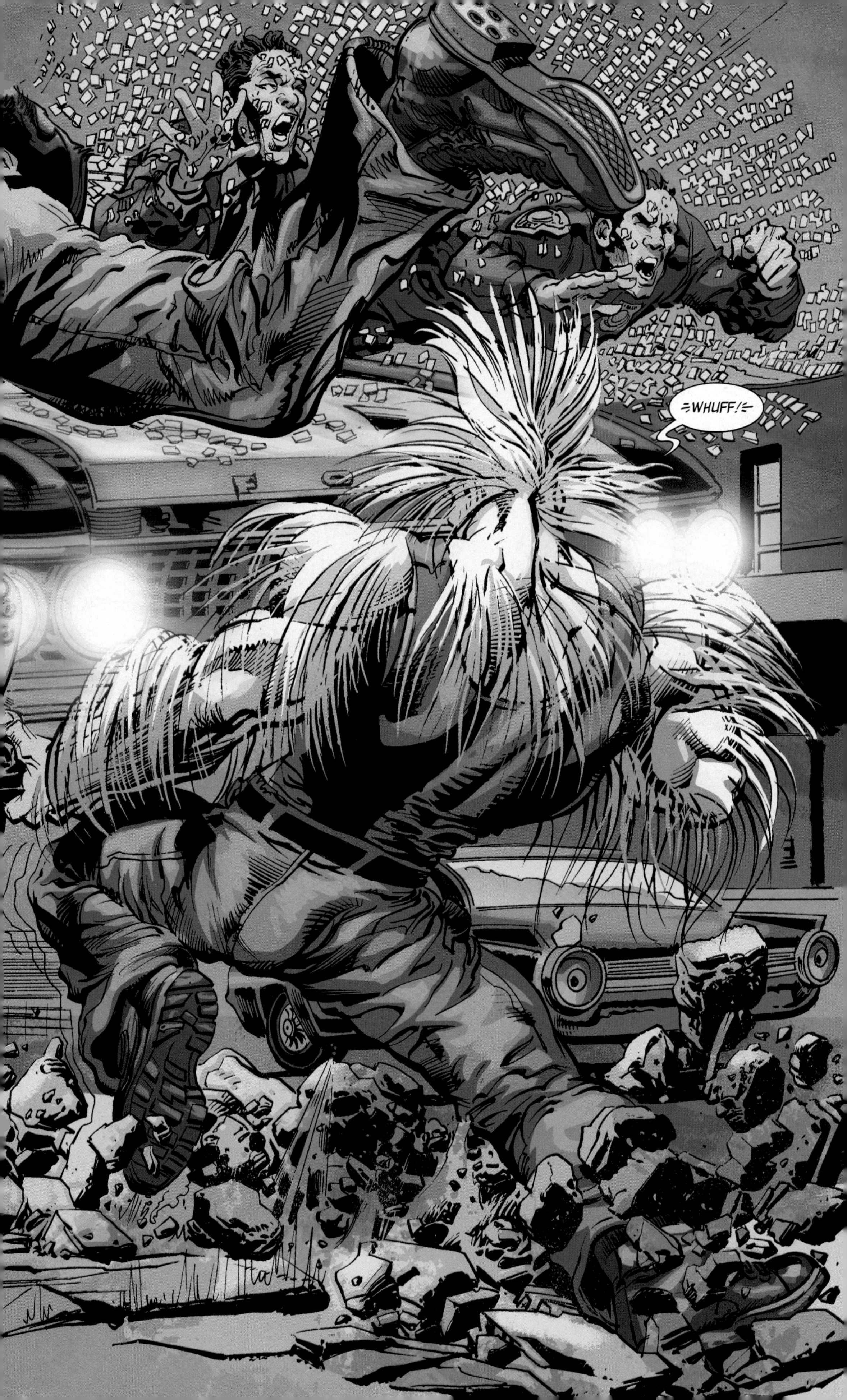
WHUFF!

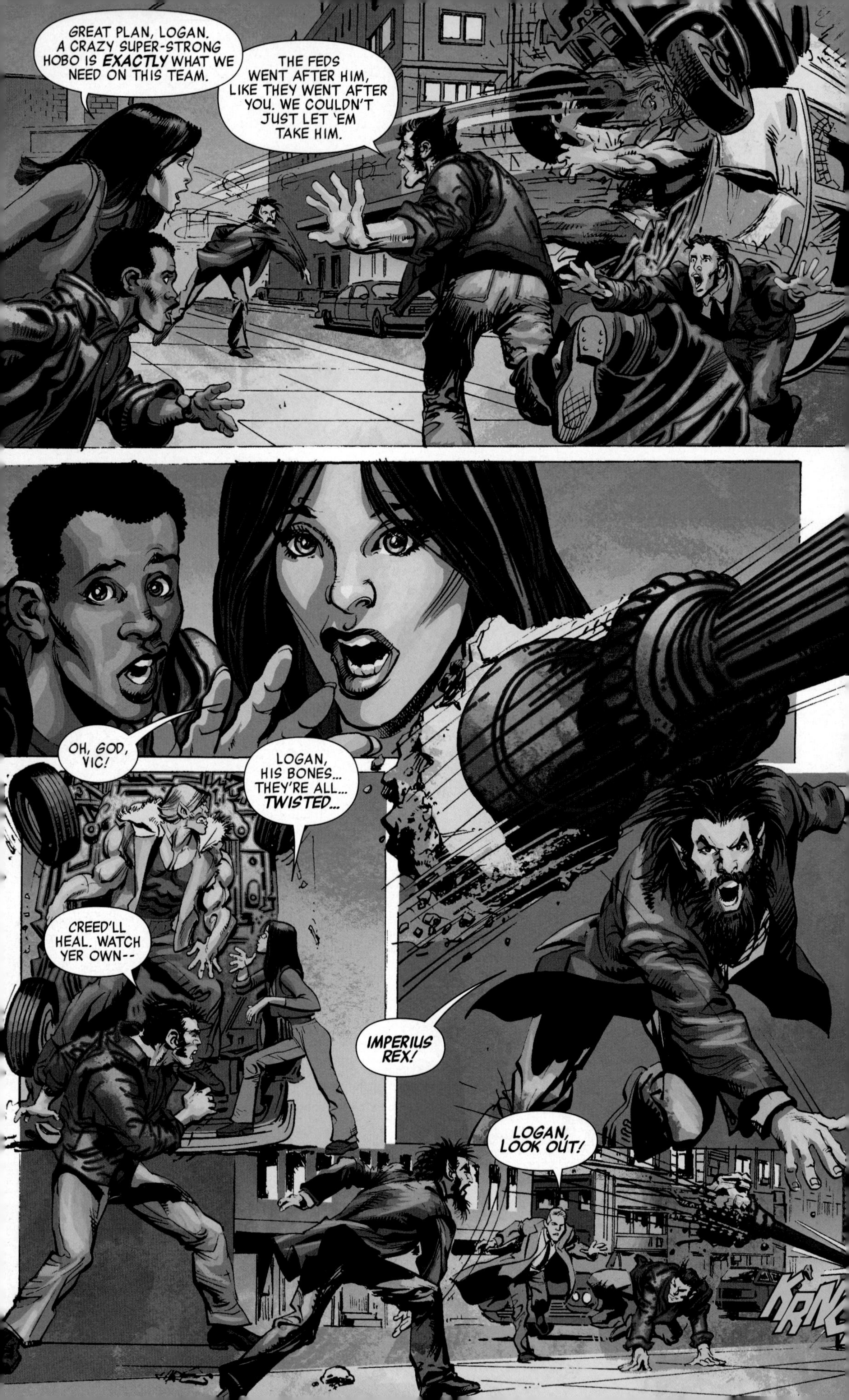
GREAT PLAN, LOGAN. A CRAZY SUPER-STRONG HOBO IS EXACTLY WHAT WE NEED ON THIS TEAM.
THE FEDS WENT AFTER HIM, LIKE THEY WENT AFTER YOU. WE COULDN'T JUST LET 'EM TAKE HIM.
OH, GOD, VIC!
LOGAN, HIS BONES... THEY'RE ALL... TWISTED...
CREED'LL HEAL. WATCH YER OWN--
IMPERIUS REX!
LOGAN, LOOK OUT!
KRN

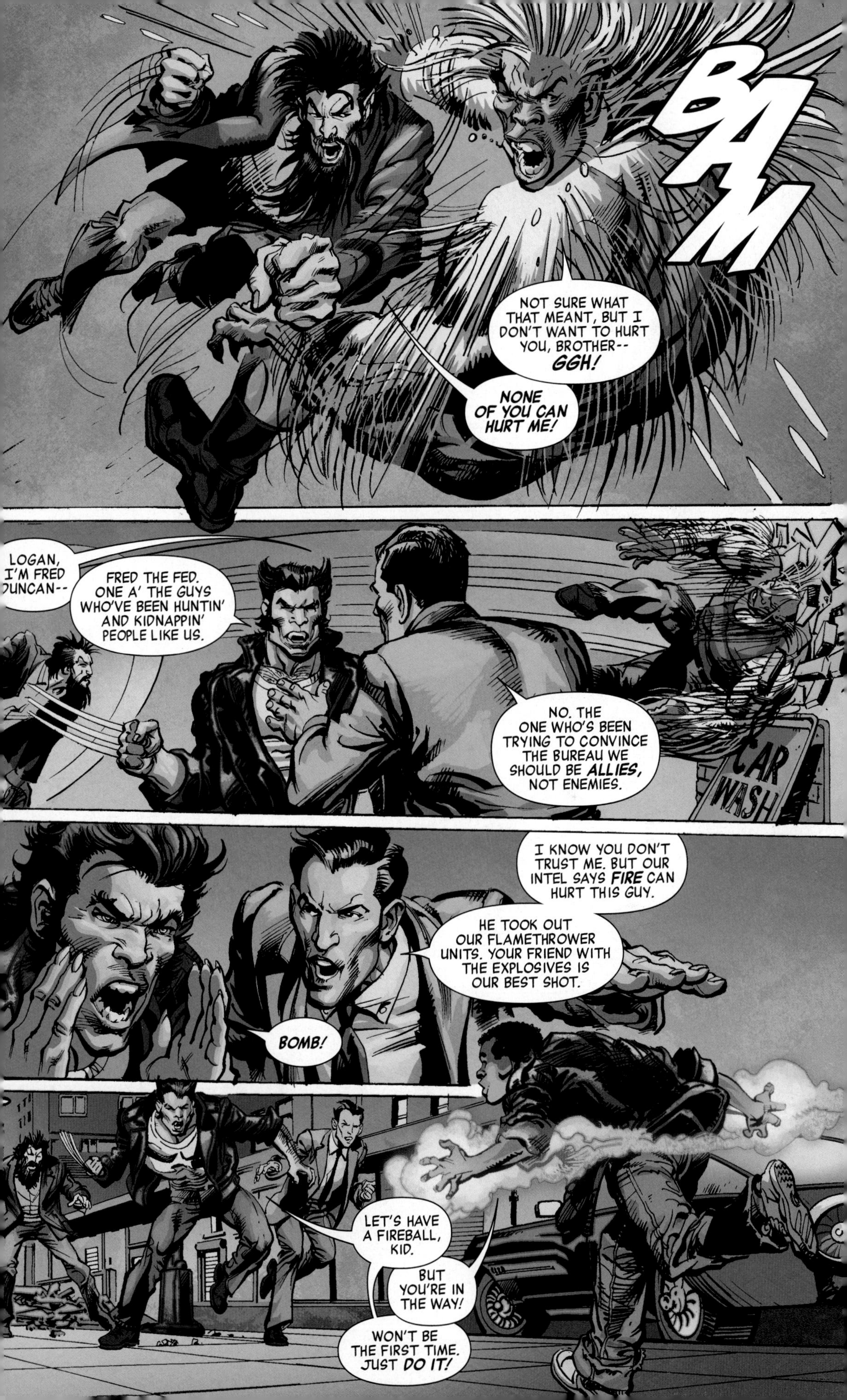
BAM
NOT SURE WHAT THAT MEANT, BUT I DON'T WANT TO HURT YOU, BROTHER-- GGH!
NONE OF YOU CAN HURT ME!
LOGAN, I'M FRED DUNCAN--
FRED THE FED. ONE A' THE GUYS WHO'VE BEEN HUNTIN' AND KIDNAPPIN' PEOPLE LIKE US.
NO. THE ONE WHO'S BEEN TRYING TO CONVINCE THE BUREAU WE SHOULD BE ALLIES, NOT ENEMIES.
CAR WASH
I KNOW YOU DON'T TRUST ME. BUT OUR INTEL SAYS FIRE CAN HURT THIS GUY.
HE TOOK OUT OUR FLAMETHROWER UNITS. YOUR FRIEND WITH THE EXPLOSIVES IS OUR BEST SHOT.
BOMB!
LET'S HAVE A FIREBALL, KID.
BUT YOU'RE IN THE WAY!
WON'T BE THE FIRST TIME. JUST DO IT!

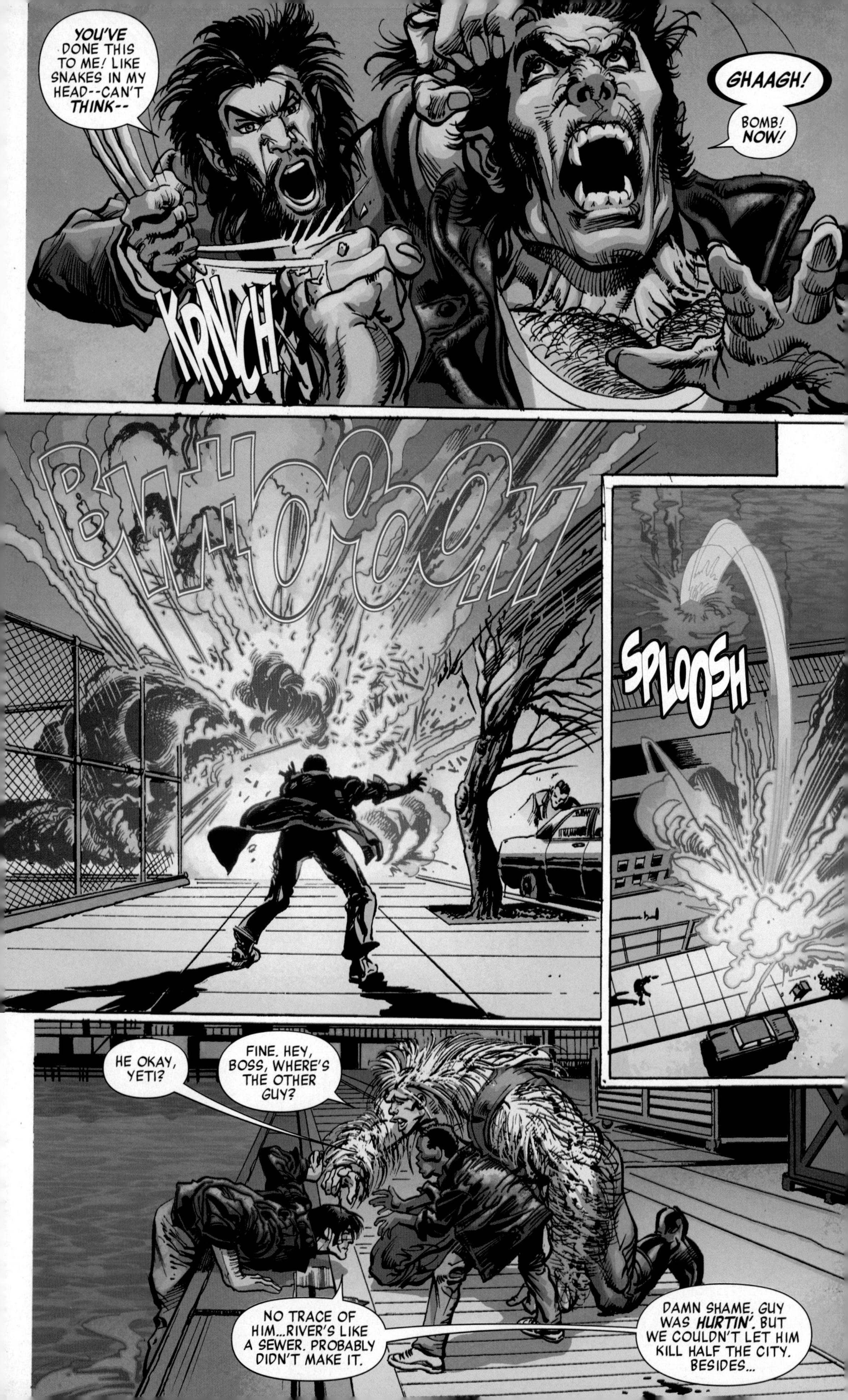
YOU'VE DONE THIS TO ME! LIKE SNAKES IN MY HEAD--CAN'T THINK--
GHAAGH!
BOMB! NOW!
KRNCH
BWHOOOOM
SPLOOSH
HE OKAY, YETI?
FINE. HEY, BOSS, WHERE'S THE OTHER GUY?
NO TRACE OF HIM...RIVER'S LIKE A SEWER. PROBABLY DIDN'T MAKE IT.
DAMN SHAME. GUY WAS HURTIN'. BUT WE COULDN'T LET HIM KILL HALF THE CITY. BESIDES...

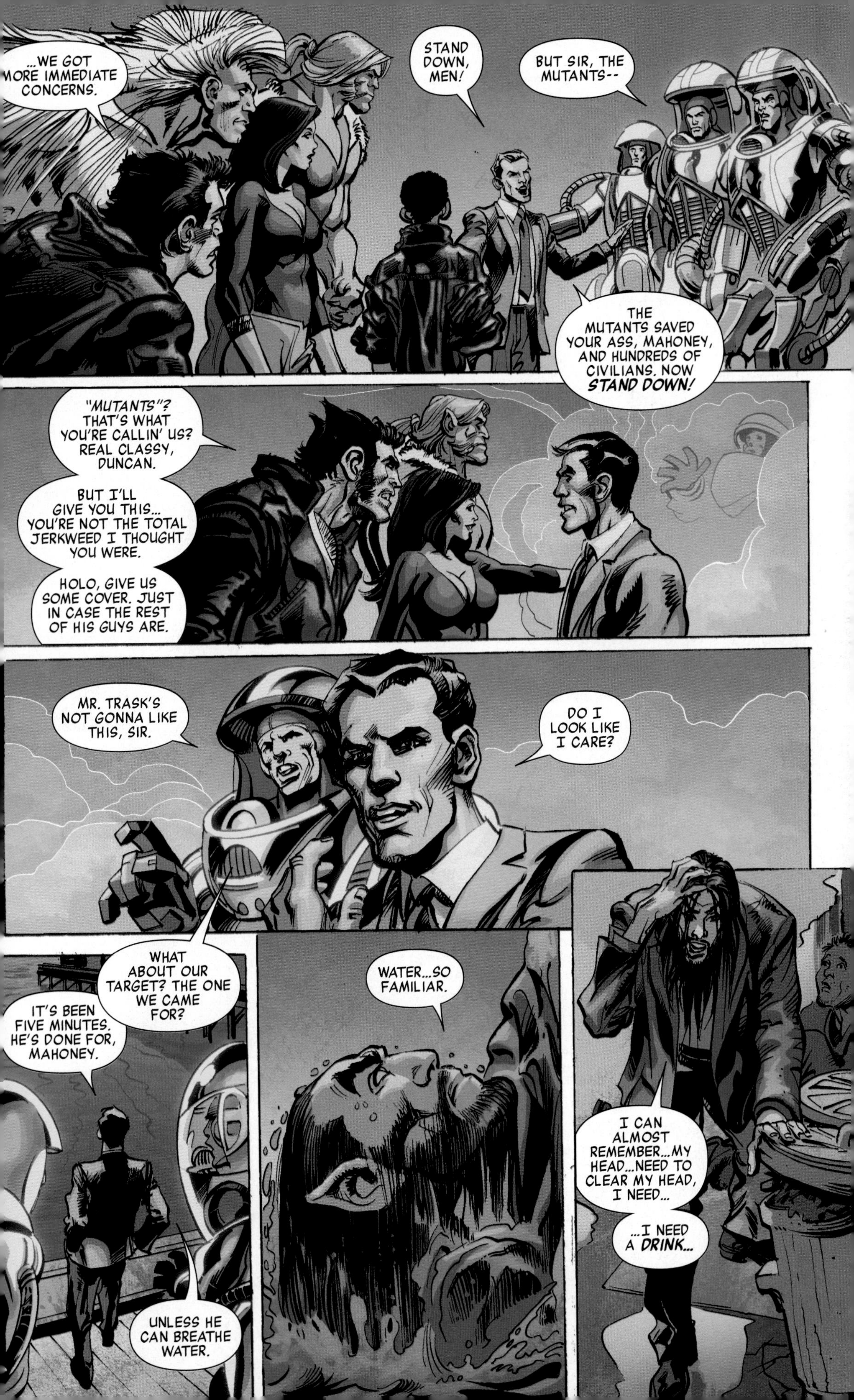
...WE GOT MORE IMMEDIATE CONCERNS.
STAND DOWN, MEN!
BUT SIR, THE MUTANTS--
THE MUTANTS SAVED YOUR ASS, MAHONEY, AND HUNDREDS OF CIVILIANS. NOW STAND DOWN!
"MUTANTS"? THAT'S WHAT YOU'RE CALLIN' US? REAL CLASSY, DUNCAN.
BUT I'LL GIVE YOU THIS... YOU'RE NOT THE TOTAL JERKWEED I THOUGHT YOU WERE.
HOLO, GIVE US SOME COVER. JUST IN CASE THE REST OF HIS GUYS ARE.
MR. TRASK'S NOT GONNA LIKE THIS, SIR.
DO I LOOK LIKE I CARE?
WHAT ABOUT OUR TARGET? THE ONE WE CAME FOR?
IT'S BEEN FIVE MINUTES. HE'S DONE FOR, MAHONEY.
UNLESS HE CAN BREATHE WATER.
WATER...SO FAMILIAR.
I CAN ALMOST REMEMBER...MY HEAD...NEED TO CLEAR MY HEAD, I NEED...
...I NEED A DRINK...

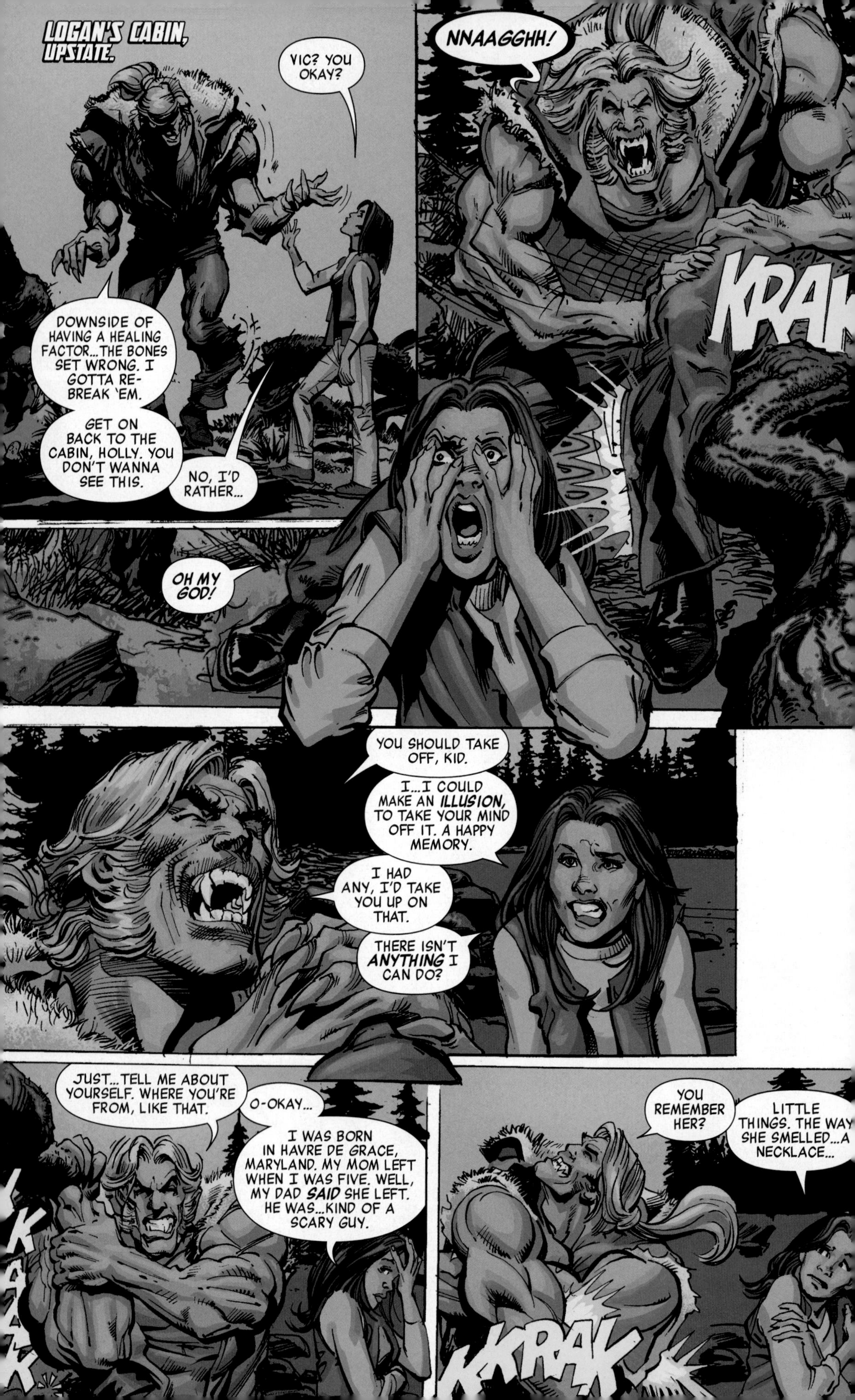
LOGAN'S CABIN, UPSTATE.
VIC? YOU OKAY?
DOWNSIDE OF HAVING A HEALING FACTOR...THE BONES SET WRONG. I GOTTA RE-BREAK 'EM.
GET ON BACK TO THE CABIN, HOLLY. YOU DON'T WANNA SEE THIS.
NO, I'D RATHER...
NNAAGGHH!
KRAK
OH MY GOD!
YOU SHOULD TAKE OFF, KID.
I...I COULD MAKE AN ILLUSION, TO TAKE YOUR MIND OFF IT. A HAPPY MEMORY.
I HAD ANY, I'D TAKE YOU UP ON THAT.
THERE ISN'T ANYTHING I CAN DO?
JUST...TELL ME ABOUT YOURSELF. WHERE YOU'RE FROM, LIKE THAT.
O-OKAY...
I WAS BORN IN HAVRE DE GRACE, MARYLAND. MY MOM LEFT WHEN I WAS FIVE. WELL, MY DAD SAID SHE LEFT. HE WAS...KIND OF A SCARY GUY.
KRAK
YOU REMEMBER HER?
LITTLE THINGS. THE WAY SHE SMELLED...A NECKLACE...
KKRAK

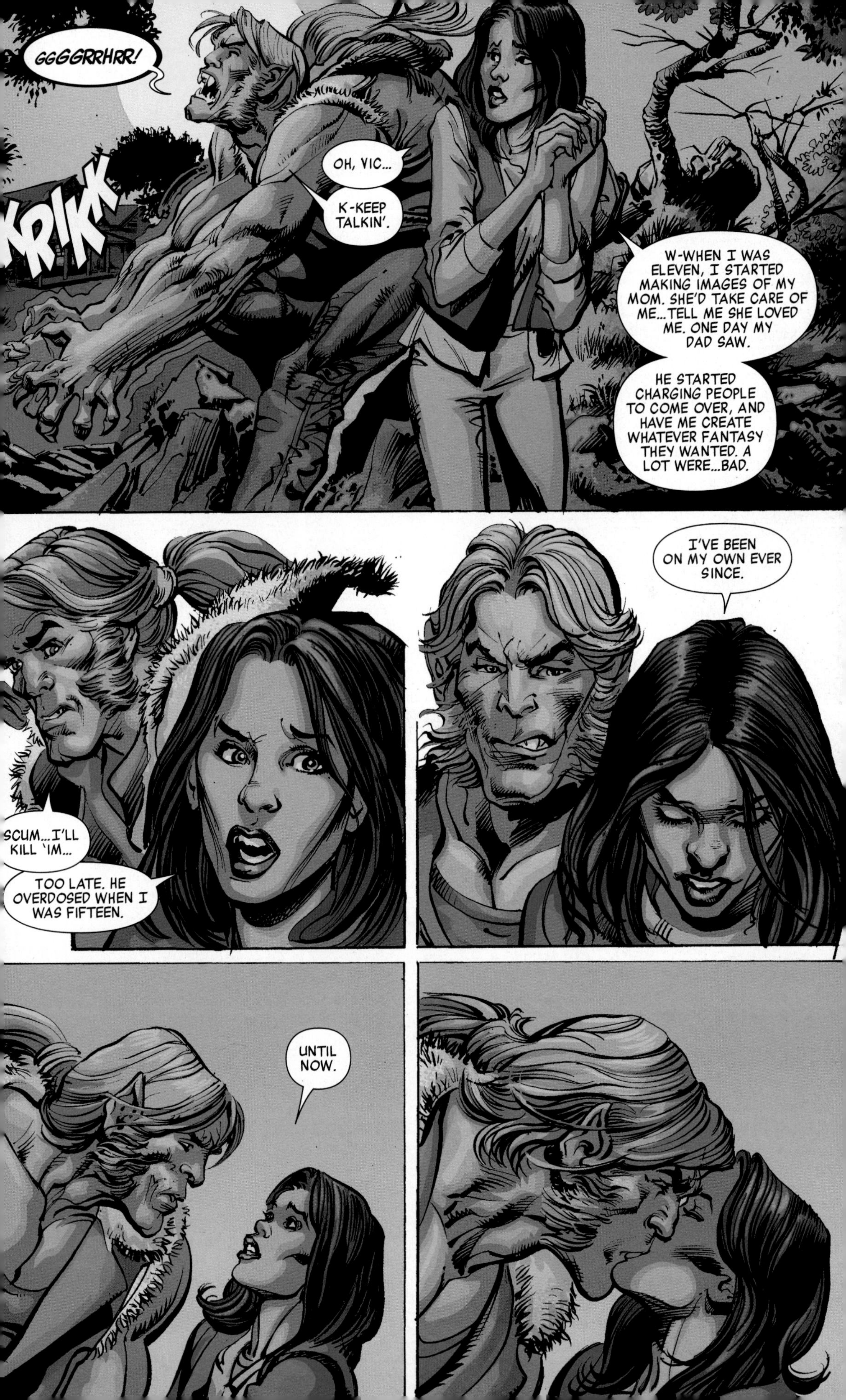
GGGGRRHRR!
KRIKK
OH, VIC...
K-KEEP TALKIN'.
W-WHEN I WAS ELEVEN, I STARTED MAKING IMAGES OF MY MOM. SHE'D TAKE CARE OF ME...TELL ME SHE LOVED ME. ONE DAY MY DAD SAW.
HE STARTED CHARGING PEOPLE TO COME OVER, AND HAVE ME CREATE WHATEVER FANTASY THEY WANTED. A LOT WERE...BAD.
SCUM...I'LL KILL 'IM...
TOO LATE. HE OVERDOSED WHEN I WAS FIFTEEN.
I'VE BEEN ON MY OWN EVER SINCE.
UNTIL NOW.

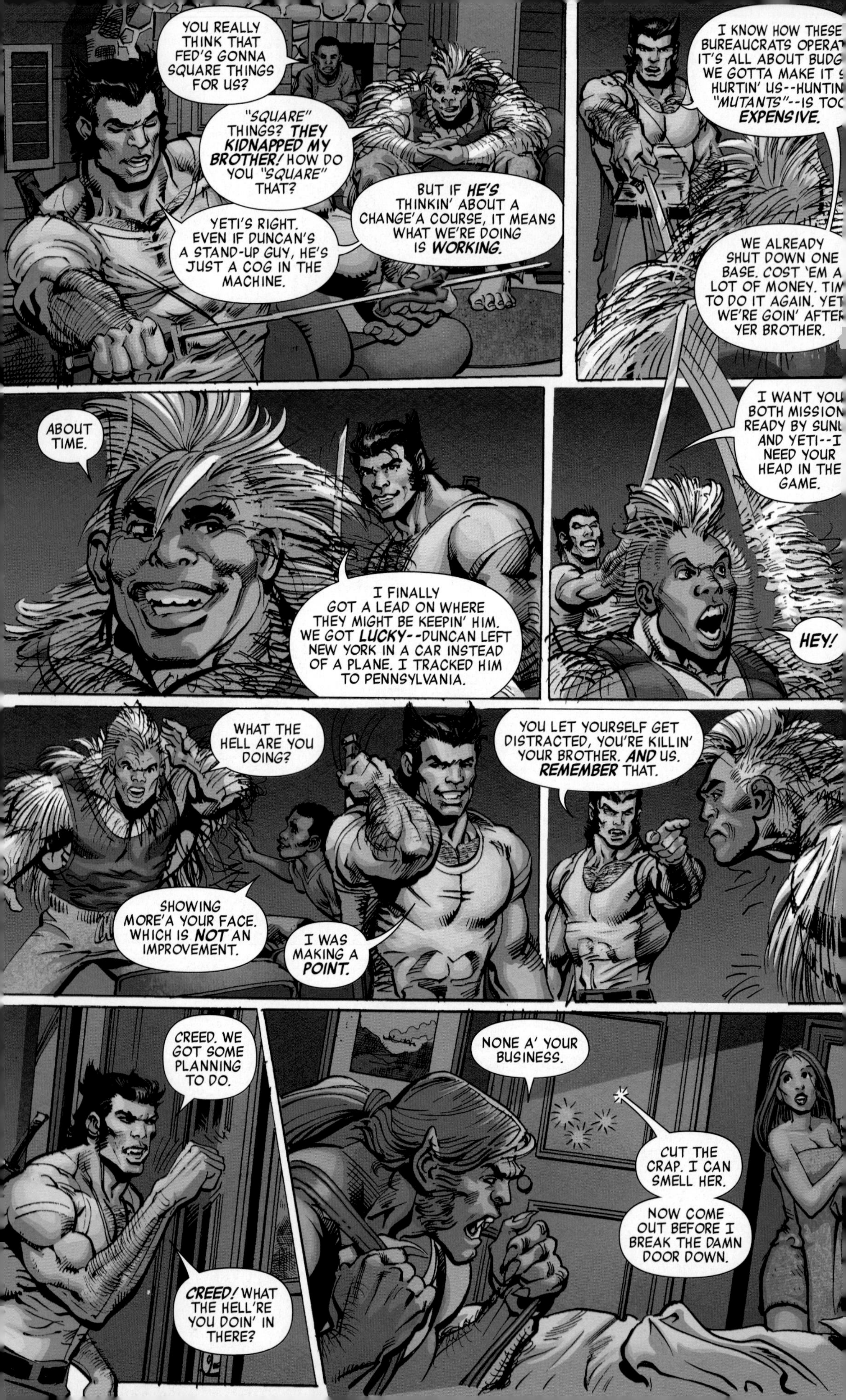
YOU REALLY THINK THAT FED'S GONNA SQUARE THINGS FOR US?
"SQUARE" THINGS? THEY KIDNAPPED MY BROTHER! HOW DO YOU "SQUARE" THAT?
YETI'S RIGHT. EVEN IF DUNCAN'S A STAND-UP GUY, HE'S JUST A COG IN THE MACHINE.
BUT IF HE'S THINKIN' ABOUT A CHANGE'A COURSE, IT MEANS WHAT WE'RE DOING IS WORKING.
I KNOW HOW THESE BUREAUCRATS OPERAT IT'S ALL ABOUT BUDG WE GOTTA MAKE IT S HURTIN' US--HUNTIN "MUTANTS"--IS TOO EXPENSIVE.
WE ALREADY SHUT DOWN ONE BASE. COST 'EM A LOT OF MONEY. TIM TO DO IT AGAIN. YET WE'RE GOIN' AFTER YER BROTHER.
ABOUT TIME.
I FINALLY GOT A LEAD ON WHERE THEY MIGHT BE KEEPIN' HIM. WE GOT LUCKY--DUNCAN LEFT NEW YORK IN A CAR INSTEAD OF A PLANE. I TRACKED HIM TO PENNSYLVANIA.
I WANT YOU BOTH MISSION READY BY SUNU AND YETI--I NEED YOUR HEAD IN THE GAME.
HEY!
WHAT THE HELL ARE YOU DOING?
SHOWING MORE'A YOUR FACE. WHICH IS NOT AN IMPROVEMENT.
I WAS MAKING A POINT.
YOU LET YOURSELF GET DISTRACTED, YOU'RE KILLIN' YOUR BROTHER. AND US. REMEMBER THAT.
CREED. WE GOT SOME PLANNING TO DO.
CREED! WHAT THE HELL'RE YOU DOIN' IN THERE?
NONE A' YOUR BUSINESS.
CUT THE CRAP. I CAN SMELL HER.
NOW COME OUT BEFORE I BREAK THE DAMN DOOR DOWN.

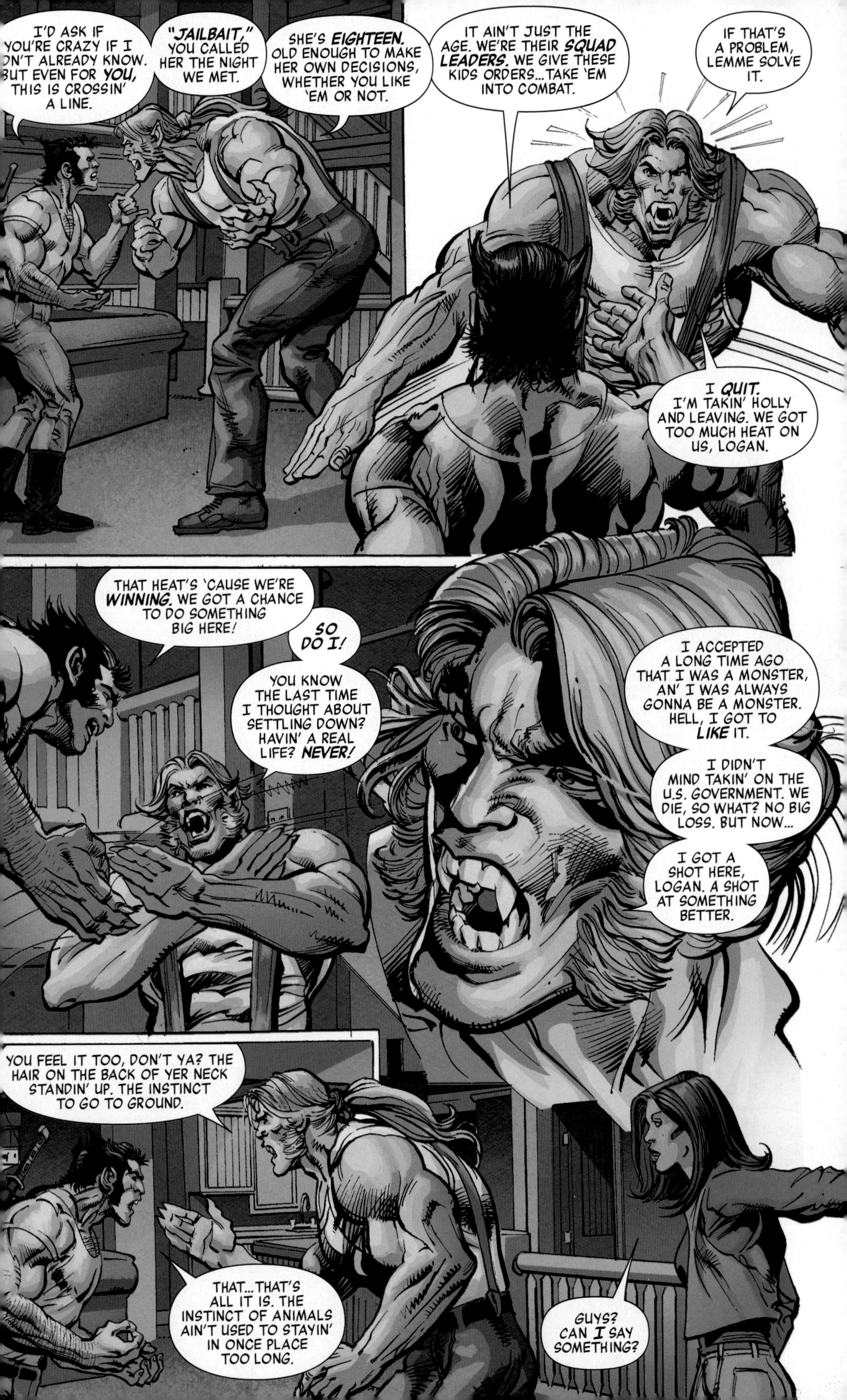
I'D ASK IF YOU'RE CRAZY IF I ON'T ALREADY KNOW. UT EVEN FOR YOU, THIS IS CROSSIN' A LINE.
"JAILBAIT," YOU CALLED HER THE NIGHT WE MET.
SHE'S EIGHTEEN. OLD ENOUGH TO MAKE HER OWN DECISIONS, WHETHER YOU LIKE 'EM OR NOT.
IT AIN'T JUST THE AGE. WE'RE THEIR SQUAD LEADERS. WE GIVE THESE KIDS ORDERS...TAKE 'EM INTO COMBAT.
IF THAT'S A PROBLEM, LEMME SOLVE IT.
I QUIT. I'M TAKIN' HOLLY AND LEAVING. WE GOT TOO MUCH HEAT ON US, LOGAN.
THAT HEAT'S 'CAUSE WE'RE WINNING. WE GOT A CHANCE TO DO SOMETHING BIG HERE!
SO DO I!
YOU KNOW THE LAST TIME I THOUGHT ABOUT SETTLING DOWN? HAVIN' A REAL LIFE? NEVER!
I ACCEPTED A LONG TIME AGO THAT I WAS A MONSTER, AN' I WAS ALWAYS GONNA BE A MONSTER. HELL, I GOT TO LIKE IT.
I DIDN'T MIND TAKIN' ON THE U.S. GOVERNMENT. WE DIE, SO WHAT? NO BIG LOSS. BUT NOW...
I GOT A SHOT HERE, LOGAN. A SHOT AT SOMETHING BETTER.
YOU FEEL IT TOO, DON'T YA? THE HAIR ON THE BACK OF YER NECK STANDIN' UP. THE INSTINCT TO GO TO GROUND.
THAT...THAT'S ALL IT IS. THE INSTINCT OF ANIMALS AIN'T USED TO STAYIN' IN ONCE PLACE TOO LONG.
GUYS? CAN I SAY SOMETHING?

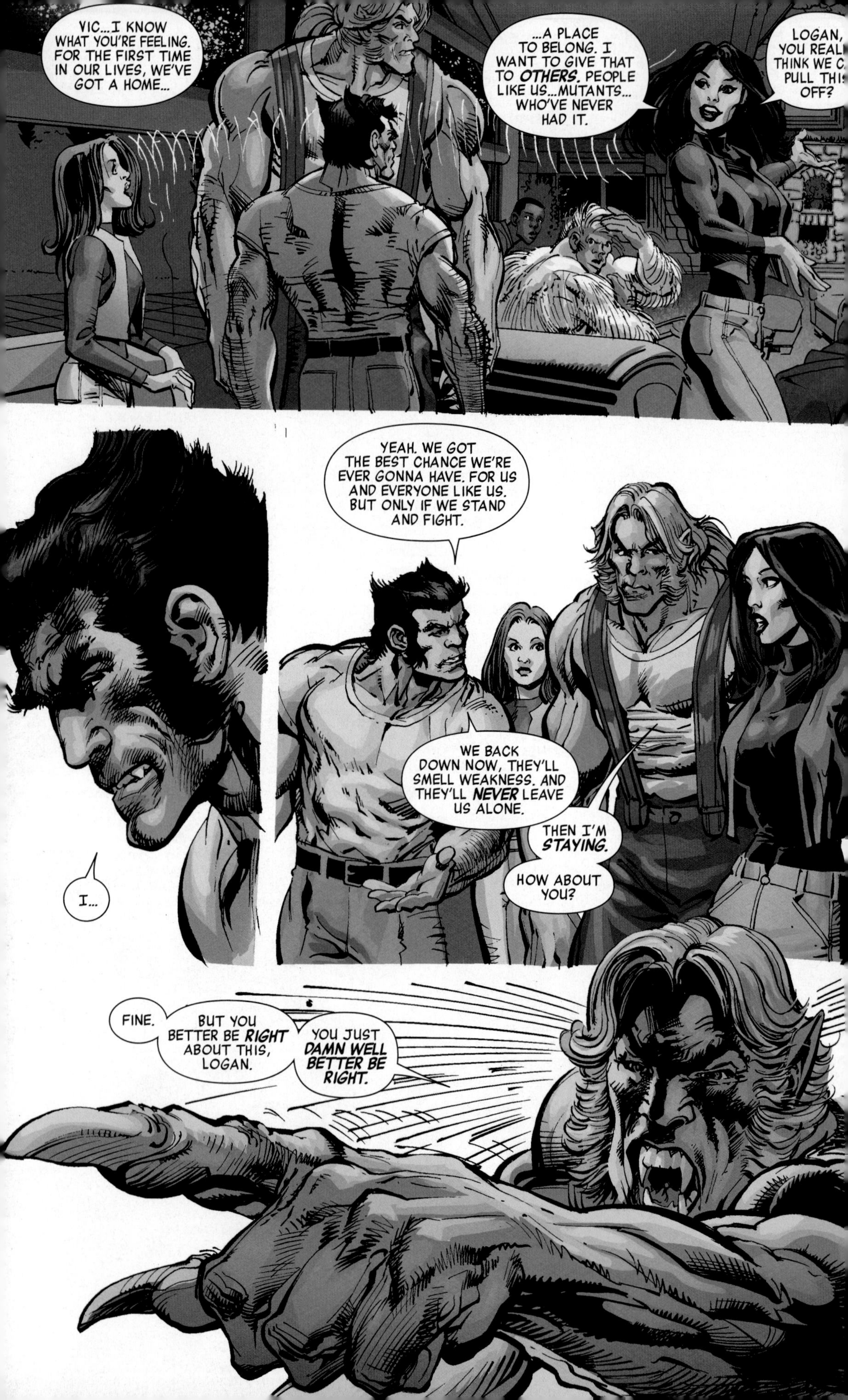
VIC...I KNOW WHAT YOU'RE FEELING. FOR THE FIRST TIME IN OUR LIVES, WE'VE GOT A HOME...
...A PLACE TO BELONG. I WANT TO GIVE THAT TO OTHERS. PEOPLE LIKE US...MUTANTS... WHO'VE NEVER HAD IT.
YEAH. WE GOT THE BEST CHANCE WE'RE EVER GONNA HAVE. FOR US AND EVERYONE LIKE US. BUT ONLY IF WE STAND AND FIGHT.
WE BACK DOWN NOW, THEY'LL SMELL WEAKNESS. AND THEY'LL NEVER LEAVE US ALONE.
THEN I'M STAYING.
HOW ABOUT YOU?
I...
FINE.
BUT YOU BETTER BE RIGHT ABOUT THIS, LOGAN.
YOU JUST DAMN WELL BETTER BE RIGHT.

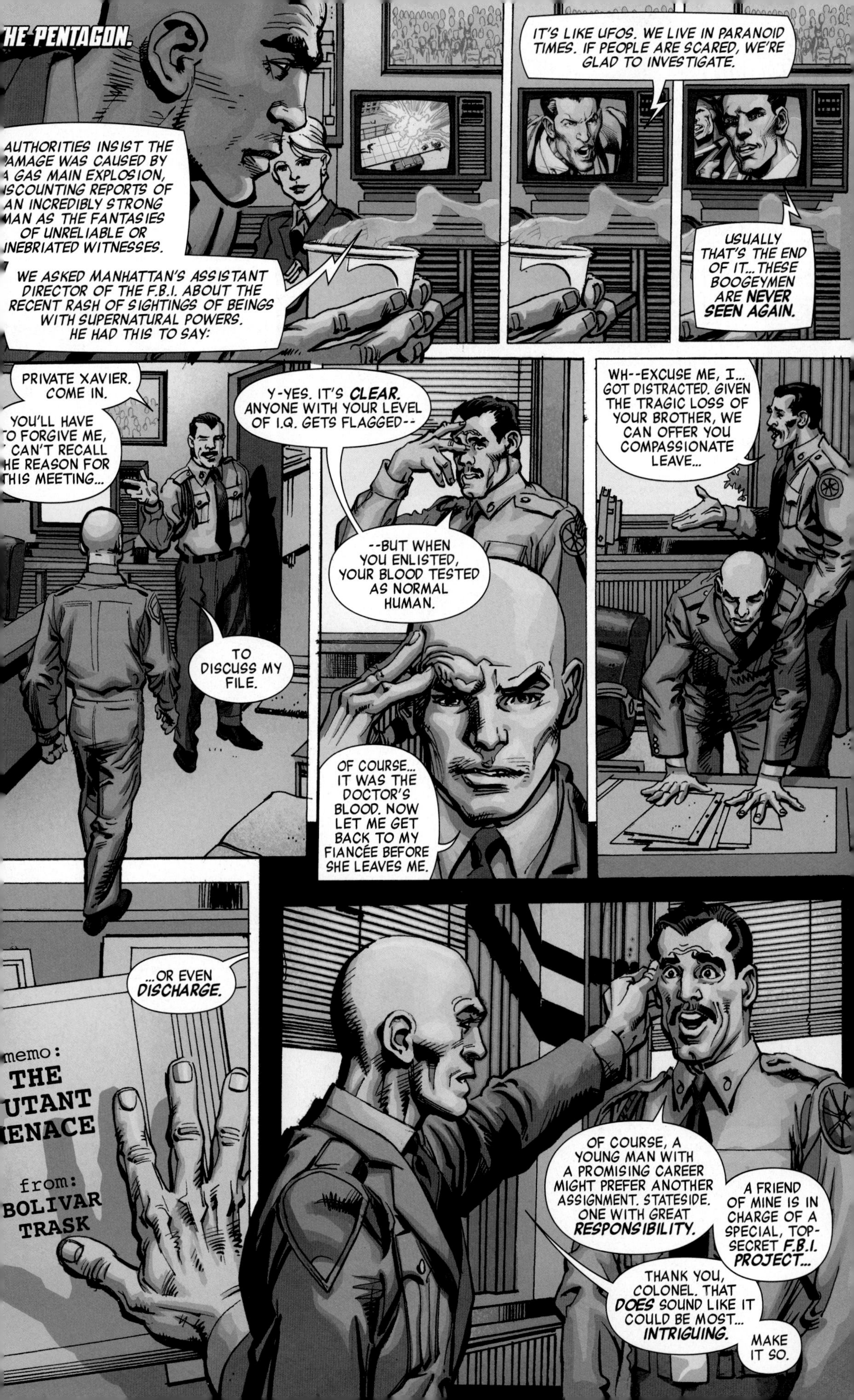

HE PENTAGON.
AUTHORITIES INSIST THE AMAGE WAS CAUSED BY A GAS MAIN EXPLOSION, ISCOUNTING REPORTS OF AN INCREDIBLY STRONG MAN AS THE FANTASIES OF UNRELIABLE OR INEBRIATED WITNESSES.
WE ASKED MANHATTAN'S ASSISTANT DIRECTOR OF THE F.B.I. ABOUT THE RECENT RASH OF SIGHTINGS OF BEINGS WITH SUPERNATURAL POWERS. HE HAD THIS TO SAY:
IT'S LIKE UFOS. WE LIVE IN PARANOID TIMES. IF PEOPLE ARE SCARED, WE'RE GLAD TO INVESTIGATE.
USUALLY THAT'S THE END OF IT...THESE BOOGEYMEN ARE NEVER SEEN AGAIN.
PRIVATE XAVIER. COME IN.
YOU'LL HAVE TO FORGIVE ME, I CAN'T RECALL THE REASON FOR THIS MEETING...
TO DISCUSS MY FILE.
Y-YES. IT'S CLEAR. ANYONE WITH YOUR LEVEL OF I.Q. GETS FLAGGED--
--BUT WHEN YOU ENLISTED, YOUR BLOOD TESTED AS NORMAL HUMAN.
OF COURSE... IT WAS THE DOCTOR'S BLOOD. NOW LET ME GET BACK TO MY FIANCÉE BEFORE SHE LEAVES ME.
WH--EXCUSE ME, I... GOT DISTRACTED. GIVEN THE TRAGIC LOSS OF YOUR BROTHER, WE CAN OFFER YOU COMPASSIONATE LEAVE...
...OR EVEN DISCHARGE.
memo: THE UTANT ENACE
from: BOLIVAR TRASK
OF COURSE, A YOUNG MAN WITH A PROMISING CAREER MIGHT PREFER ANOTHER ASSIGNMENT. STATESIDE. ONE WITH GREAT RESPONSIBILITY.
A FRIEND OF MINE IS IN CHARGE OF A SPECIAL, TOP-SECRET F.B.I. PROJECT...
THANK YOU, COLONEL. THAT DOES SOUND LIKE IT COULD BE MOST... INTRIGUING.
MAKE IT SO.

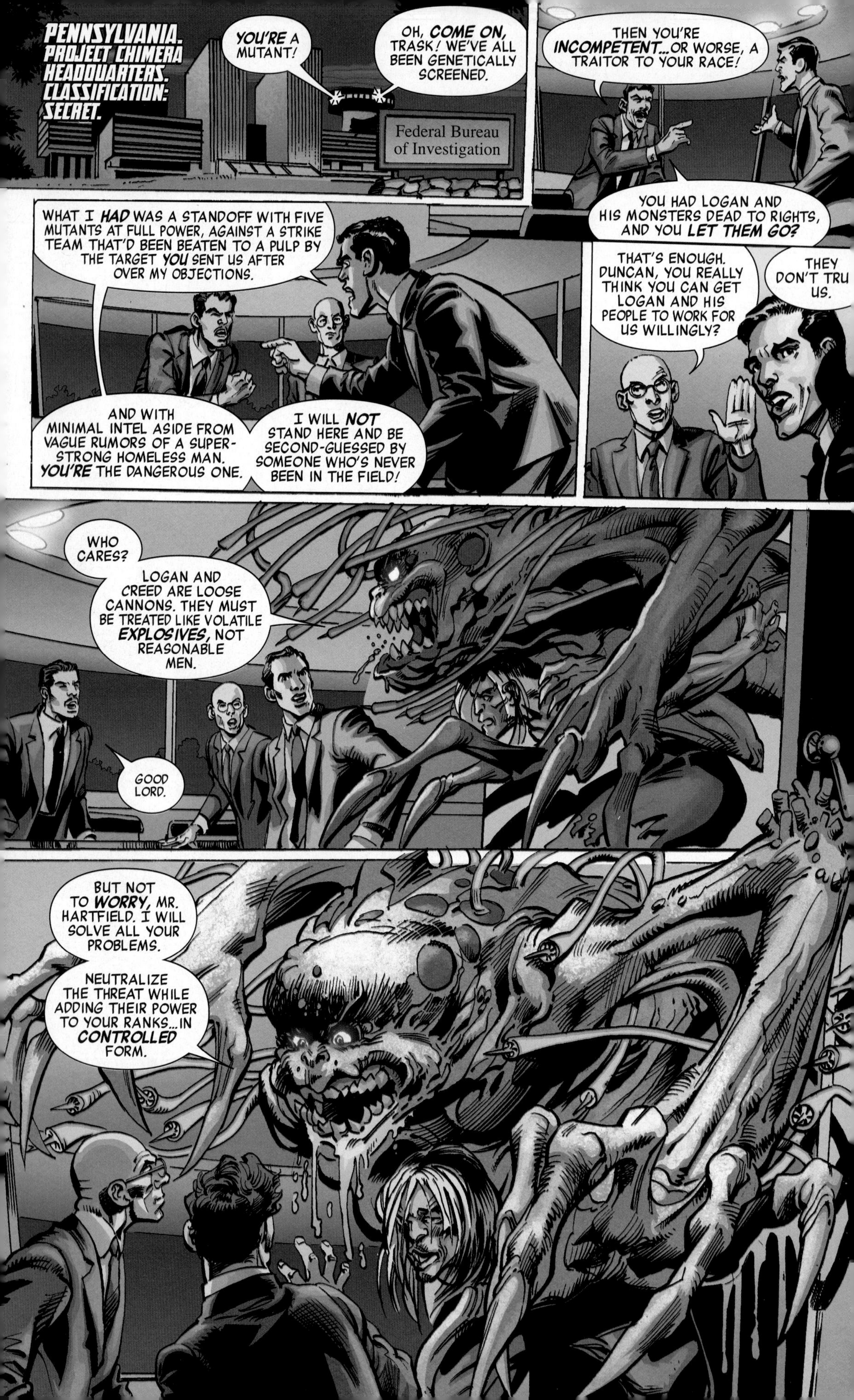
PENNSYLVANIA. PROJECT CHIMERA HEADQUARTERS. CLASSIFICATION: SECRET.
Federal Bureau of Investigation
YOU'RE A MUTANT!
OH, COME ON, TRASK! WE'VE ALL BEEN GENETICALLY SCREENED.
THEN YOU'RE INCOMPETENT...OR WORSE, A TRAITOR TO YOUR RACE!
YOU HAD LOGAN AND HIS MONSTERS DEAD TO RIGHTS, AND YOU LET THEM GO?
WHAT I HAD WAS A STANDOFF WITH FIVE MUTANTS AT FULL POWER, AGAINST A STRIKE TEAM THAT'D BEEN BEATEN TO A PULP BY THE TARGET YOU SENT US AFTER OVER MY OBJECTIONS.
AND WITH MINIMAL INTEL ASIDE FROM VAGUE RUMORS OF A SUPER-STRONG HOMELESS MAN. YOU'RE THE DANGEROUS ONE.
I WILL NOT STAND HERE AND BE SECOND-GUESSED BY SOMEONE WHO'S NEVER BEEN IN THE FIELD!
THAT'S ENOUGH. DUNCAN, YOU REALLY THINK YOU CAN GET LOGAN AND HIS PEOPLE TO WORK FOR US WILLINGLY?
THEY DON'T TRU US.
WHO CARES?
LOGAN AND CREED ARE LOOSE CANNONS. THEY MUST BE TREATED LIKE VOLATILE EXPLOSIVES, NOT REASONABLE MEN.
GOOD LORD.
BUT NOT TO WORRY, MR. HARTFIELD. I WILL SOLVE ALL YOUR PROBLEMS.
NEUTRALIZE THE THREAT WHILE ADDING THEIR POWER TO YOUR RANKS...IN CONTROLLED FORM.

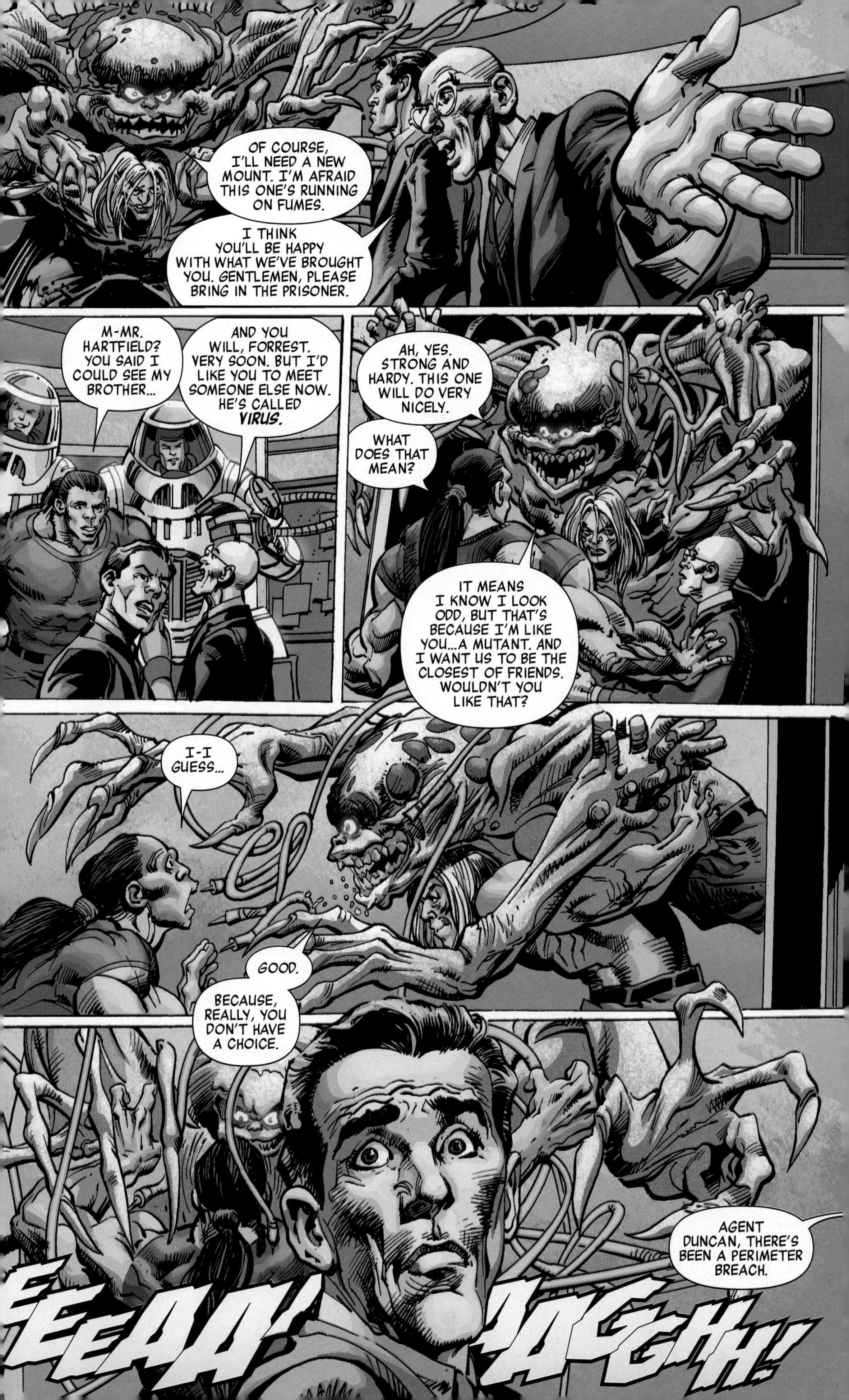
OF COURSE, I'LL NEED A NEW MOUNT. I'M AFRAID THIS ONE'S RUNNING ON FUMES.
I THINK YOU'LL BE HAPPY WITH WHAT WE'VE BROUGHT YOU. GENTLEMEN, PLEASE BRING IN THE PRISONER.
M-MR. HARTFIELD? YOU SAID I COULD SEE MY BROTHER...
AND YOU WILL, FORREST. VERY SOON. BUT I'D LIKE YOU TO MEET SOMEONE ELSE NOW. HE'S CALLED VIRUS.
AH, YES. STRONG AND HARDY. THIS ONE WILL DO VERY NICELY.
WHAT DOES THAT MEAN?
IT MEANS I KNOW I LOOK ODD, BUT THAT'S BECAUSE I'M LIKE YOU...A MUTANT. AND I WANT US TO BE THE CLOSEST OF FRIENDS. WOULDN'T YOU LIKE THAT?
I-I GUESS...
GOOD.
BECAUSE, REALLY, YOU DON'T HAVE A CHOICE.
AGENT DUNCAN, THERE'S BEEN A PERIMETER BREACH.

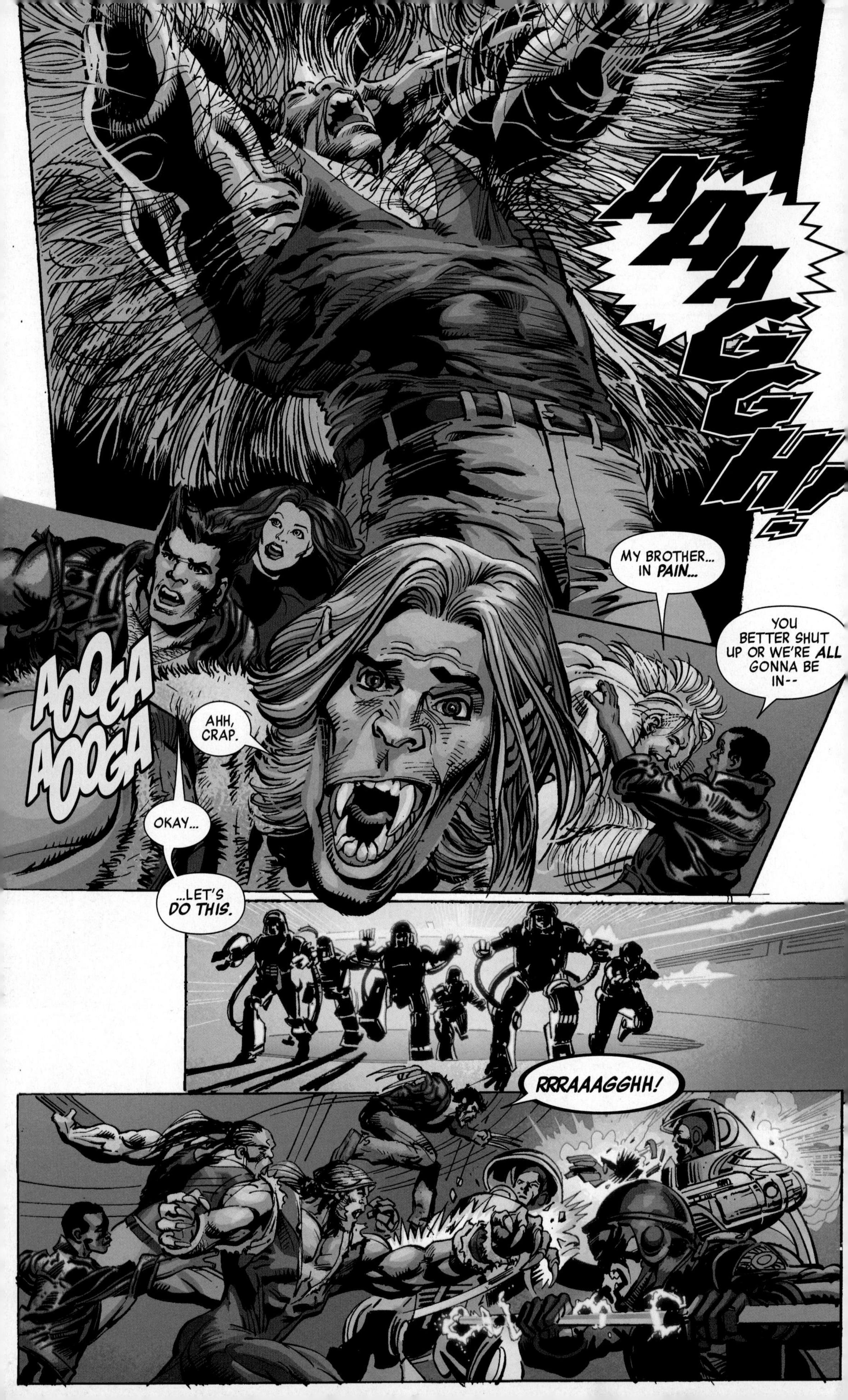
AAAGGH!
MY BROTHER... IN PAIN...
YOU BETTER SHUT UP OR WE'RE ALL GONNA BE IN--
AOOGA AOOGA
AHH, CRAP.
OKAY...
...LET'S DO THIS.
RRRAAAGGHH!

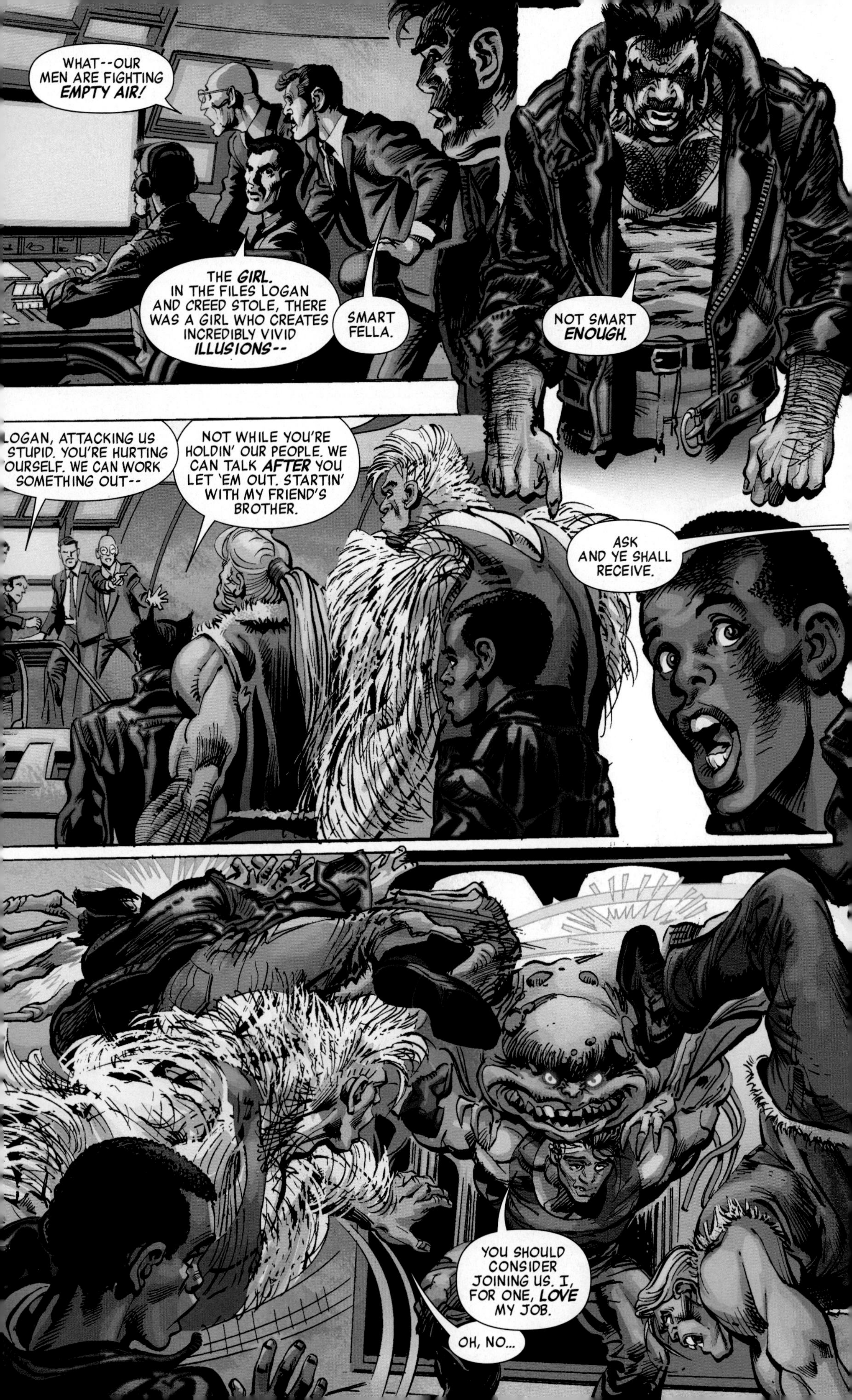
WHAT--OUR MEN ARE FIGHTING EMPTY AIR!
THE GIRL. IN THE FILES LOGAN AND CREED STOLE, THERE WAS A GIRL WHO CREATES INCREDIBLY VIVID ILLUSIONS--
SMART FELLA.
NOT SMART ENOUGH.
LOGAN, ATTACKING US STUPID. YOU'RE HURTING OURSELF. WE CAN WORK SOMETHING OUT--
NOT WHILE YOU'RE HOLDIN' OUR PEOPLE. WE CAN TALK AFTER YOU LET 'EM OUT. STARTIN' WITH MY FRIEND'S BROTHER.
ASK AND YE SHALL RECEIVE.
YOU SHOULD CONSIDER JOINING US. I, FOR ONE, LOVE MY JOB.
OH, NO...

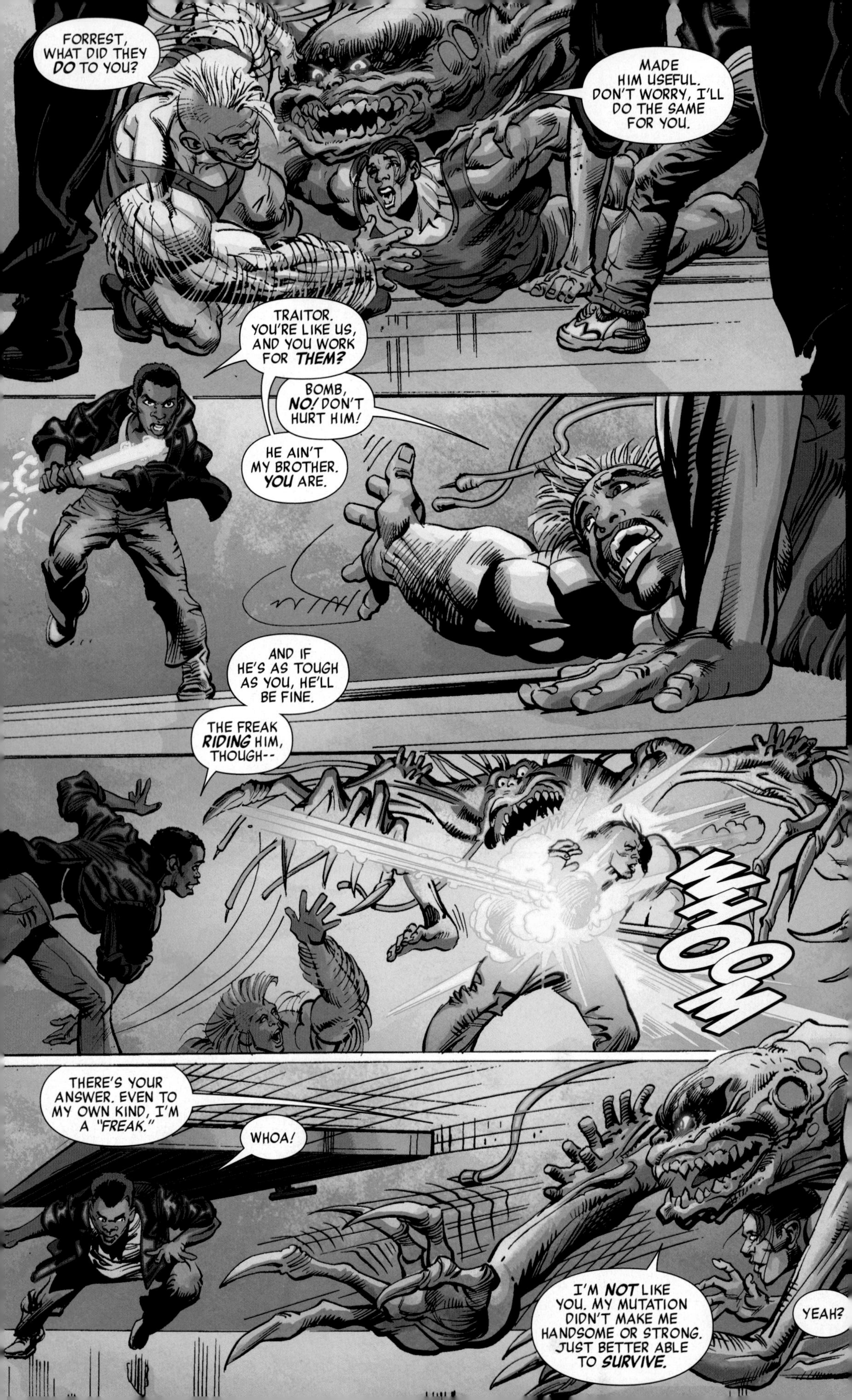
FORREST, WHAT DID THEY DO TO YOU?
MADE HIM USEFUL. DON'T WORRY, I'LL DO THE SAME FOR YOU.
TRAITOR. YOU'RE LIKE US, AND YOU WORK FOR THEM?
BOMB, NO! DON'T HURT HIM!
HE AIN'T MY BROTHER. YOU ARE.
AND IF HE'S AS TOUGH AS YOU, HE'LL BE FINE.
THE FREAK RIDING HIM, THOUGH--
WHOOM
THERE'S YOUR ANSWER. EVEN TO MY OWN KIND, I'M A "FREAK."
WHOA!
I'M NOT LIKE YOU. MY MUTATION DIDN'T MAKE ME HANDSOME OR STRONG. JUST BETTER ABLE TO SURVIVE.
YEAH?

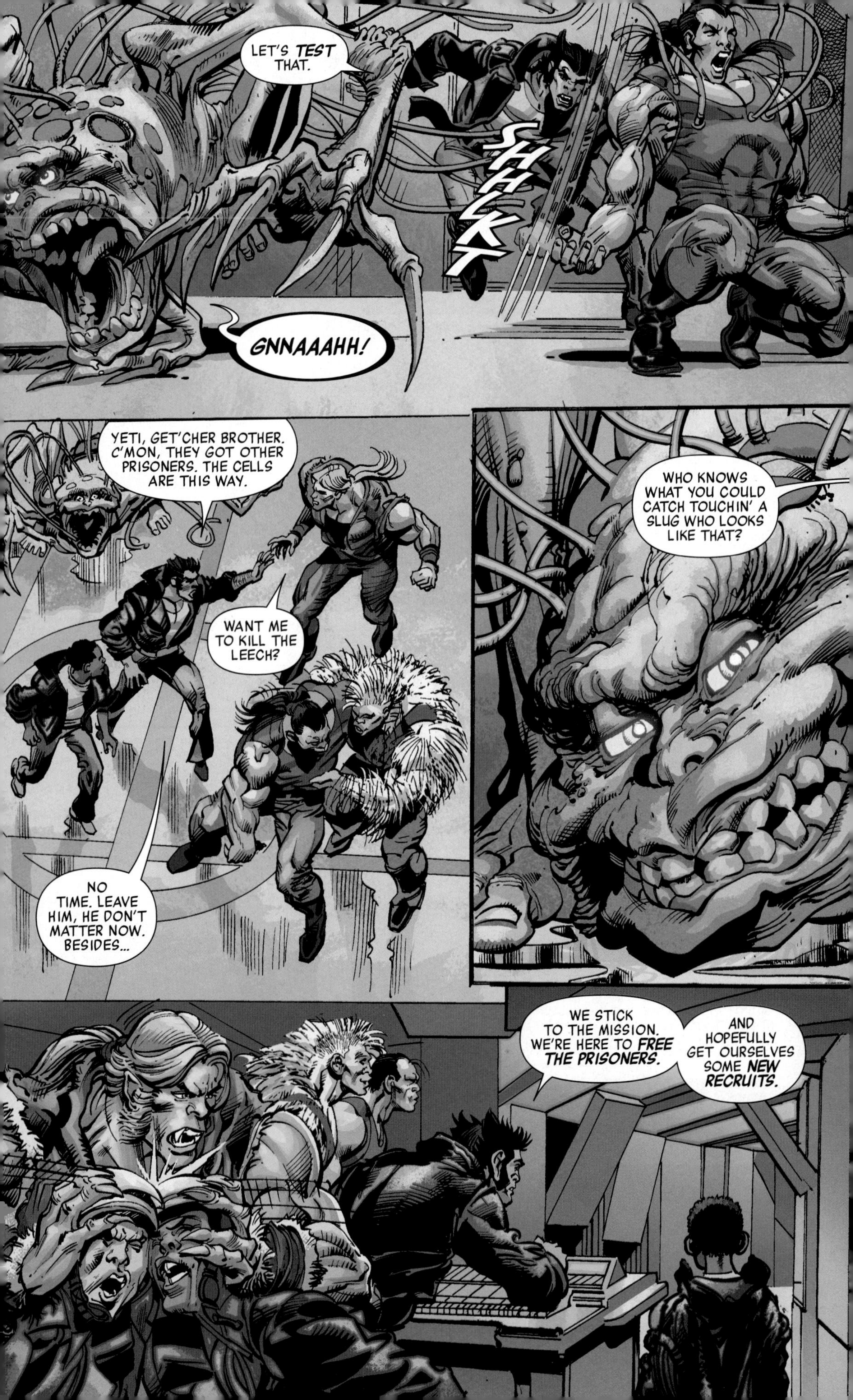
LET'S TEST THAT.
SHHLKT
GNNAAAHH!
YETI, GET'CHER BROTHER. C'MON, THEY GOT OTHER PRISONERS. THE CELLS ARE THIS WAY.
WANT ME TO KILL THE LEECH?
NO TIME. LEAVE HIM, HE DON'T MATTER NOW. BESIDES...
WHO KNOWS WHAT YOU COULD CATCH TOUCHIN' A SLUG WHO LOOKS LIKE THAT?
WE STICK TO THE MISSION. WE'RE HERE TO FREE THE PRISONERS.
AND HOPEFULLY GET OURSELVES SOME NEW RECRUITS.

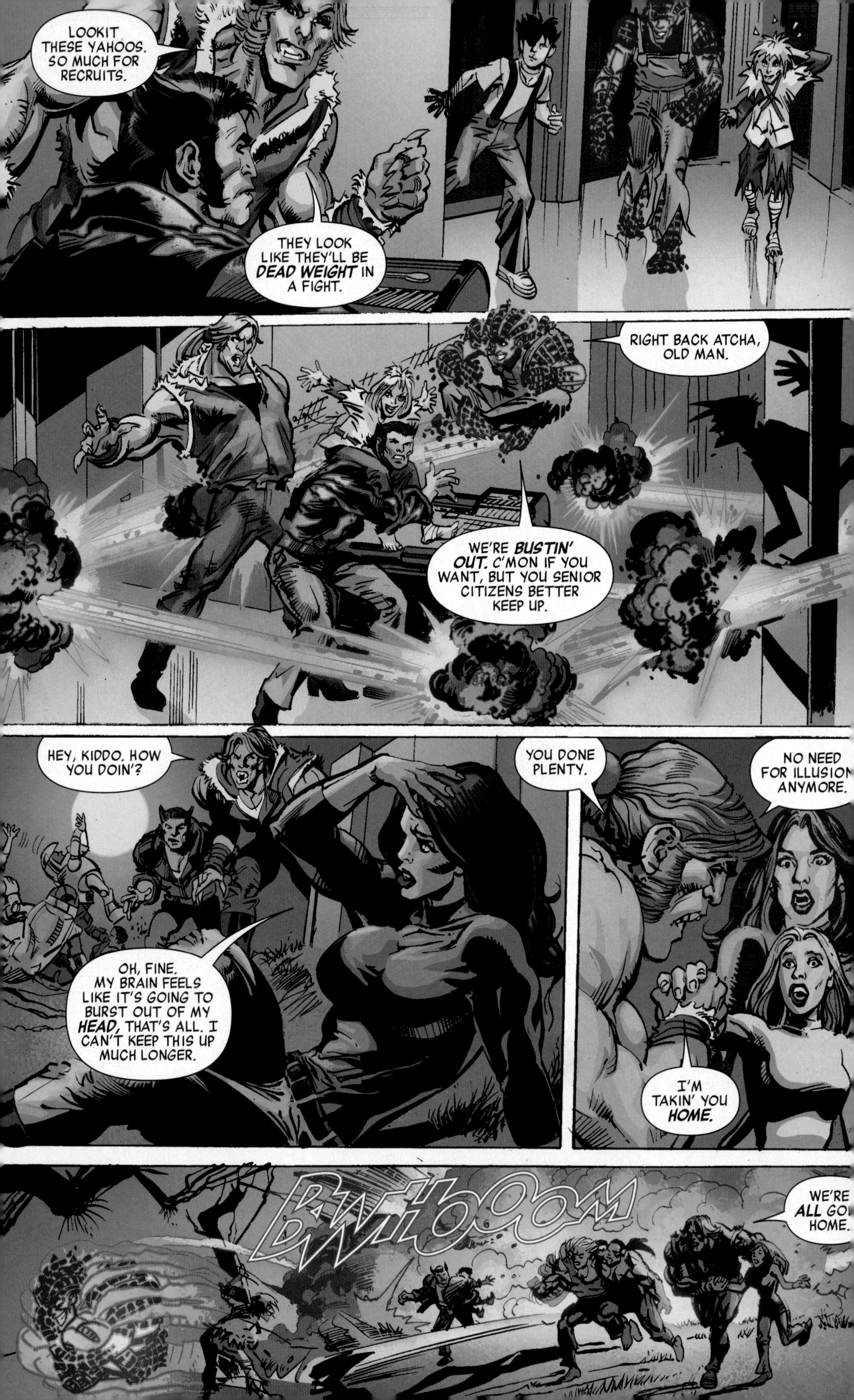
LOOKIT THESE YAHOOS. SO MUCH FOR RECRUITS.
THEY LOOK LIKE THEY'LL BE DEAD WEIGHT IN A FIGHT.
RIGHT BACK ATCHA, OLD MAN.
WE'RE BUSTIN' OUT. C'MON IF YOU WANT, BUT YOU SENIOR CITIZENS BETTER KEEP UP.
HEY, KIDDO. HOW YOU DOIN'?
OH, FINE. MY BRAIN FEELS LIKE IT'S GOING TO BURST OUT OF MY HEAD, THAT'S ALL. I CAN'T KEEP THIS UP MUCH LONGER.
YOU DONE PLENTY.
NO NEED FOR ILLUSION ANYMORE.
I'M TAKIN' YOU HOME.
BWHOOOM
WE'RE ALL GO HOME.

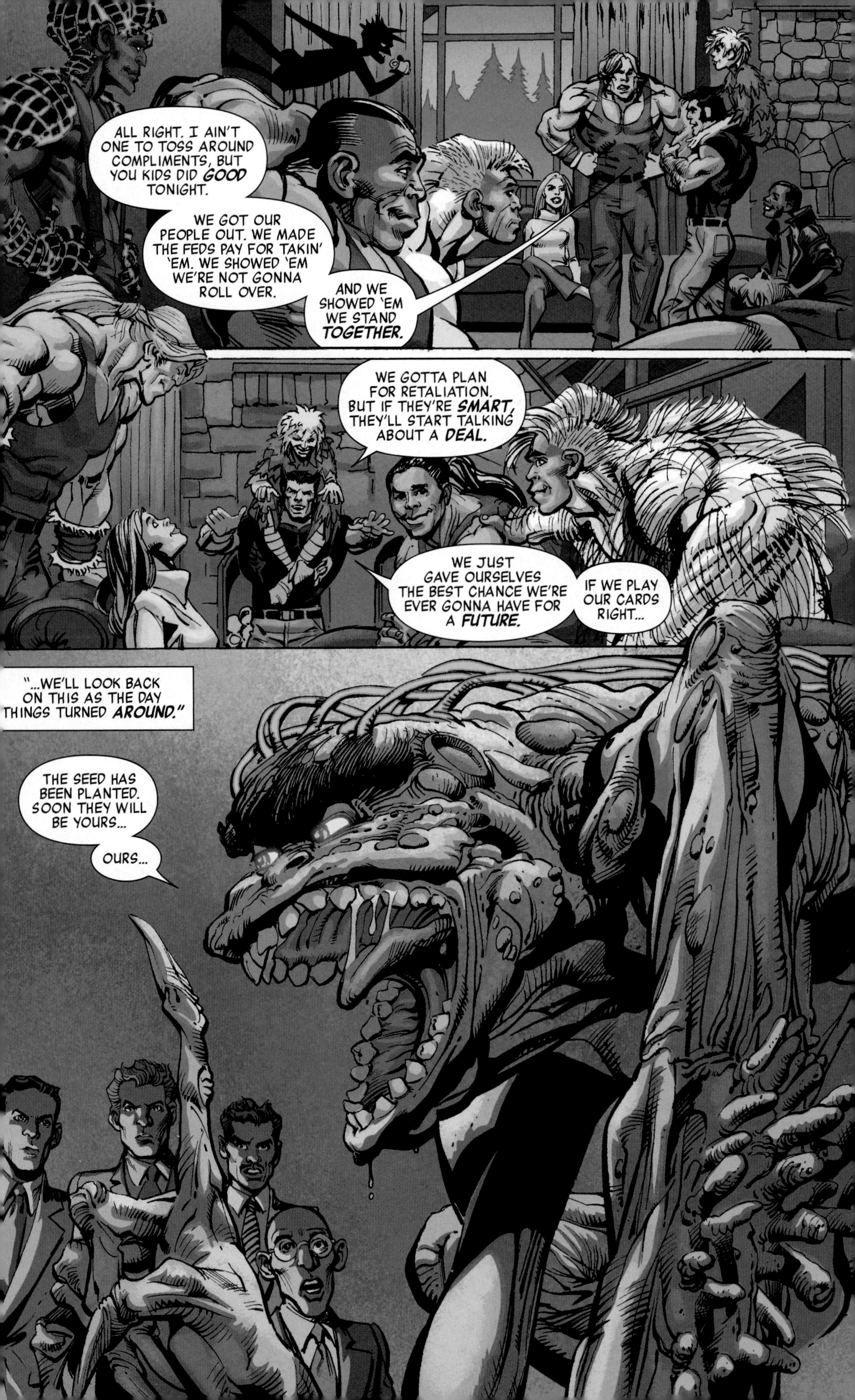
ALL RIGHT. I AIN'T ONE TO TOSS AROUND COMPLIMENTS, BUT YOU KIDS DID GOOD TONIGHT.
WE GOT OUR PEOPLE OUT. WE MADE THE FEDS PAY FOR TAKIN' 'EM. WE SHOWED 'EM WE'RE NOT GONNA ROLL OVER.
AND WE SHOWED 'EM WE STAND TOGETHER.
WE GOTTA PLAN FOR RETALIATION. BUT IF THEY'RE SMART, THEY'LL START TALKING ABOUT A DEAL.
WE JUST GAVE OURSELVES THE BEST CHANCE WE'RE EVER GONNA HAVE FOR A FUTURE.
IF WE PLAY OUR CARDS RIGHT...
"...WE'LL LOOK BACK ON THIS AS THE DAY THINGS TURNED AROUND."
THE SEED HAS BEEN PLANTED. SOON THEY WILL BE YOURS...
OURS...

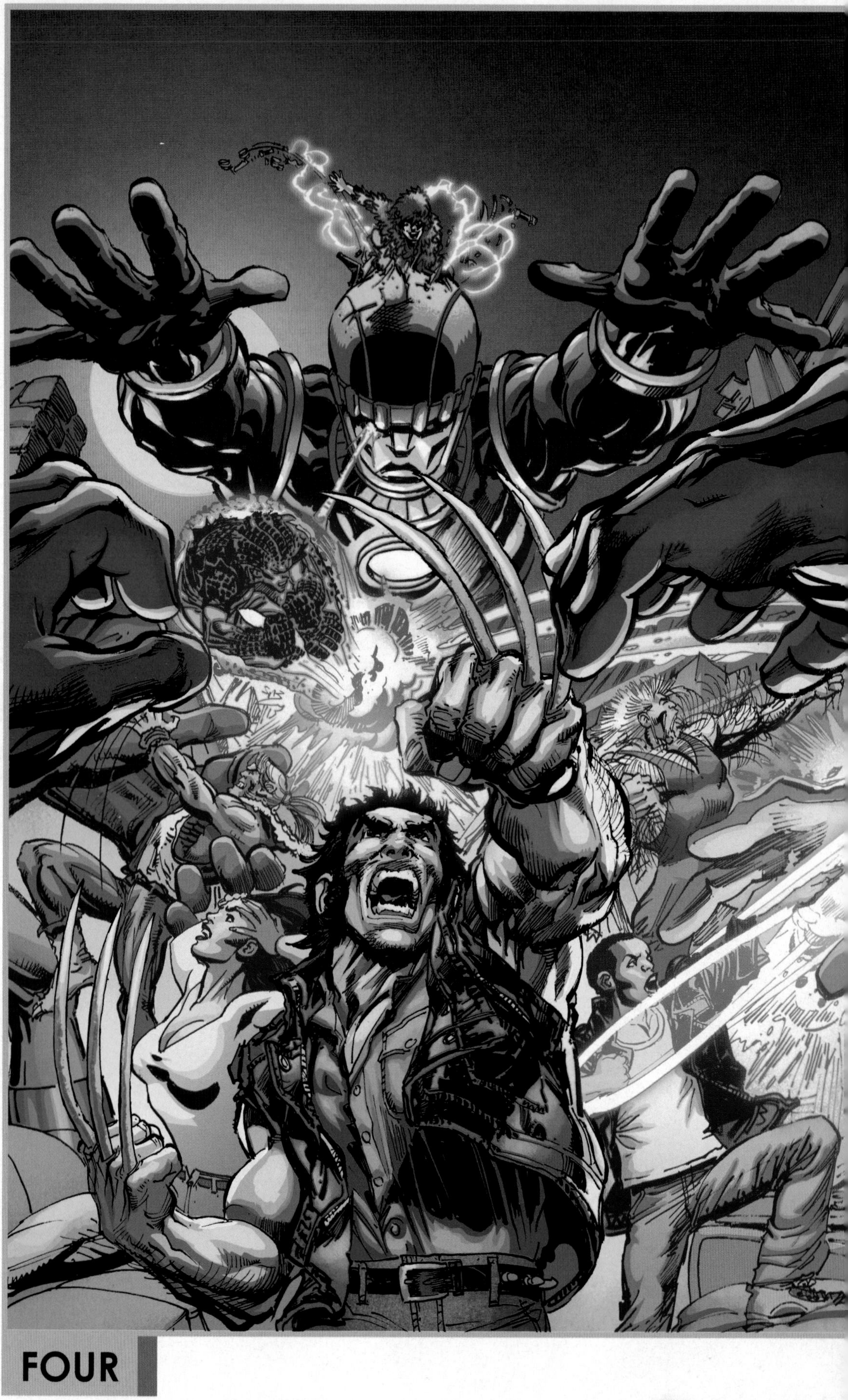

FOUR

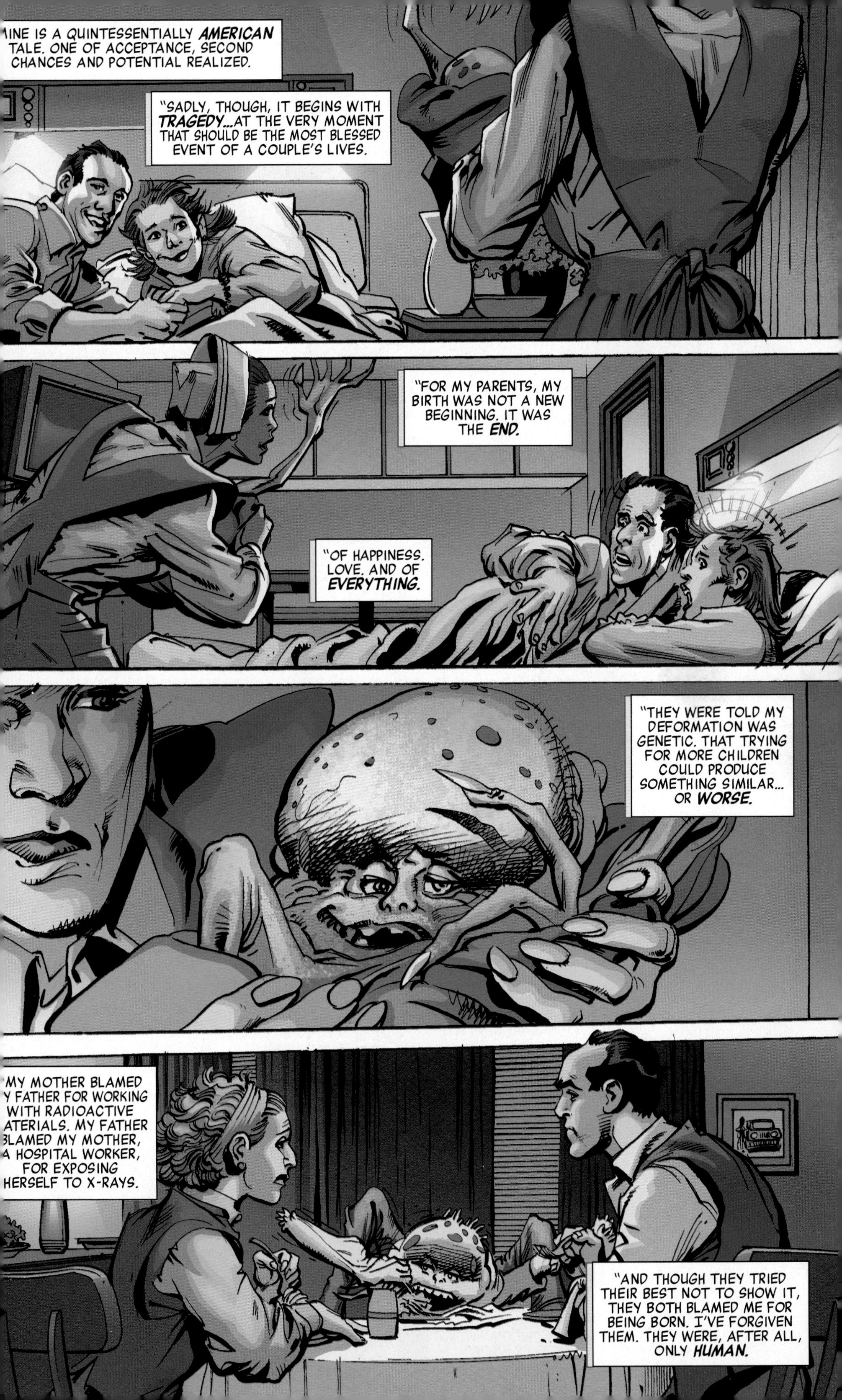
MINE IS A QUINTESSENTIALLY AMERICAN TALE. ONE OF ACCEPTANCE, SECOND CHANCES AND POTENTIAL REALIZED.
"SADLY, THOUGH, IT BEGINS WITH TRAGEDY...AT THE VERY MOMENT THAT SHOULD BE THE MOST BLESSED EVENT OF A COUPLE'S LIVES.
"FOR MY PARENTS, MY BIRTH WAS NOT A NEW BEGINNING. IT WAS THE END.
"OF HAPPINESS. LOVE. AND OF EVERYTHING.
"THEY WERE TOLD MY DEFORMATION WAS GENETIC. THAT TRYING FOR MORE CHILDREN COULD PRODUCE SOMETHING SIMILAR... OR WORSE.
"MY MOTHER BLAMED MY FATHER FOR WORKING WITH RADIOACTIVE MATERIALS. MY FATHER BLAMED MY MOTHER, A HOSPITAL WORKER, FOR EXPOSING HERSELF TO X-RAYS.
"AND THOUGH THEY TRIED THEIR BEST NOT TO SHOW IT, THEY BOTH BLAMED ME FOR BEING BORN. I'VE FORGIVEN THEM. THEY WERE, AFTER ALL, ONLY HUMAN.

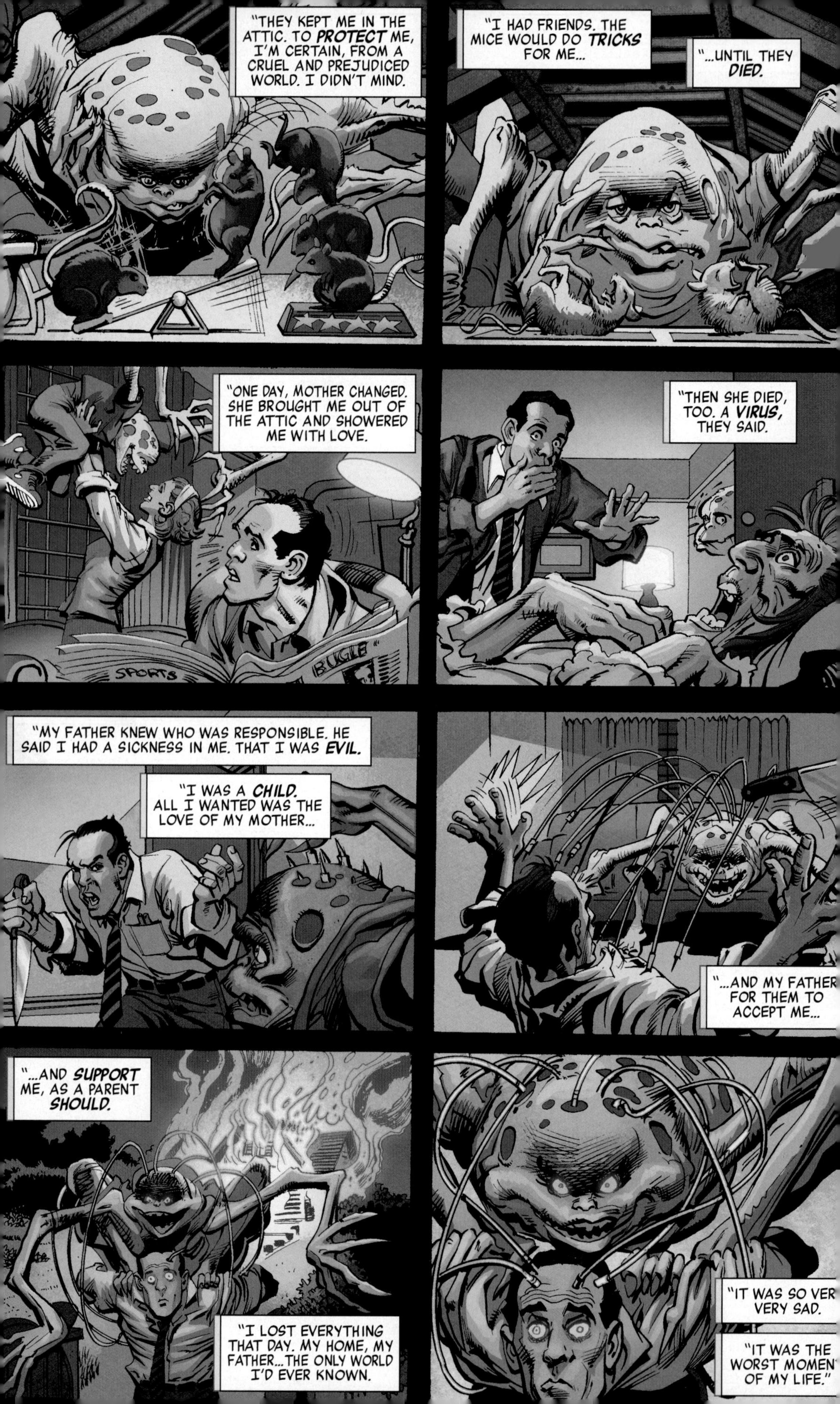
"THEY KEPT ME IN THE ATTIC. TO PROTECT ME, I'M CERTAIN, FROM A CRUEL AND PREJUDICED WORLD. I DIDN'T MIND.
"I HAD FRIENDS. THE MICE WOULD DO TRICKS FOR ME...
"...UNTIL THEY DIED.
"ONE DAY, MOTHER CHANGED. SHE BROUGHT ME OUT OF THE ATTIC AND SHOWERED ME WITH LOVE.
SPORTS
BUGLE
"THEN SHE DIED, TOO. A VIRUS, THEY SAID.
"MY FATHER KNEW WHO WAS RESPONSIBLE. HE SAID I HAD A SICKNESS IN ME. THAT I WAS EVIL.
"I WAS A CHILD. ALL I WANTED WAS THE LOVE OF MY MOTHER...
"...AND MY FATHER FOR THEM TO ACCEPT ME...
"...AND SUPPORT ME, AS A PARENT SHOULD.
"I LOST EVERYTHING THAT DAY. MY HOME, MY FATHER... THE ONLY WORLD I'D EVER KNOWN.
"IT WAS SO VER VERY SAD.
"IT WAS THE WORST MOMEN OF MY LIFE."

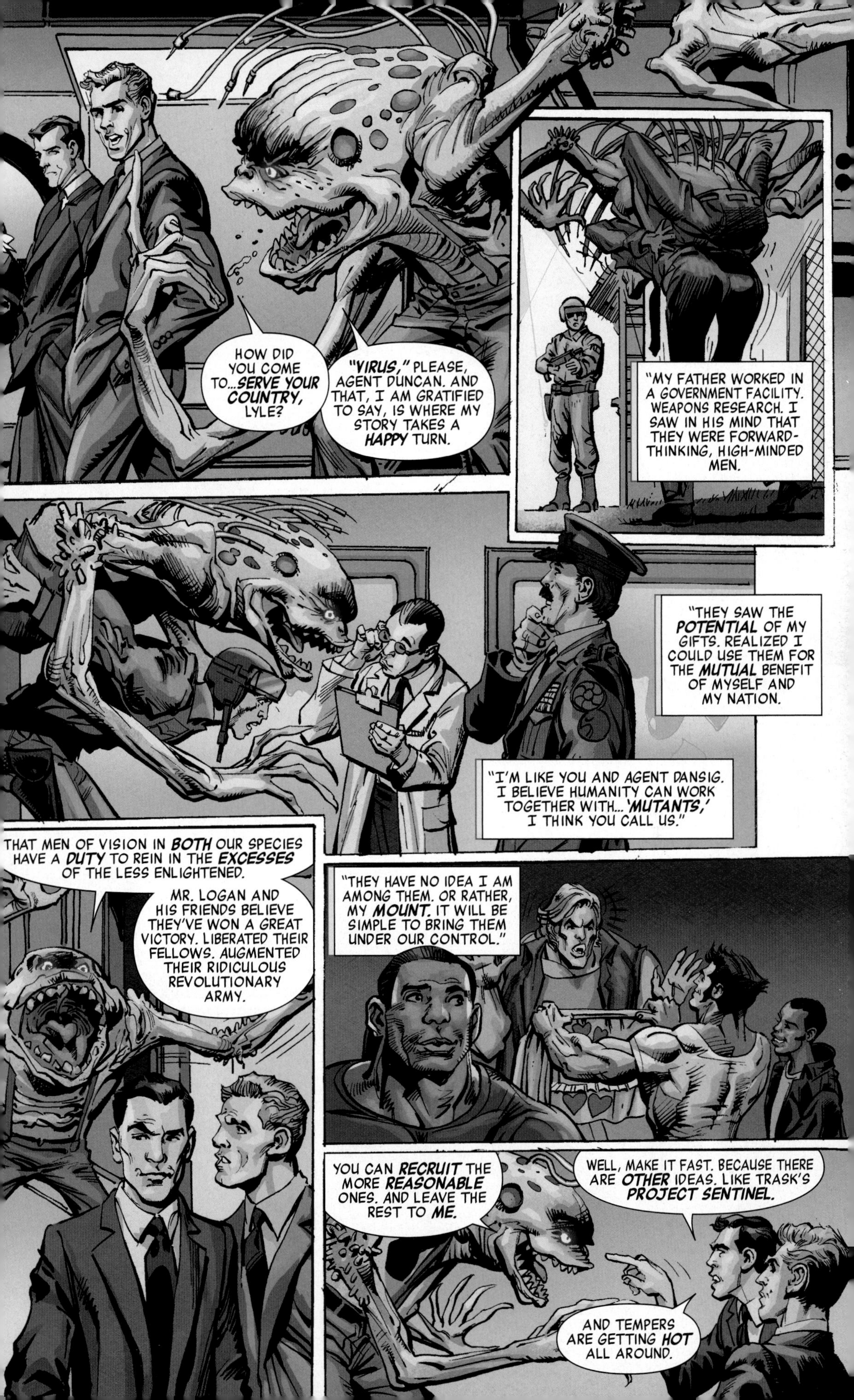

HOW DID YOU COME TO...SERVE YOUR COUNTRY, LYLE?
"VIRUS," PLEASE, AGENT DUNCAN. AND THAT, I AM GRATIFIED TO SAY, IS WHERE MY STORY TAKES A HAPPY TURN.
"MY FATHER WORKED IN A GOVERNMENT FACILITY. WEAPONS RESEARCH. I SAW IN HIS MIND THAT THEY WERE FORWARD-THINKING, HIGH-MINDED MEN.
"THEY SAW THE POTENTIAL OF MY GIFTS. REALIZED I COULD USE THEM FOR THE MUTUAL BENEFIT OF MYSELF AND MY NATION.
"I'M LIKE YOU AND AGENT DANSIG. I BELIEVE HUMANITY CAN WORK TOGETHER WITH... 'MUTANTS,' I THINK YOU CALL US."
THAT MEN OF VISION IN BOTH OUR SPECIES HAVE A DUTY TO REIN IN THE EXCESSES OF THE LESS ENLIGHTENED.
MR. LOGAN AND HIS FRIENDS BELIEVE THEY'VE WON A GREAT VICTORY. LIBERATED THEIR FELLOWS. AUGMENTED THEIR RIDICULOUS REVOLUTIONARY ARMY.
"THEY HAVE NO IDEA I AM AMONG THEM. OR RATHER, MY MOUNT. IT WILL BE SIMPLE TO BRING THEM UNDER OUR CONTROL."
YOU CAN RECRUIT THE MORE REASONABLE ONES. AND LEAVE THE REST TO ME.
WELL, MAKE IT FAST. BECAUSE THERE ARE OTHER IDEAS. LIKE TRASK'S PROJECT SENTINEL.
AND TEMPERS ARE GETTING HOT ALL AROUND.

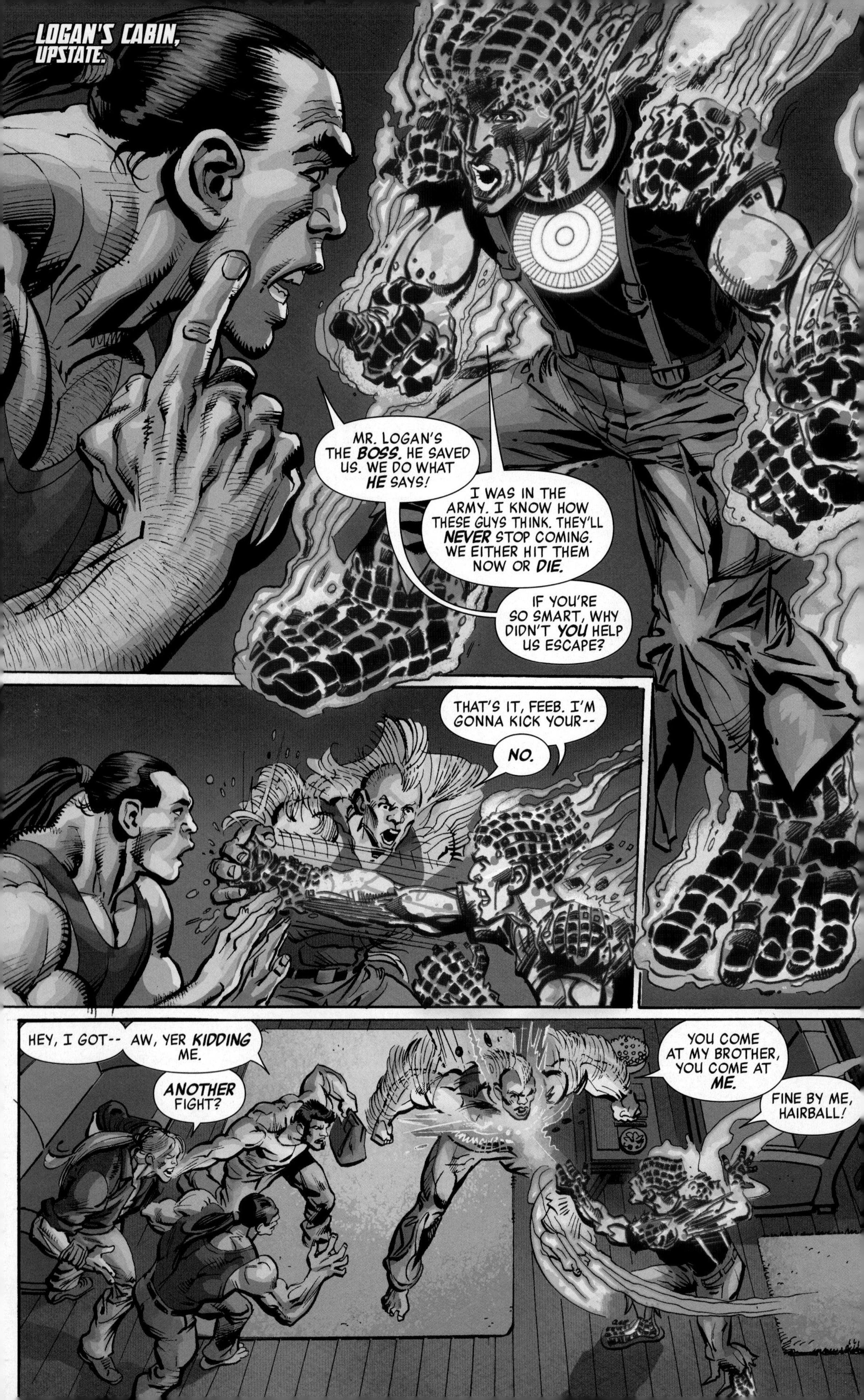
LOGAN'S CABIN, UPSTATE.
MR. LOGAN'S THE BOSS. HE SAVED US. WE DO WHAT HE SAYS!
I WAS IN THE ARMY. I KNOW HOW THESE GUYS THINK. THEY'LL NEVER STOP COMING. WE EITHER HIT THEM NOW OR DIE.
IF YOU'RE SO SMART, WHY DIDN'T YOU HELP US ESCAPE?
THAT'S IT, FEEB. I'M GONNA KICK YOUR--
NO.
HEY, I GOT--
AW, YER KIDDING ME.
ANOTHER FIGHT?
YOU COME AT MY BROTHER, YOU COME AT ME.
FINE BY ME, HAIRBALL!

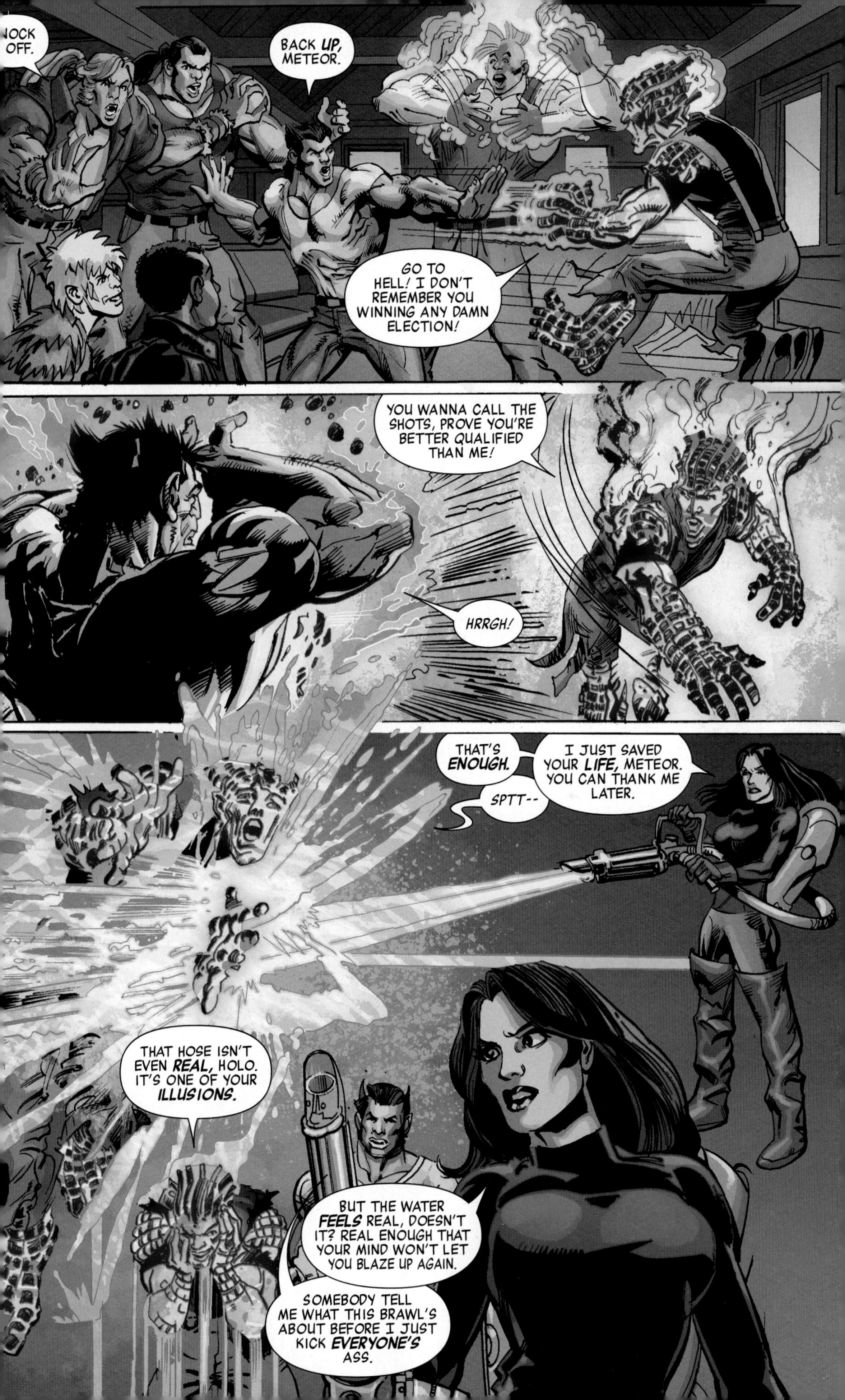

NOCK OFF.
BACK UP, METEOR.
GO TO HELL! I DON'T REMEMBER YOU WINNING ANY DAMN ELECTION!
YOU WANNA CALL THE SHOTS, PROVE YOU'RE BETTER QUALIFIED THAN ME!
HRRGH!
THAT'S ENOUGH.
I JUST SAVED YOUR LIFE, METEOR. YOU CAN THANK ME LATER.
SPTT--
THAT HOSE ISN'T EVEN REAL, HOLO. IT'S ONE OF YOUR ILLUSIONS.
BUT THE WATER FEELS REAL, DOESN'T IT? REAL ENOUGH THAT YOUR MIND WON'T LET YOU BLAZE UP AGAIN.
SOMEBODY TELL ME WHAT THIS BRAWL'S ABOUT BEFORE I JUST KICK EVERYONE'S ASS.

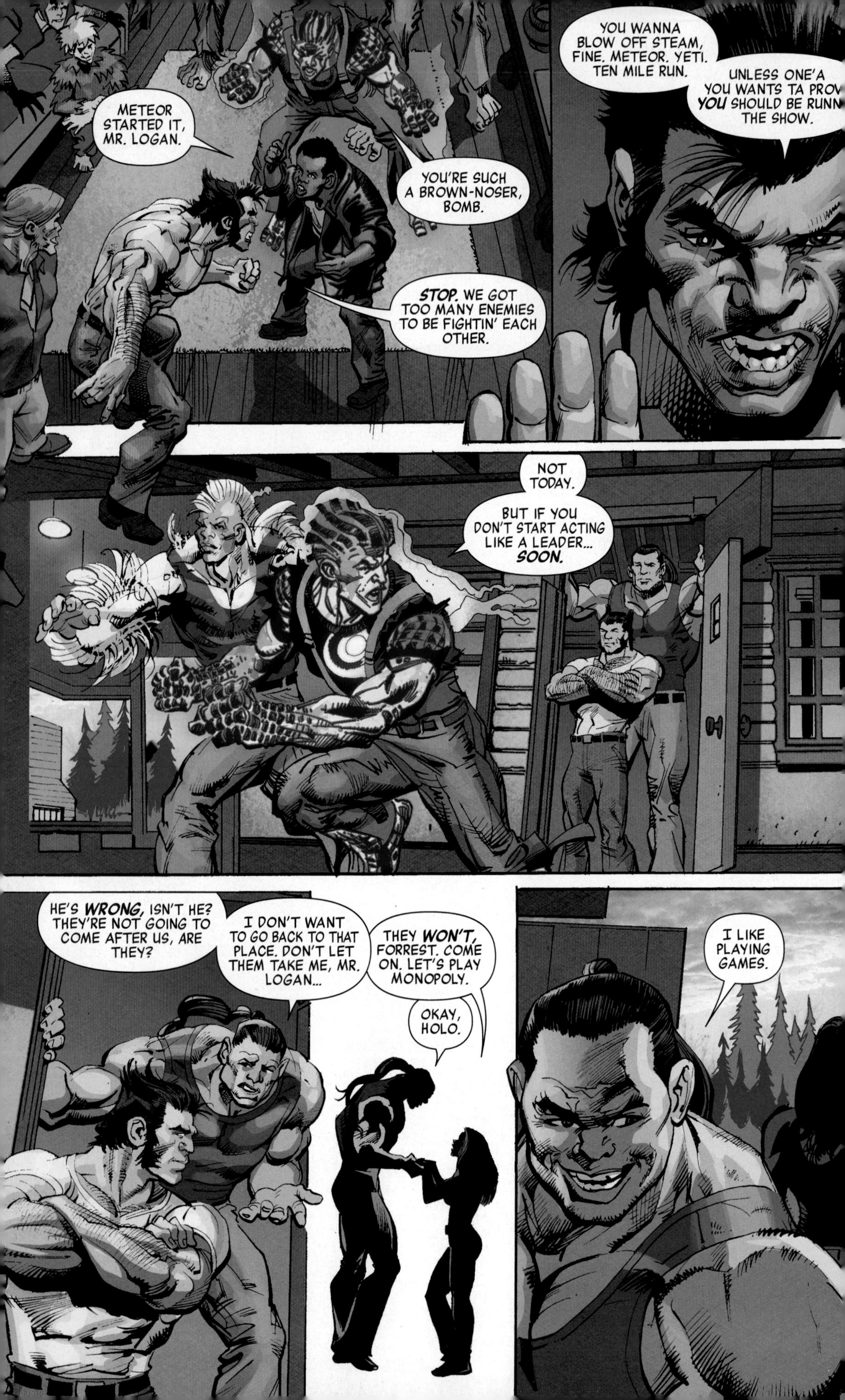

METEOR STARTED IT, MR. LOGAN.
YOU'RE SUCH A BROWN-NOSER, BOMB.
STOP. WE GOT TOO MANY ENEMIES TO BE FIGHTIN' EACH OTHER.
YOU WANNA BLOW OFF STEAM, FINE. METEOR. YETI. TEN MILE RUN.
UNLESS ONE'A YOU WANTS TA PROV YOU SHOULD BE RUNN THE SHOW.
NOT TODAY.
BUT IF YOU DON'T START ACTING LIKE A LEADER... SOON.
HE'S WRONG, ISN'T HE? THEY'RE NOT GOING TO COME AFTER US, ARE THEY?
I DON'T WANT TO GO BACK TO THAT PLACE. DON'T LET THEM TAKE ME, MR. LOGAN...
THEY WON'T, FORREST. COME ON. LET'S PLAY MONOPOLY.
OKAY, HOLO.
I LIKE PLAYING GAMES.

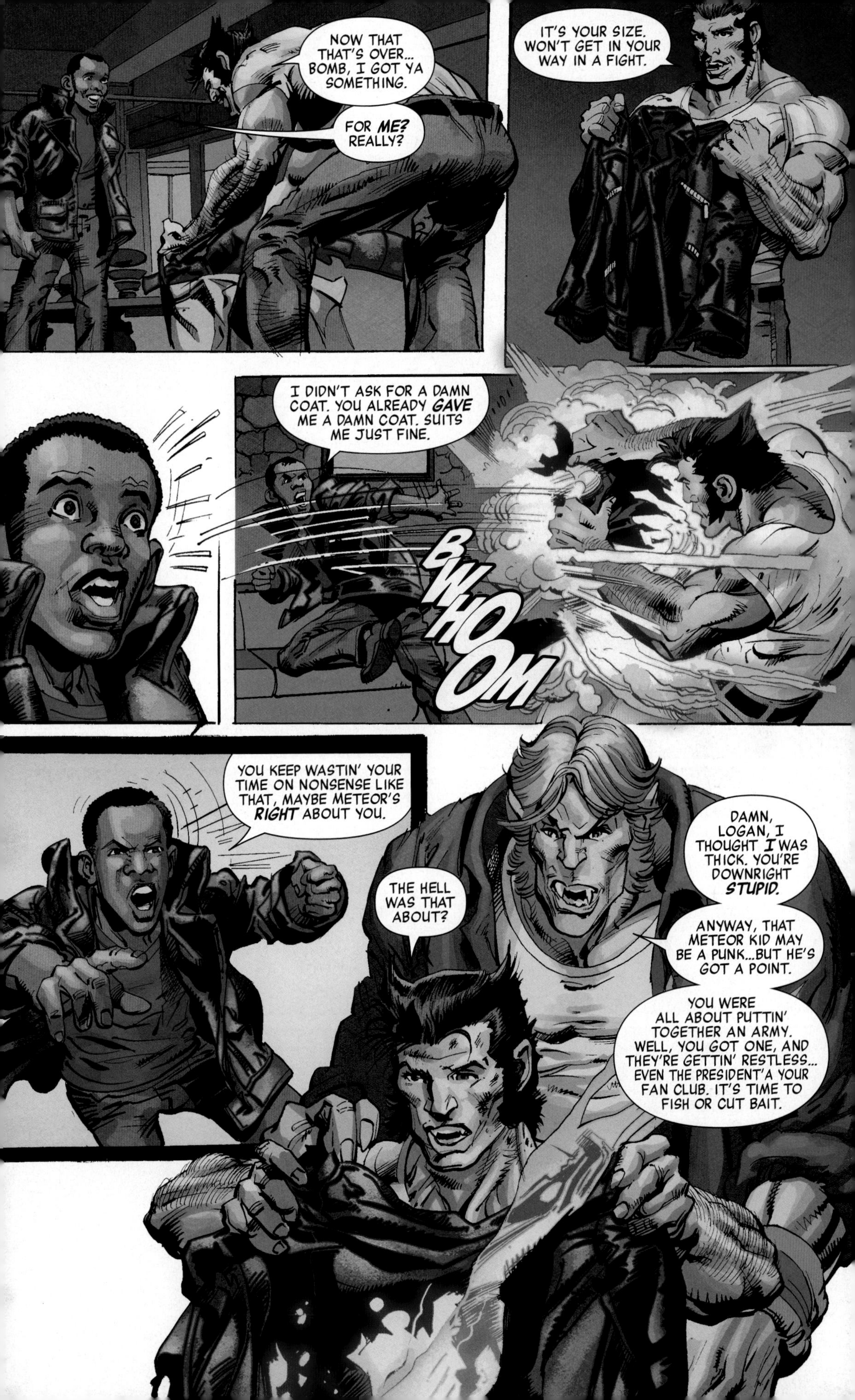
NOW THAT THAT'S OVER... BOMB, I GOT YA SOMETHING.
FOR ME? REALLY?
IT'S YOUR SIZE. WON'T GET IN YOUR WAY IN A FIGHT.
I DIDN'T ASK FOR A DAMN COAT. YOU ALREADY GAVE ME A DAMN COAT. SUITS ME JUST FINE.
BWHOOM
YOU KEEP WASTIN' YOUR TIME ON NONSENSE LIKE THAT, MAYBE METEOR'S RIGHT ABOUT YOU.
THE HELL WAS THAT ABOUT?
DAMN, LOGAN, I THOUGHT I WAS THICK. YOU'RE DOWNRIGHT STUPID.
ANYWAY, THAT METEOR KID MAY BE A PUNK...BUT HE'S GOT A POINT.
YOU WERE ALL ABOUT PUTTIN' TOGETHER AN ARMY. WELL, YOU GOT ONE, AND THEY'RE GETTIN' RESTLESS... EVEN THE PRESIDENT'A YOUR FAN CLUB. IT'S TIME TO FISH OR CUT BAIT.

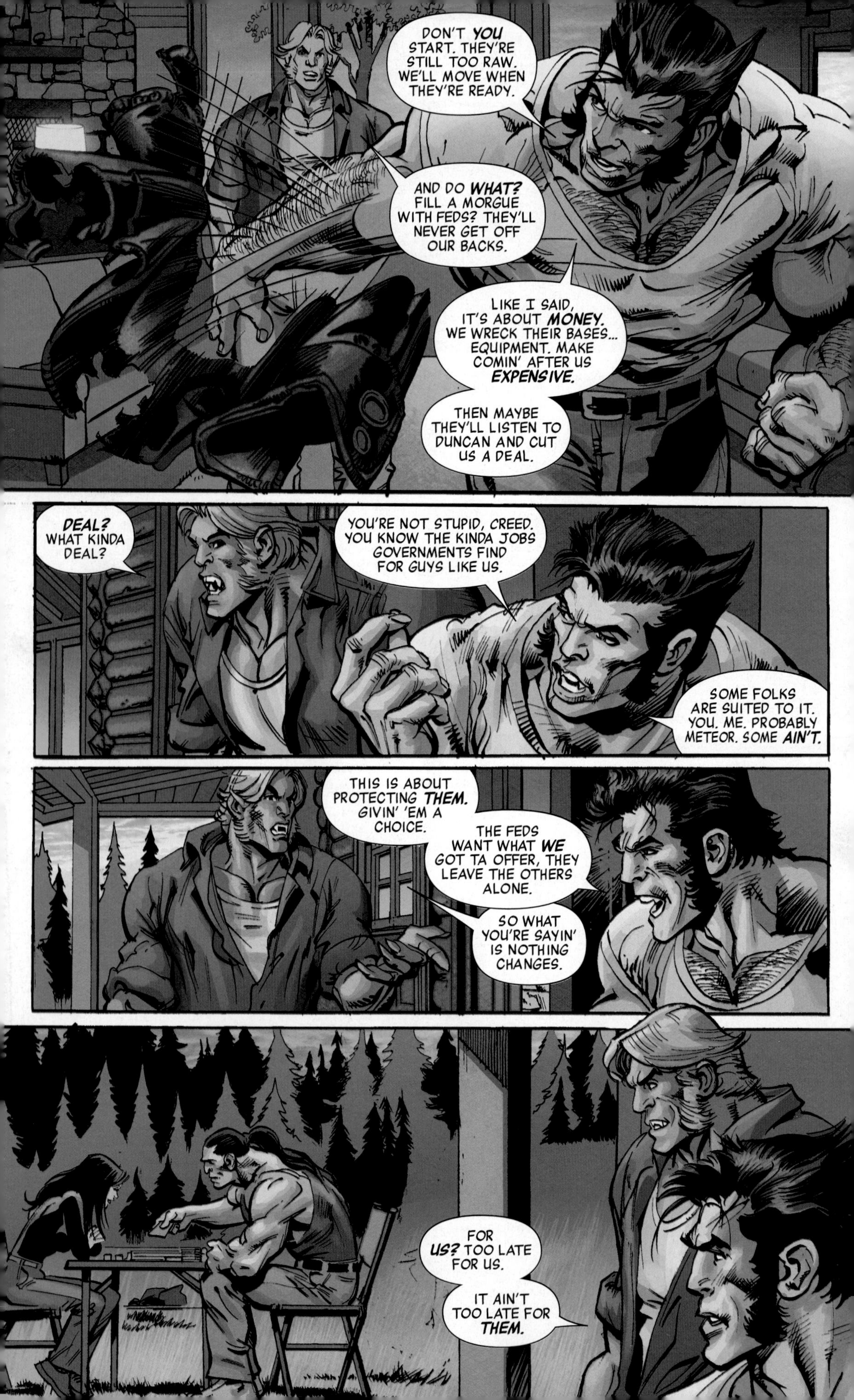
DON'T YOU START. THEY'RE STILL TOO RAW. WE'LL MOVE WHEN THEY'RE READY.
AND DO WHAT? FILL A MORGUE WITH FEDS? THEY'LL NEVER GET OFF OUR BACKS.
LIKE I SAID, IT'S ABOUT MONEY. WE WRECK THEIR BASES... EQUIPMENT. MAKE COMIN' AFTER US EXPENSIVE.
THEN MAYBE THEY'LL LISTEN TO DUNCAN AND CUT US A DEAL.
DEAL? WHAT KINDA DEAL?
YOU'RE NOT STUPID, CREED. YOU KNOW THE KINDA JOBS GOVERNMENTS FIND FOR GUYS LIKE US.
SOME FOLKS ARE SUITED TO IT. YOU. ME. PROBABLY METEOR. SOME AIN'T.
THIS IS ABOUT PROTECTING THEM. GIVIN' 'EM A CHOICE.
THE FEDS WANT WHAT WE GOT TA OFFER, THEY LEAVE THE OTHERS ALONE.
SO WHAT YOU'RE SAYIN' IS NOTHING CHANGES.
FOR US? TOO LATE FOR US.
IT AIN'T TOO LATE FOR THEM.

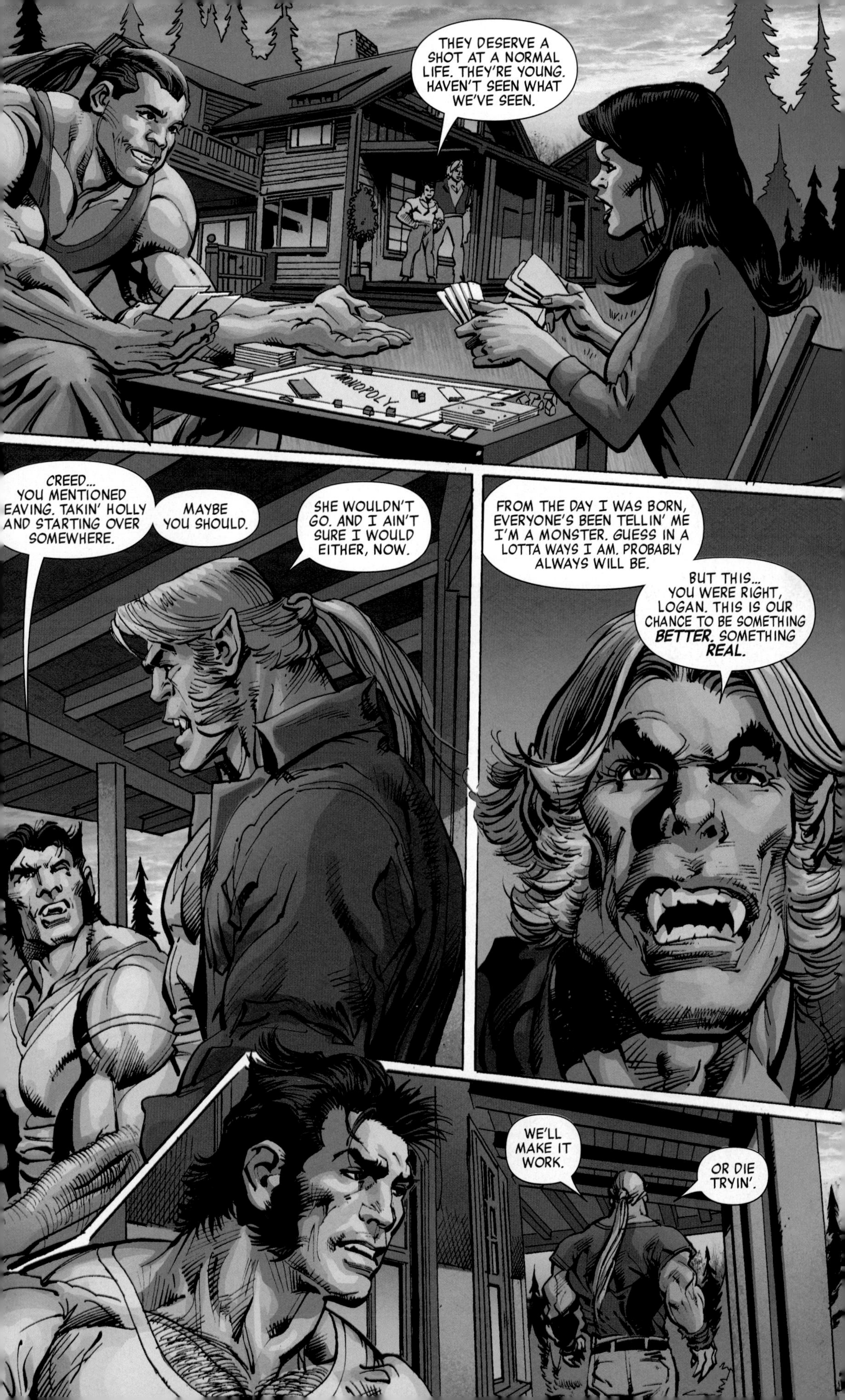
THEY DESERVE A SHOT AT A NORMAL LIFE. THEY'RE YOUNG. HAVEN'T SEEN WHAT WE'VE SEEN.
CREED... YOU MENTIONED EAVING. TAKIN' HOLLY AND STARTING OVER SOMEWHERE.
MAYBE YOU SHOULD.
SHE WOULDN'T GO. AND I AIN'T SURE I WOULD EITHER, NOW.
FROM THE DAY I WAS BORN, EVERYONE'S BEEN TELLIN' ME I'M A MONSTER. GUESS IN A LOTTA WAYS I AM. PROBABLY ALWAYS WILL BE.
BUT THIS... YOU WERE RIGHT, LOGAN. THIS IS OUR CHANCE TO BE SOMETHING BETTER. SOMETHING REAL.
WE'LL MAKE IT WORK.
OR DIE TRYIN'.

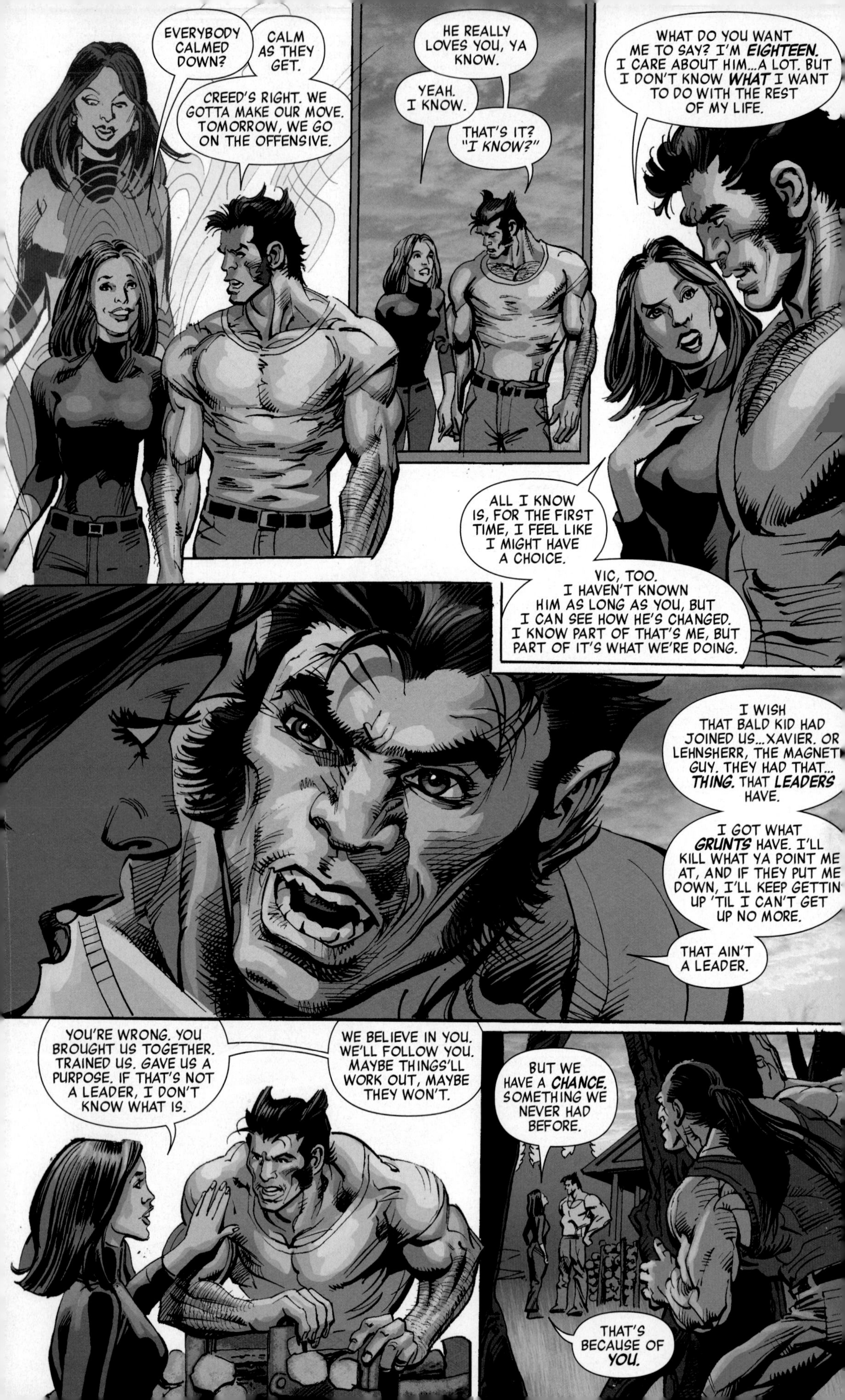
EVERYBODY CALMED DOWN?
CALM AS THEY GET.
CREED'S RIGHT. WE GOTTA MAKE OUR MOVE. TOMORROW, WE GO ON THE OFFENSIVE.
HE REALLY LOVES YOU, YA KNOW.
YEAH. I KNOW.
THAT'S IT? "I KNOW?"
WHAT DO YOU WANT ME TO SAY? I'M EIGHTEEN. I CARE ABOUT HIM...A LOT. BUT I DON'T KNOW WHAT I WANT TO DO WITH THE REST OF MY LIFE.
ALL I KNOW IS, FOR THE FIRST TIME, I FEEL LIKE I MIGHT HAVE A CHOICE.
VIC, TOO. I HAVEN'T KNOWN HIM AS LONG AS YOU, BUT I CAN SEE HOW HE'S CHANGED. I KNOW PART OF THAT'S ME, BUT PART OF IT'S WHAT WE'RE DOING.
I WISH THAT BALD KID HAD JOINED US...XAVIER. OR LEHNSHERR, THE MAGNET GUY. THEY HAD THAT... THING. THAT LEADERS HAVE.
I GOT WHAT GRUNTS HAVE. I'LL KILL WHAT YA POINT ME AT, AND IF THEY PUT ME DOWN, I'LL KEEP GETTIN UP 'TIL I CAN'T GET UP NO MORE.
THAT AIN'T A LEADER.
YOU'RE WRONG. YOU BROUGHT US TOGETHER. TRAINED US. GAVE US A PURPOSE. IF THAT'S NOT A LEADER, I DON'T KNOW WHAT IS.
WE BELIEVE IN YOU. WE'LL FOLLOW YOU. MAYBE THINGS'LL WORK OUT, MAYBE THEY WON'T.
BUT WE HAVE A CHANCE. SOMETHING WE NEVER HAD BEFORE.
THAT'S BECAUSE OF YOU.

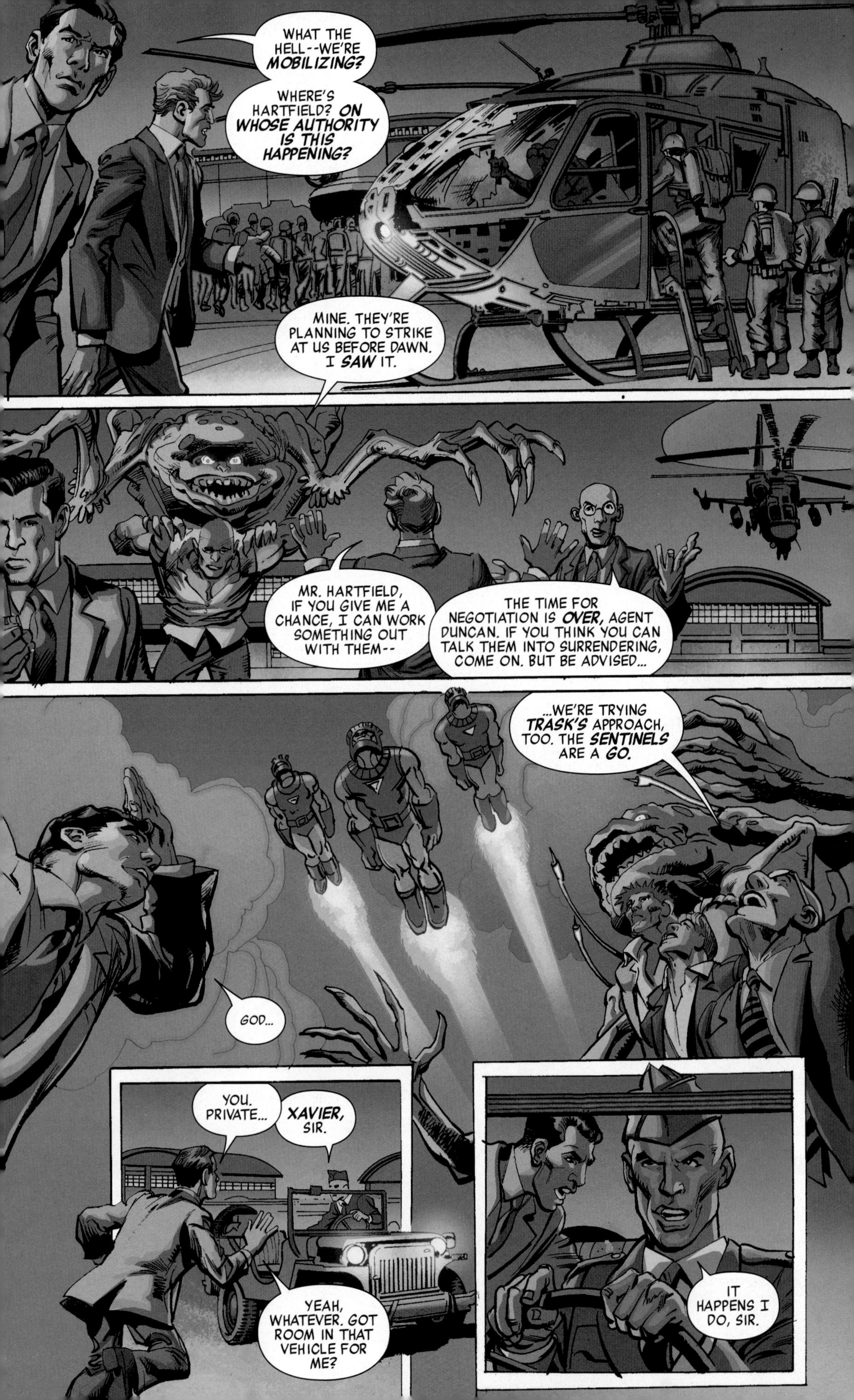
WHAT THE HELL--WE'RE MOBILIZING?
WHERE'S HARTFIELD? ON WHOSE AUTHORITY IS THIS HAPPENING?
MINE. THEY'RE PLANNING TO STRIKE AT US BEFORE DAWN. I SAW IT.
MR. HARTFIELD, IF YOU GIVE ME A CHANCE, I CAN WORK SOMETHING OUT WITH THEM--
THE TIME FOR NEGOTIATION IS OVER, AGENT DUNCAN. IF YOU THINK YOU CAN TALK THEM INTO SURRENDERING, COME ON. BUT BE ADVISED...
...WE'RE TRYING TRASK'S APPROACH, TOO. THE SENTINELS ARE A GO.
GOD...
YOU. PRIVATE...
XAVIER, SIR.
YEAH, WHATEVER. GOT ROOM IN THAT VEHICLE FOR ME?
IT HAPPENS I DO, SIR.

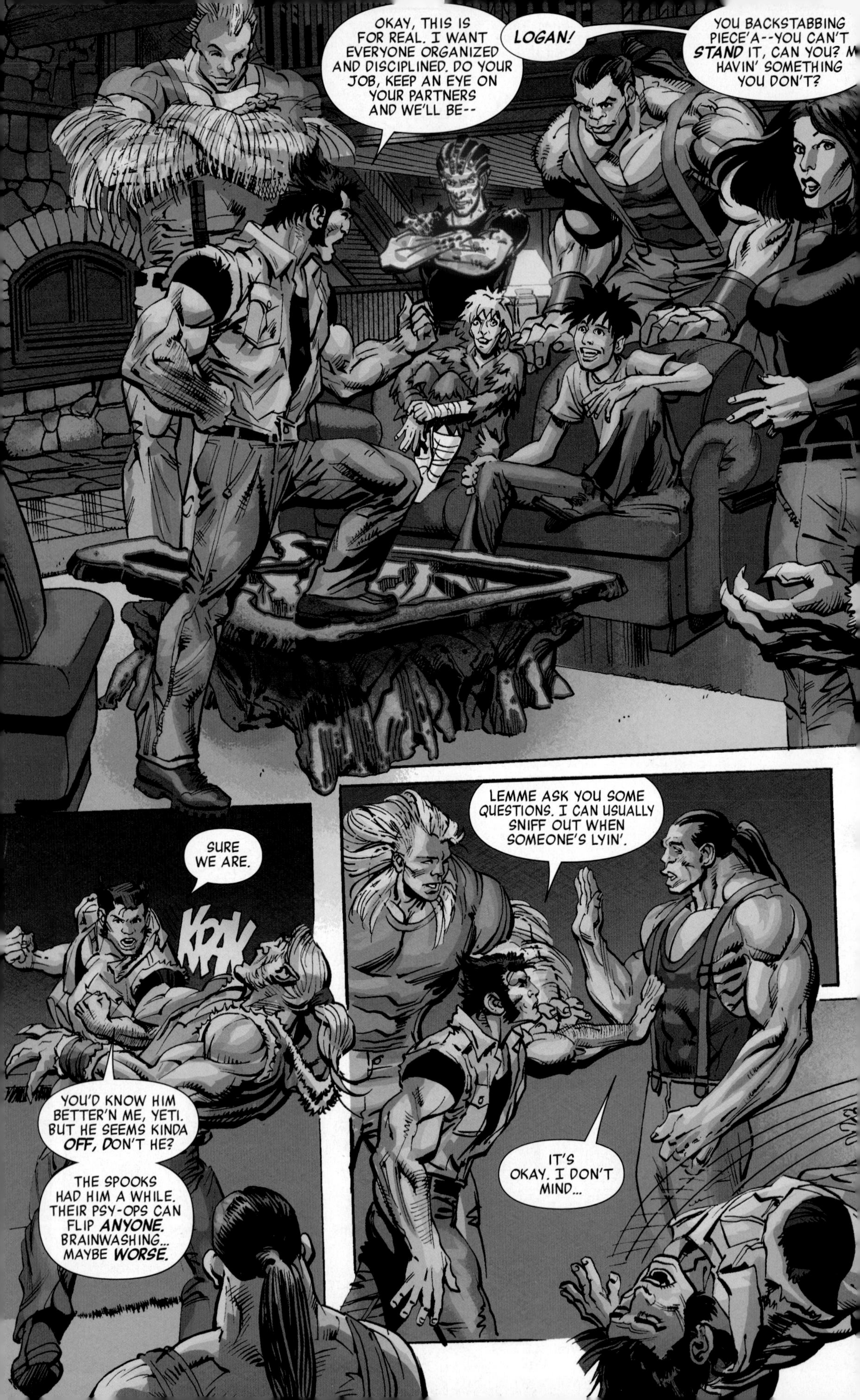
OKAY, THIS IS FOR REAL. I WANT EVERYONE ORGANIZED AND DISCIPLINED. DO YOUR JOB, KEEP AN EYE ON YOUR PARTNERS AND WE'LL BE--
LOGAN!
YOU BACKSTABBING PIECE'A--YOU CAN'T STAND IT, CAN YOU? M HAVIN' SOMETHING YOU DON'T?
SURE WE ARE.
KRAK
YOU'D KNOW HIM BETTER'N ME, YETI. BUT HE SEEMS KINDA OFF, DON'T HE?
THE SPOOKS HAD HIM A WHILE. THEIR PSY-OPS CAN FLIP ANYONE. BRAINWASHING... MAYBE WORSE.
LEMME ASK YOU SOME QUESTIONS. I CAN USUALLY SNIFF OUT WHEN SOMEONE'S LYIN'.
IT'S OKAY. I DON'T MIND...

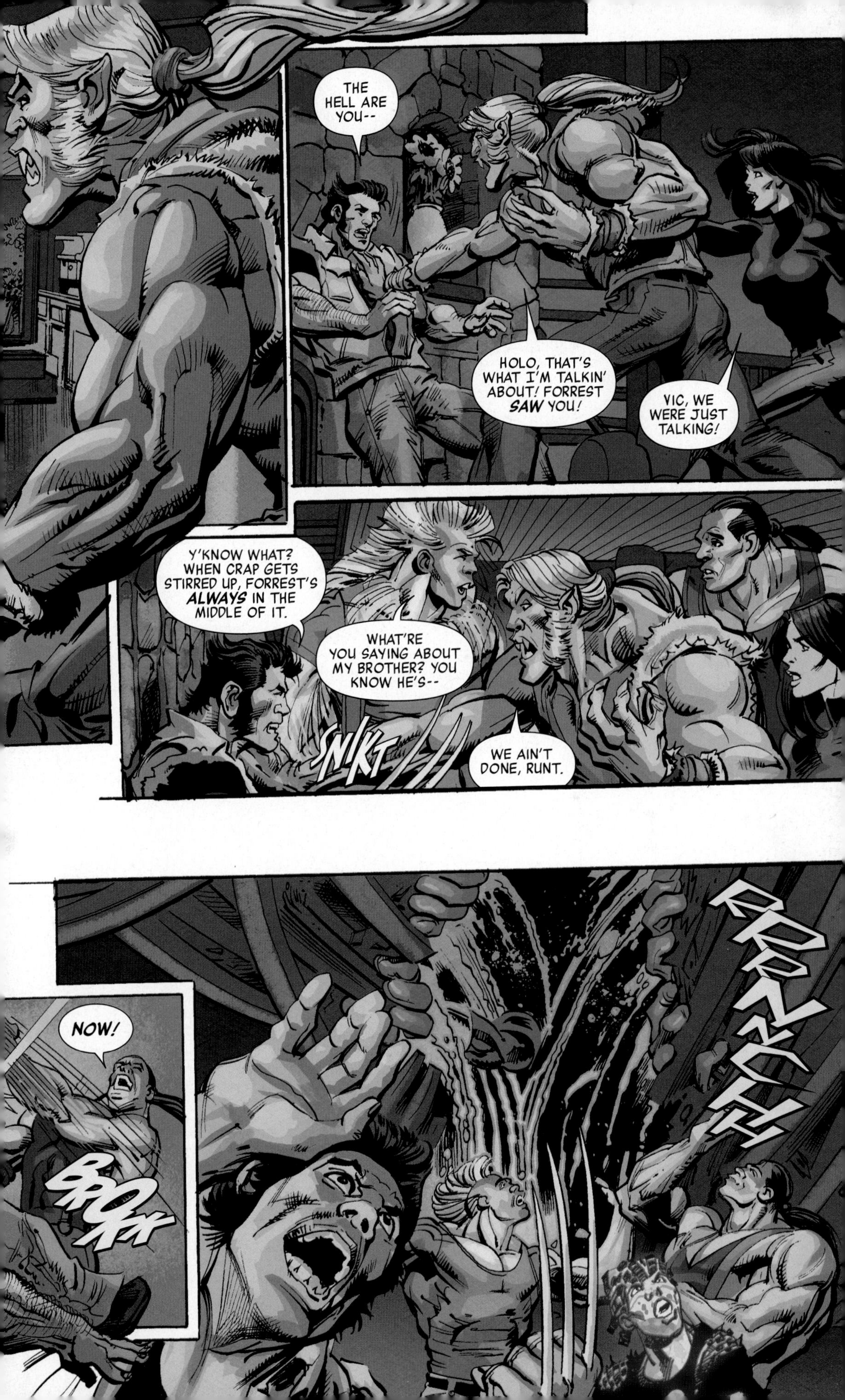
THE HELL ARE YOU--
HOLO, THAT'S WHAT I'M TALKIN' ABOUT! FORREST SAW YOU!
VIC, WE WERE JUST TALKING!
Y'KNOW WHAT? WHEN CRAP GETS STIRRED UP, FORREST'S ALWAYS IN THE MIDDLE OF IT.
WHAT'RE YOU SAYING ABOUT MY BROTHER? YOU KNOW HE'S--
SNIKT
WE AIN'T DONE, RUNT.
RRRNNCHH
NOW!
BROK

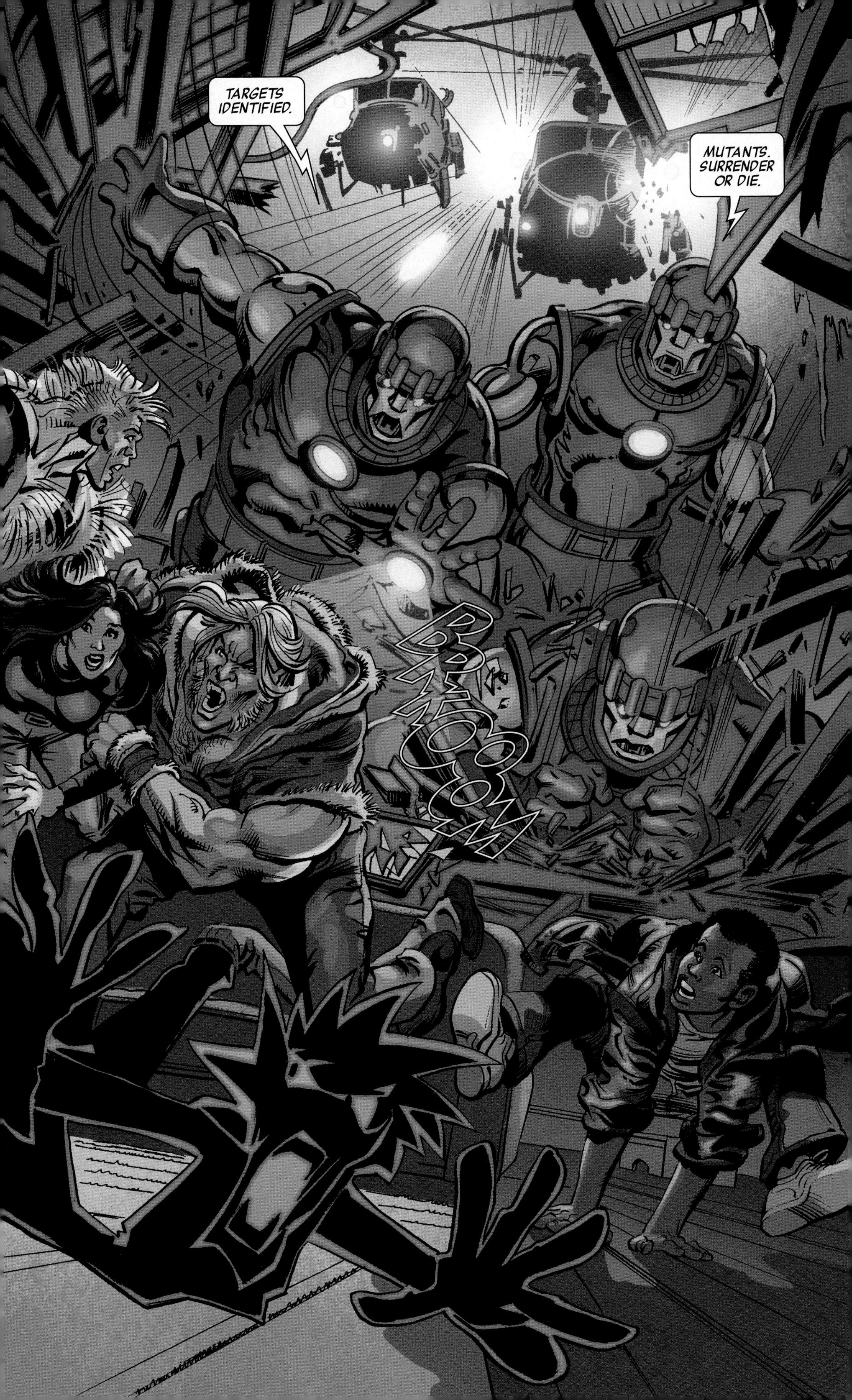
TARGETS IDENTIFIED.
MUTANTS. SURRENDER OR DIE.
BBRROOOOM

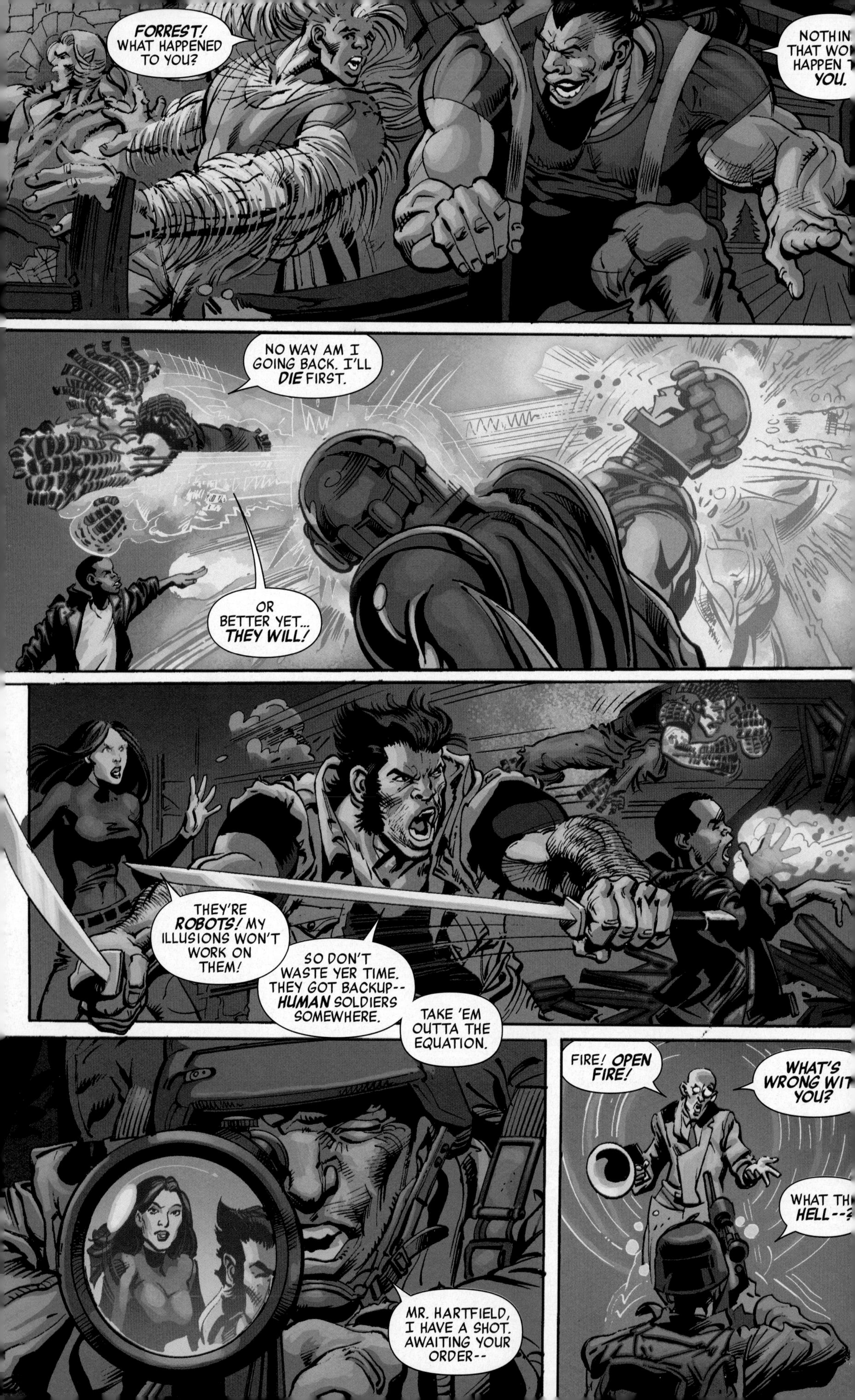
FORREST! WHAT HAPPENED TO YOU?
NOTHIN THAT WO HAPPEN T YOU.
NO WAY AM I GOING BACK. I'LL DIE FIRST.
OR BETTER YET... THEY WILL!
THEY'RE ROBOTS! MY ILLUSIONS WON'T WORK ON THEM!
SO DON'T WASTE YER TIME. THEY GOT BACKUP-- HUMAN SOLDIERS SOMEWHERE.
TAKE 'EM OUTTA THE EQUATION.
MR. HARTFIELD, I HAVE A SHOT. AWAITING YOUR ORDER--
FIRE! OPEN FIRE!
WHAT'S WRONG WIT YOU?
WHAT TH HELL--?

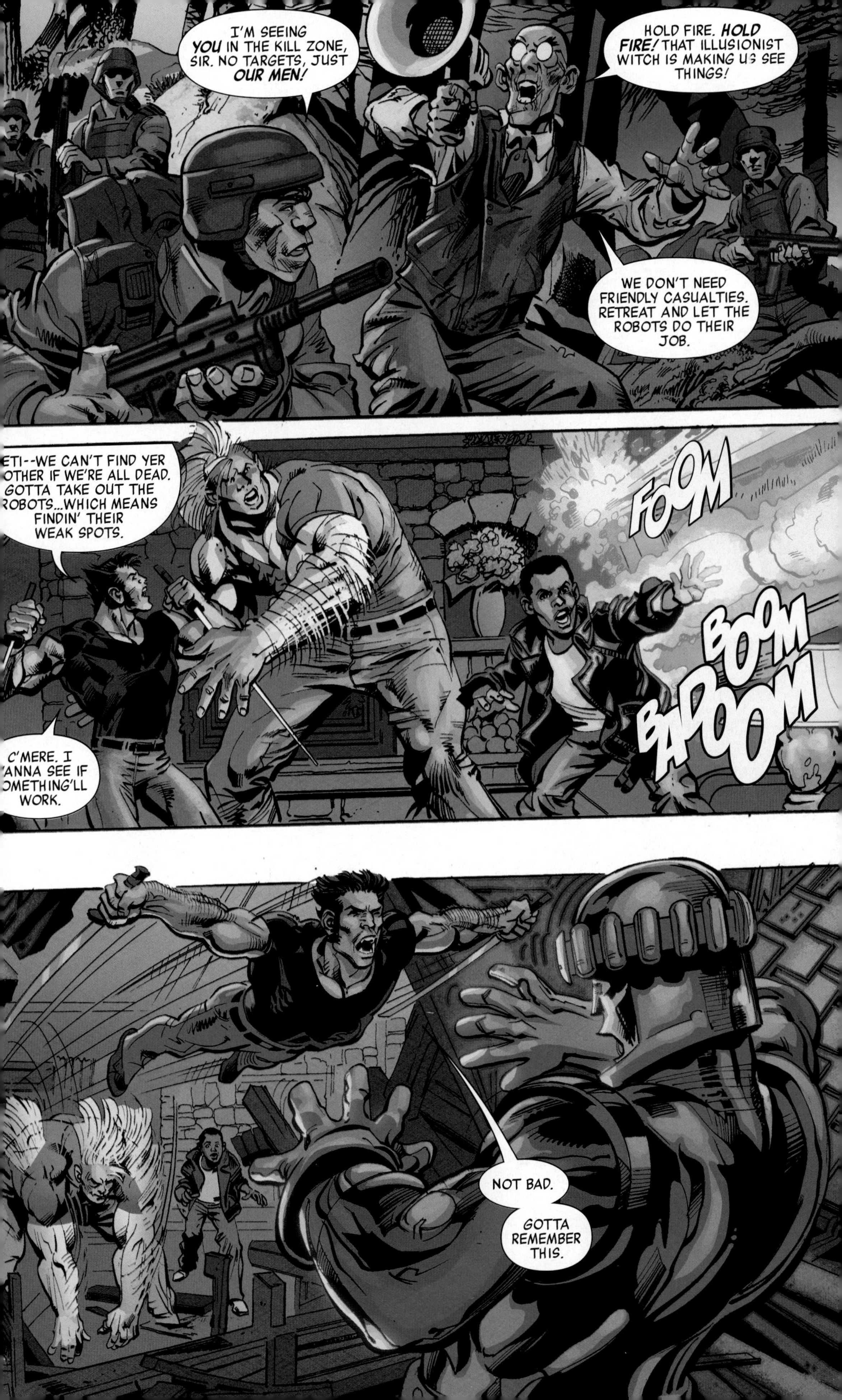

I'M SEEING YOU IN THE KILL ZONE, SIR. NO TARGETS, JUST OUR MEN!
HOLD FIRE. HOLD FIRE! THAT ILLUSIONIST WITCH IS MAKING US SEE THINGS!
WE DON'T NEED FRIENDLY CASUALTIES. RETREAT AND LET THE ROBOTS DO THEIR JOB.
ETI--WE CAN'T FIND YER OTHER IF WE'RE ALL DEAD. GOTTA TAKE OUT THE ROBOTS...WHICH MEANS FINDIN' THEIR WEAK SPOTS.
FOOM
BOOM
BADOOM
C'MERE. I ANNA SEE IF OMETHING'LL WORK.
NOT BAD.
GOTTA REMEMBER THIS.

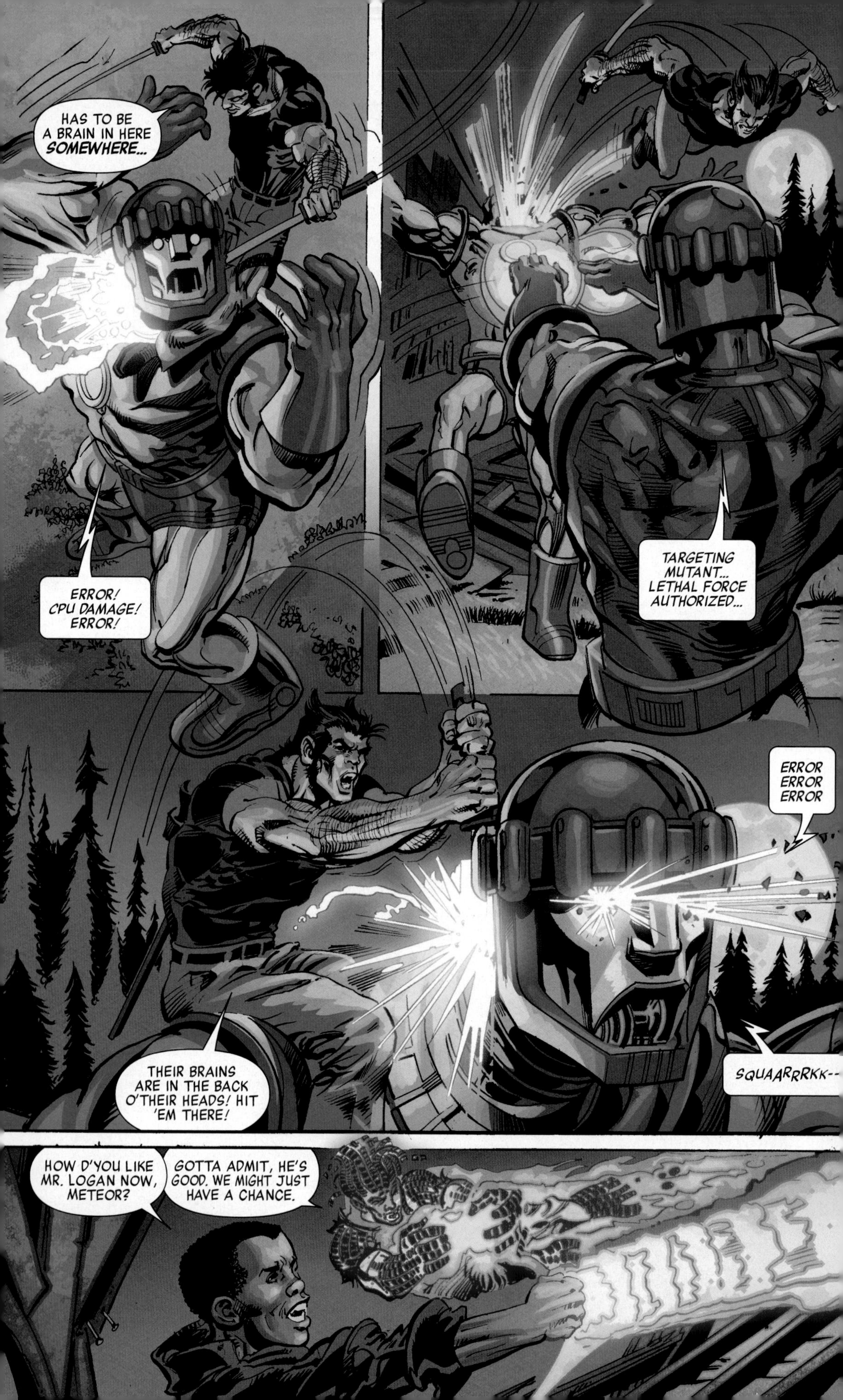
HAS TO BE A BRAIN IN HERE SOMEWHERE...
ERROR! CPU DAMAGE! ERROR!
TARGETING MUTANT... LETHAL FORCE AUTHORIZED...
ERROR ERROR ERROR
THEIR BRAINS ARE IN THE BACK O'THEIR HEADS! HIT 'EM THERE!
SQUAARRRKK--
HOW D'YOU LIKE MR. LOGAN NOW, METEOR?
GOTTA ADMIT, HE'S GOOD. WE MIGHT JUST HAVE A CHANCE.

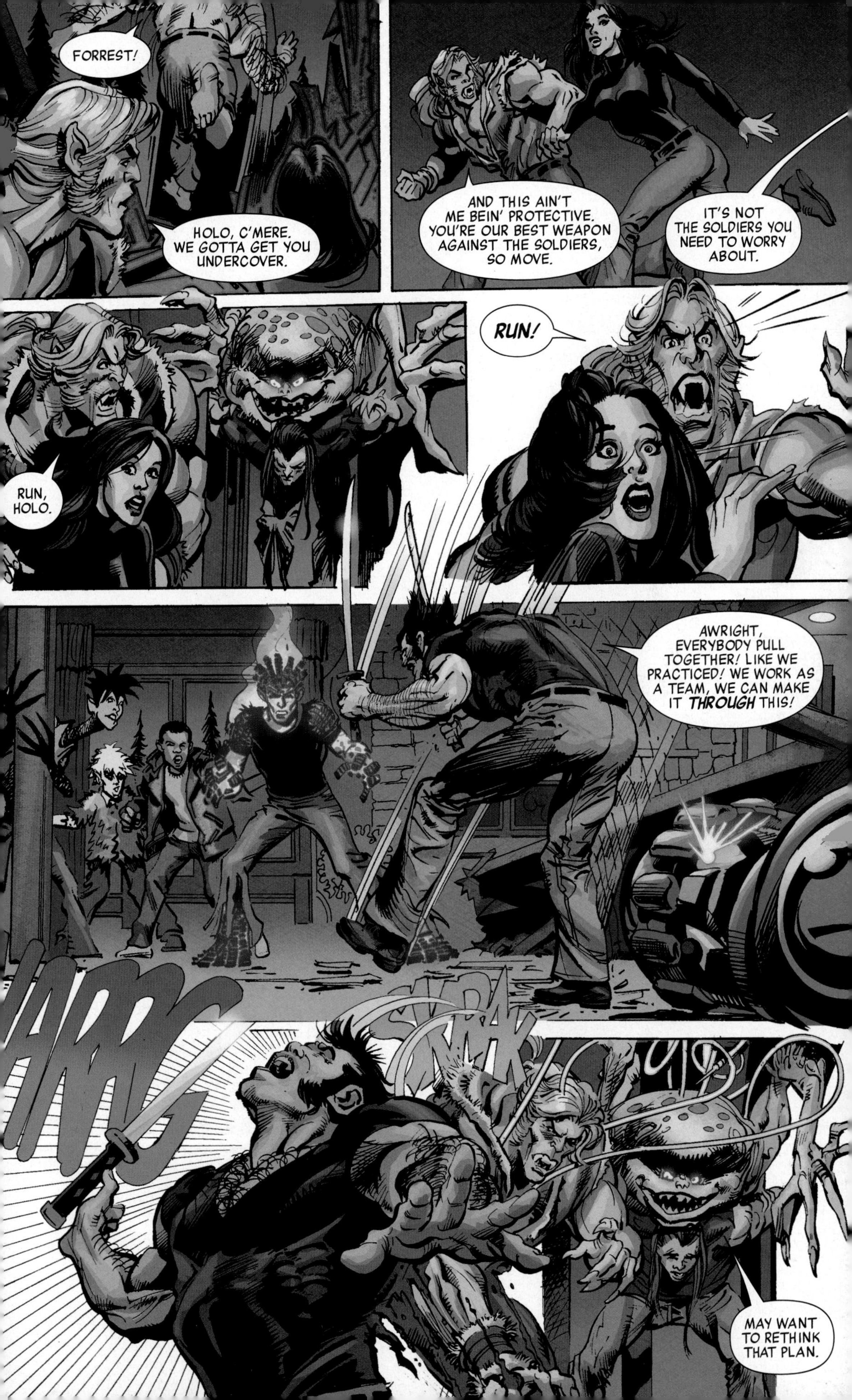
FORREST!
HOLO, C'MERE. WE GOTTA GET YOU UNDERCOVER.
AND THIS AIN'T ME BEIN' PROTECTIVE. YOU'RE OUR BEST WEAPON AGAINST THE SOLDIERS, SO MOVE.
IT'S NOT THE SOLDIERS YOU NEED TO WORRY ABOUT.
RUN, HOLO.
RUN!
AWRIGHT, EVERYBODY PULL TOGETHER! LIKE WE PRACTICED! WE WORK AS A TEAM, WE CAN MAKE IT THROUGH THIS!
MAY WANT TO RETHINK THAT PLAN.

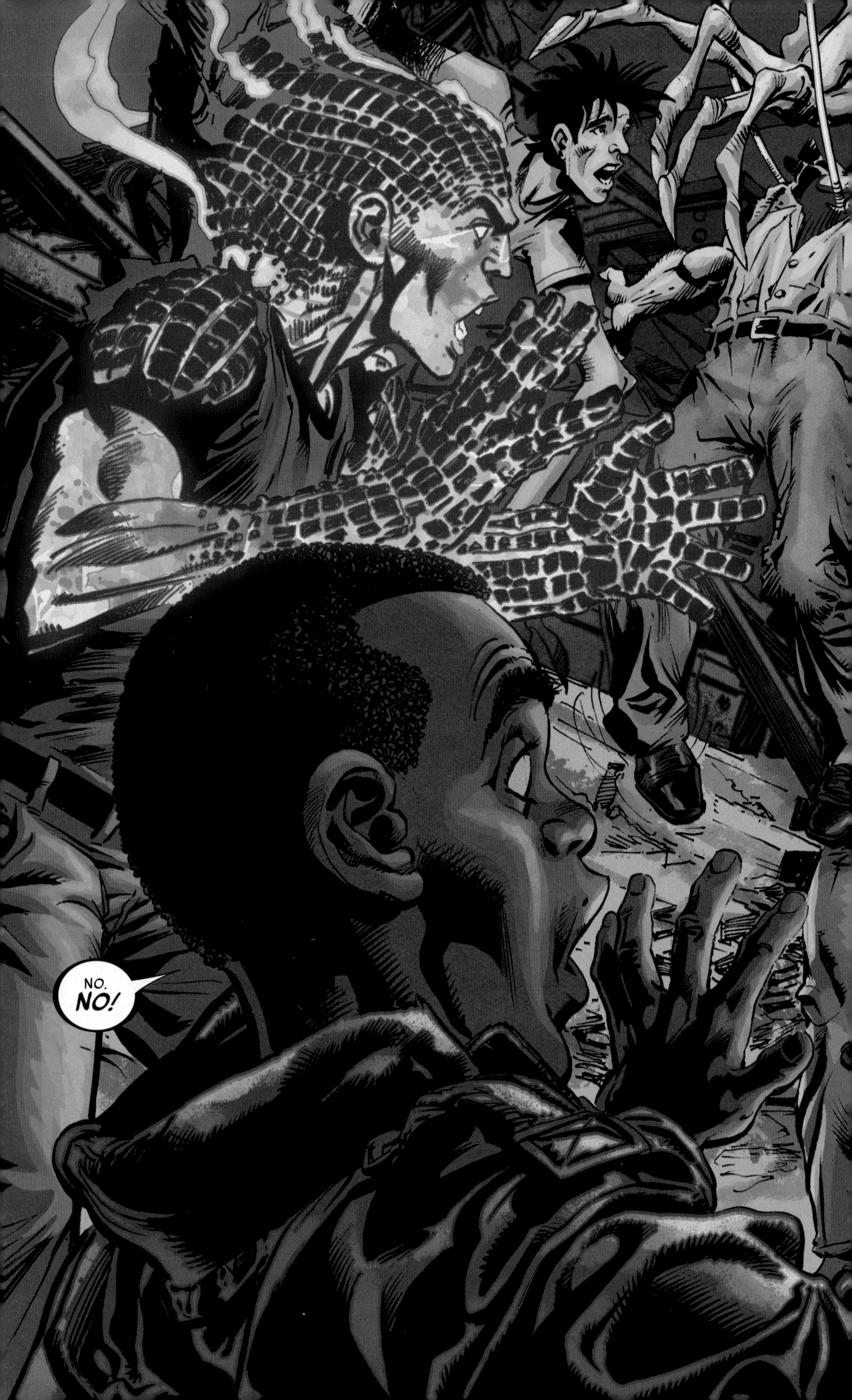
NO. NO!

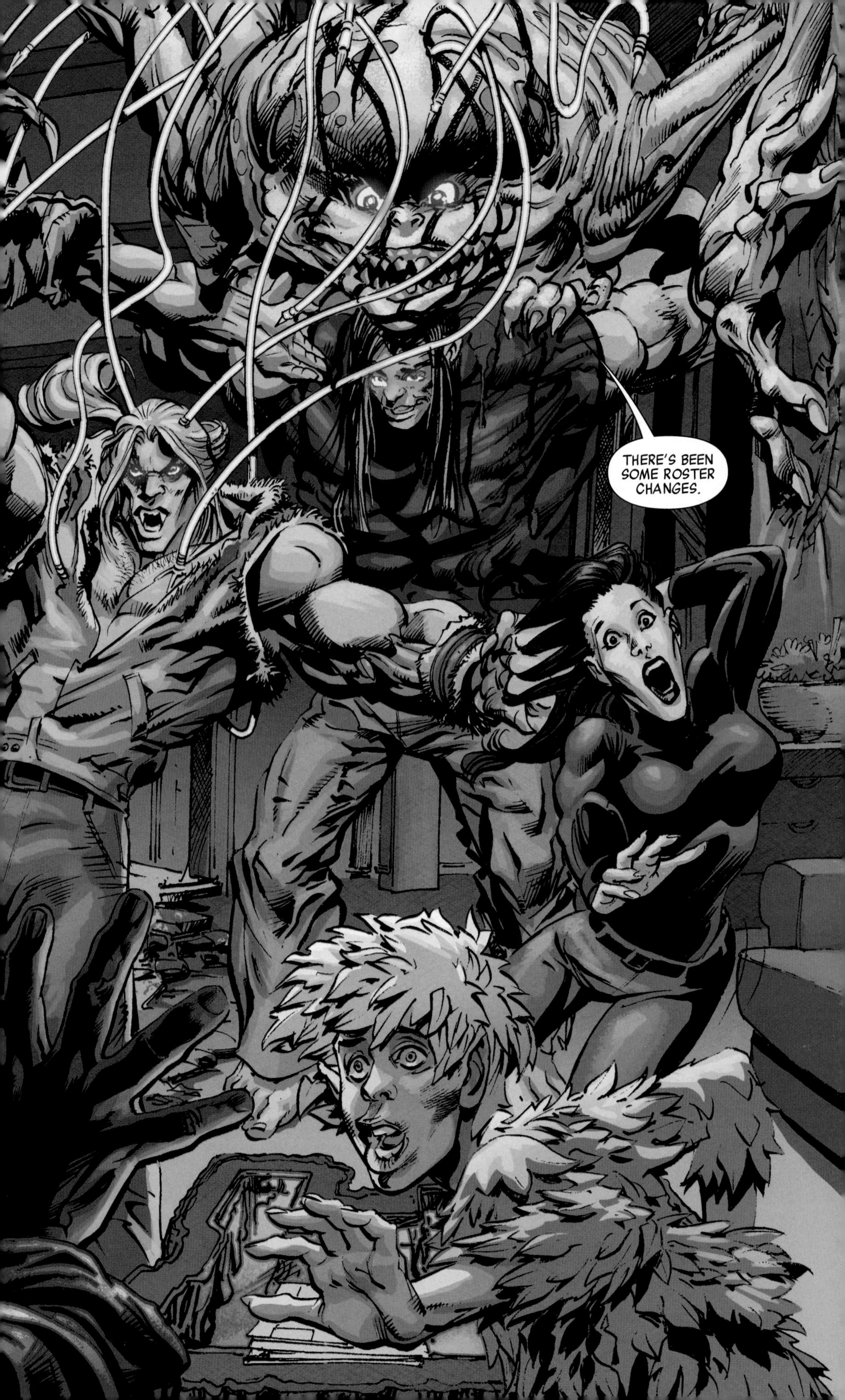
THERE'S BEEN SOME ROSTER CHANGES.

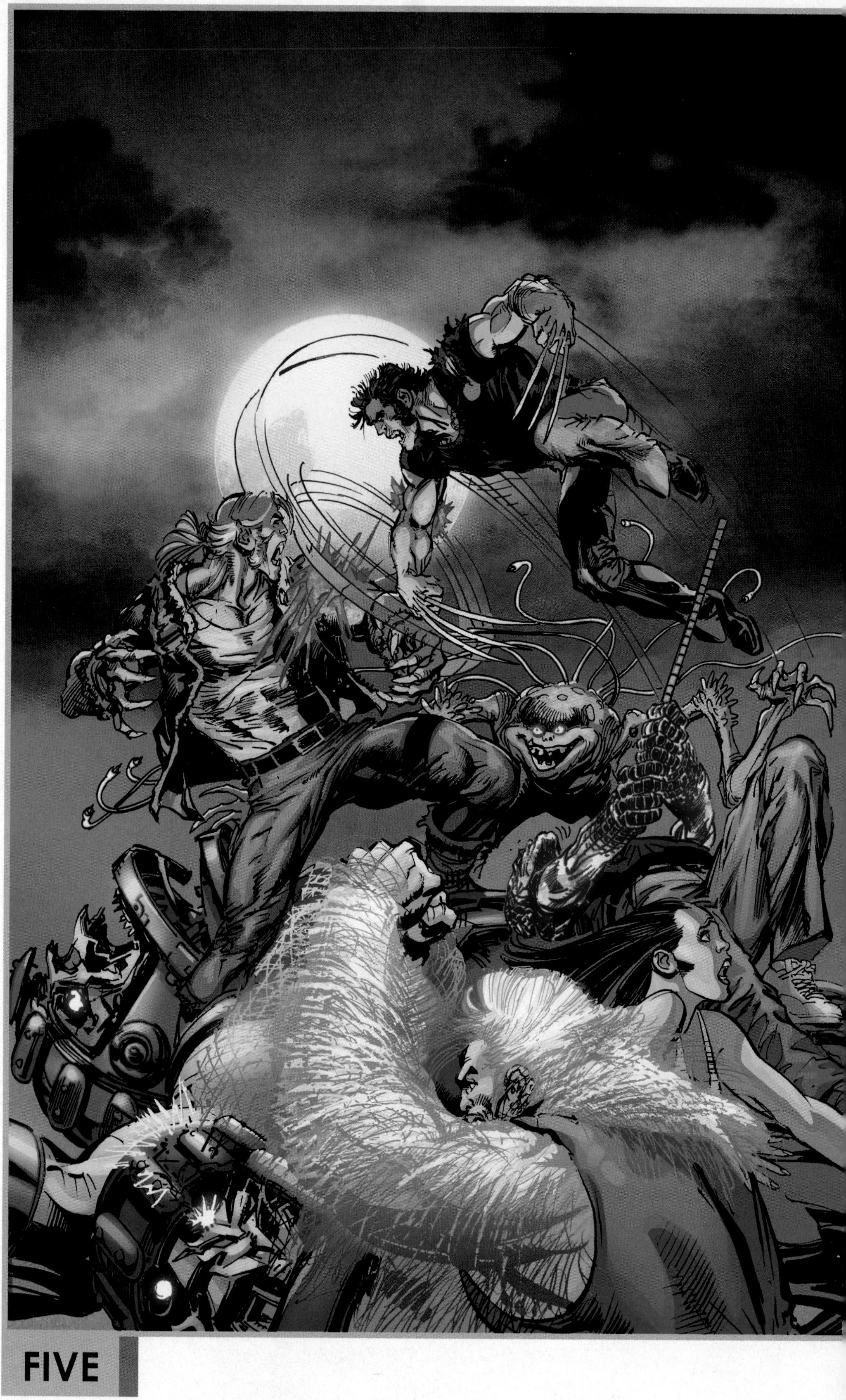

FIVE

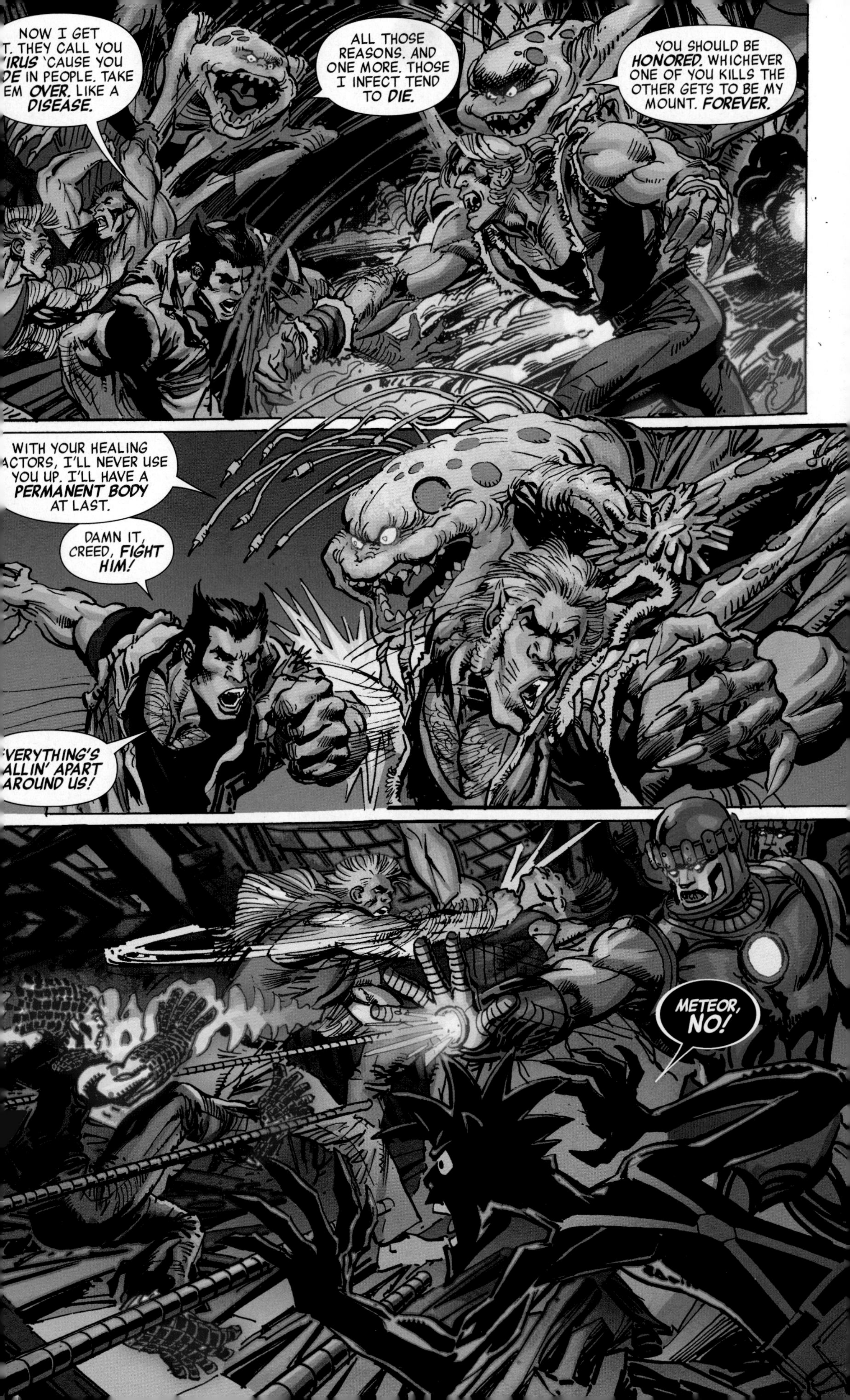
NOW I GET T. THEY CALL YOU *IRUS* 'CAUSE YOU *DE* IN PEOPLE. TAKE EM *OVER.* LIKE A *DISEASE.*
ALL THOSE REASONS. AND ONE MORE. THOSE I INFECT TEND TO *DIE.*
YOU SHOULD BE *HONORED.* WHICHEVER ONE OF YOU KILLS THE OTHER GETS TO BE MY MOUNT. *FOREVER.*
WITH YOUR HEALING ACTORS, I'LL NEVER USE YOU UP. I'LL HAVE A *PERMANENT BODY* AT LAST.
DAMN IT, CREED, *FIGHT HIM!*
VERYTHING'S ALLIN' APART AROUND US!
METEOR, NO!

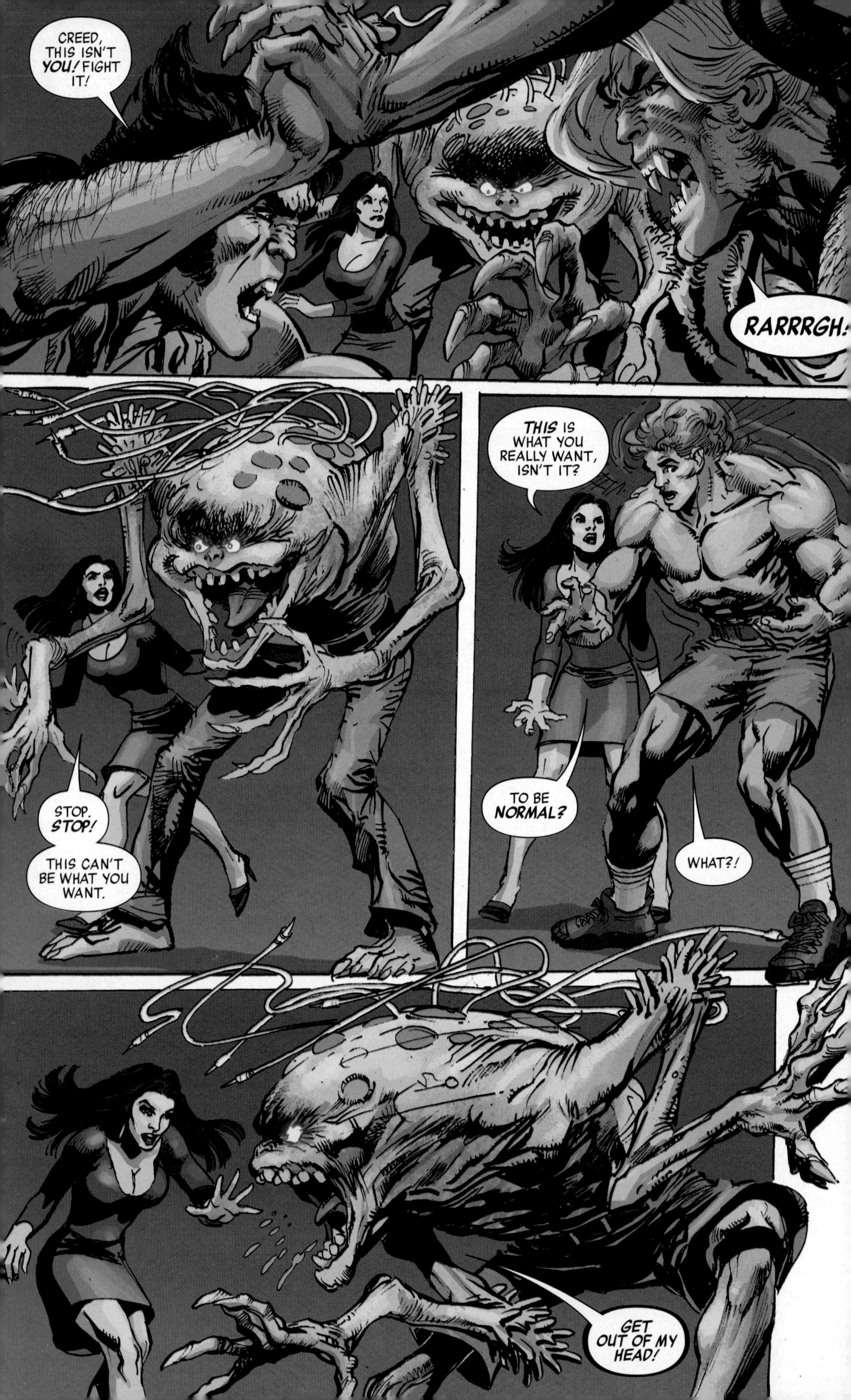
CREED, THIS ISN'T YOU! FIGHT IT!
RARRRGH!
STOP. STOP!
THIS CAN'T BE WHAT YOU WANT.
THIS IS WHAT YOU REALLY WANT, ISN'T IT?
TO BE NORMAL?
WHAT?!
GET OUT OF MY HEAD!

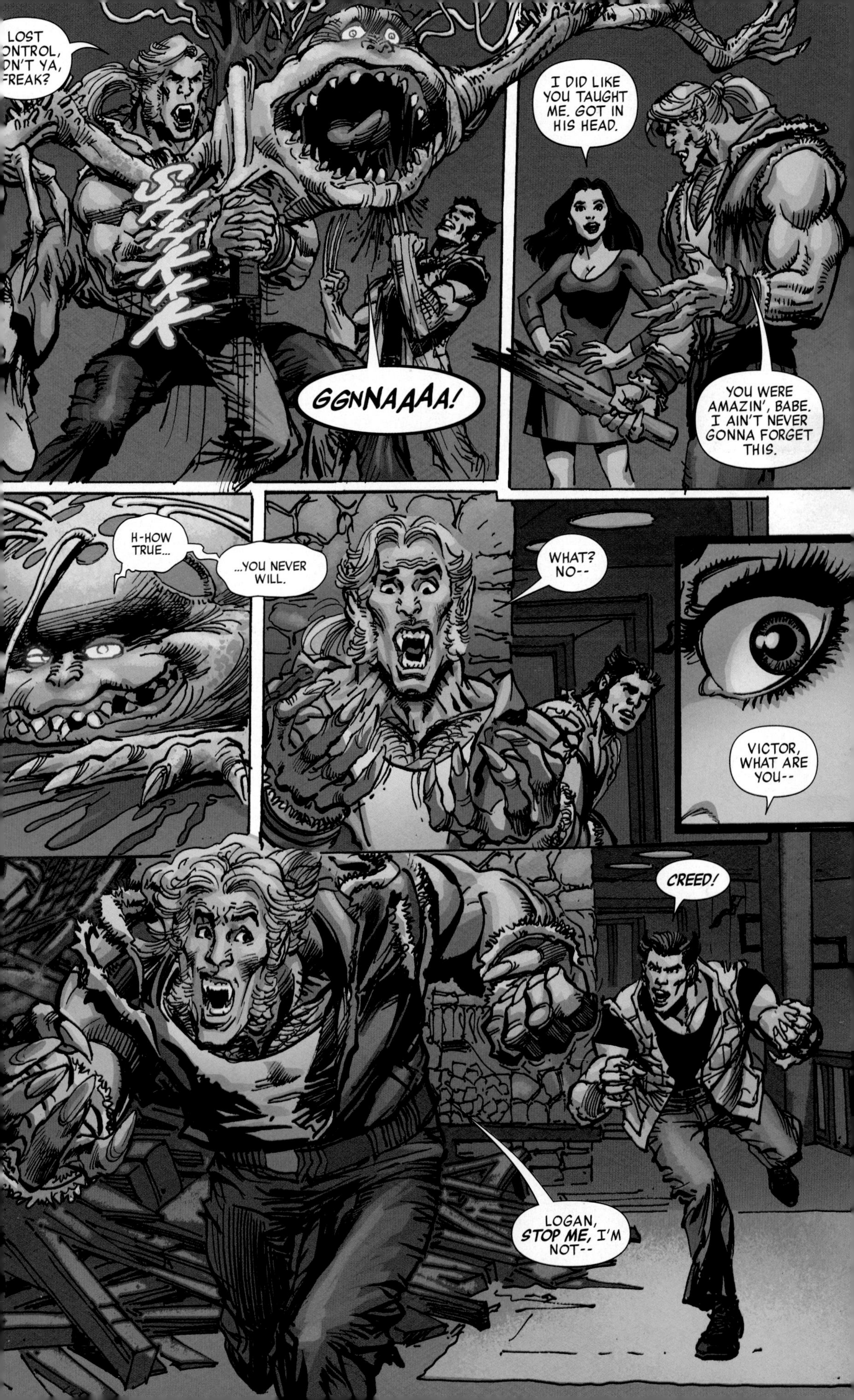

LOST CONTROL, DON'T YA, FREAK?
SHKKKK
GGNNAAAA!
I DID LIKE YOU TAUGHT ME. GOT IN HIS HEAD.
YOU WERE AMAZIN', BABE. I AIN'T NEVER GONNA FORGET THIS.
H-HOW TRUE...
...YOU NEVER WILL.
WHAT? NO--
VICTOR, WHAT ARE YOU--
CREED!
LOGAN, STOP ME, I'M NOT--

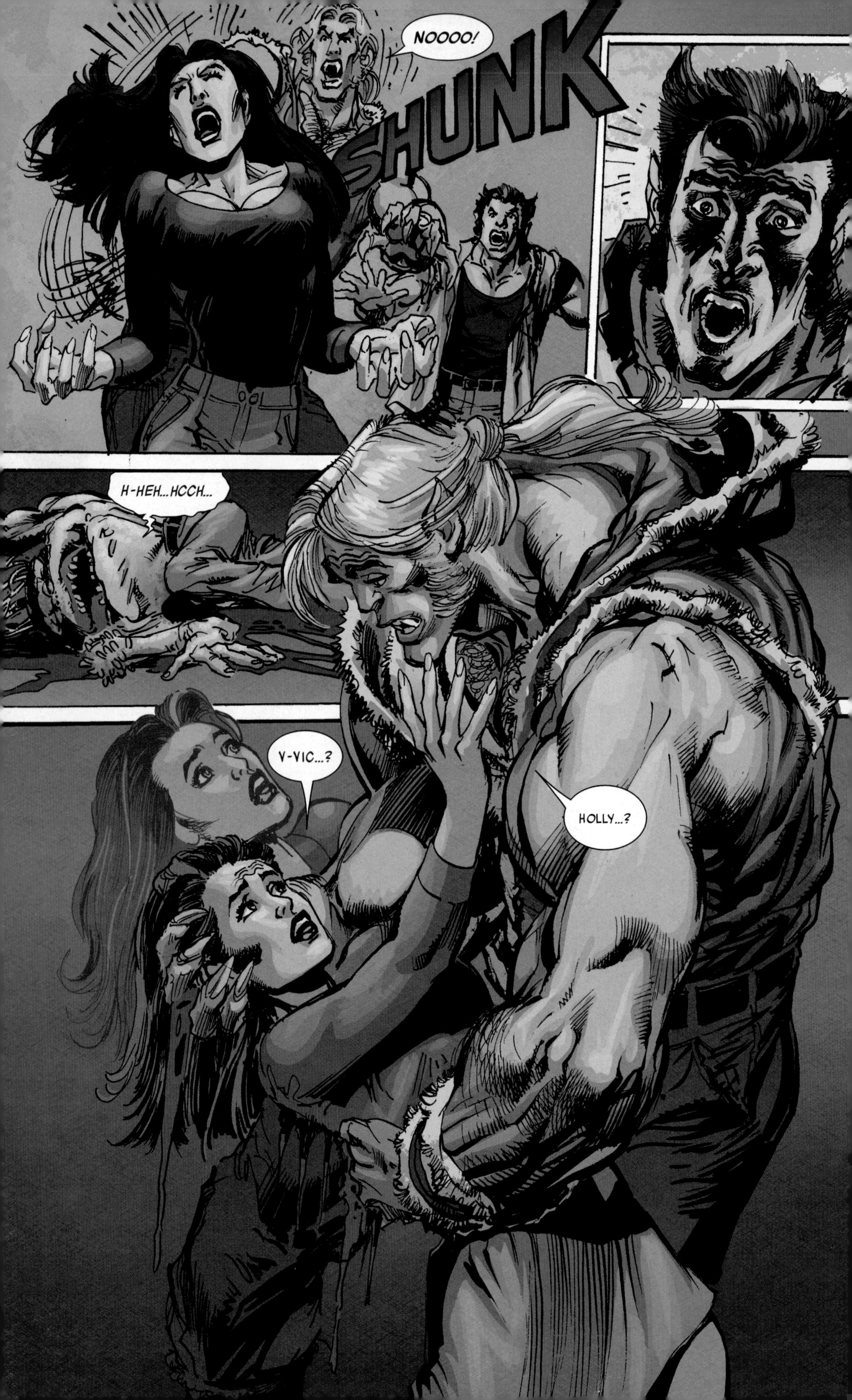
NOOOO!
SHUNK
H-HEH...HCCH...
V-VIC...?
HOLLY...?

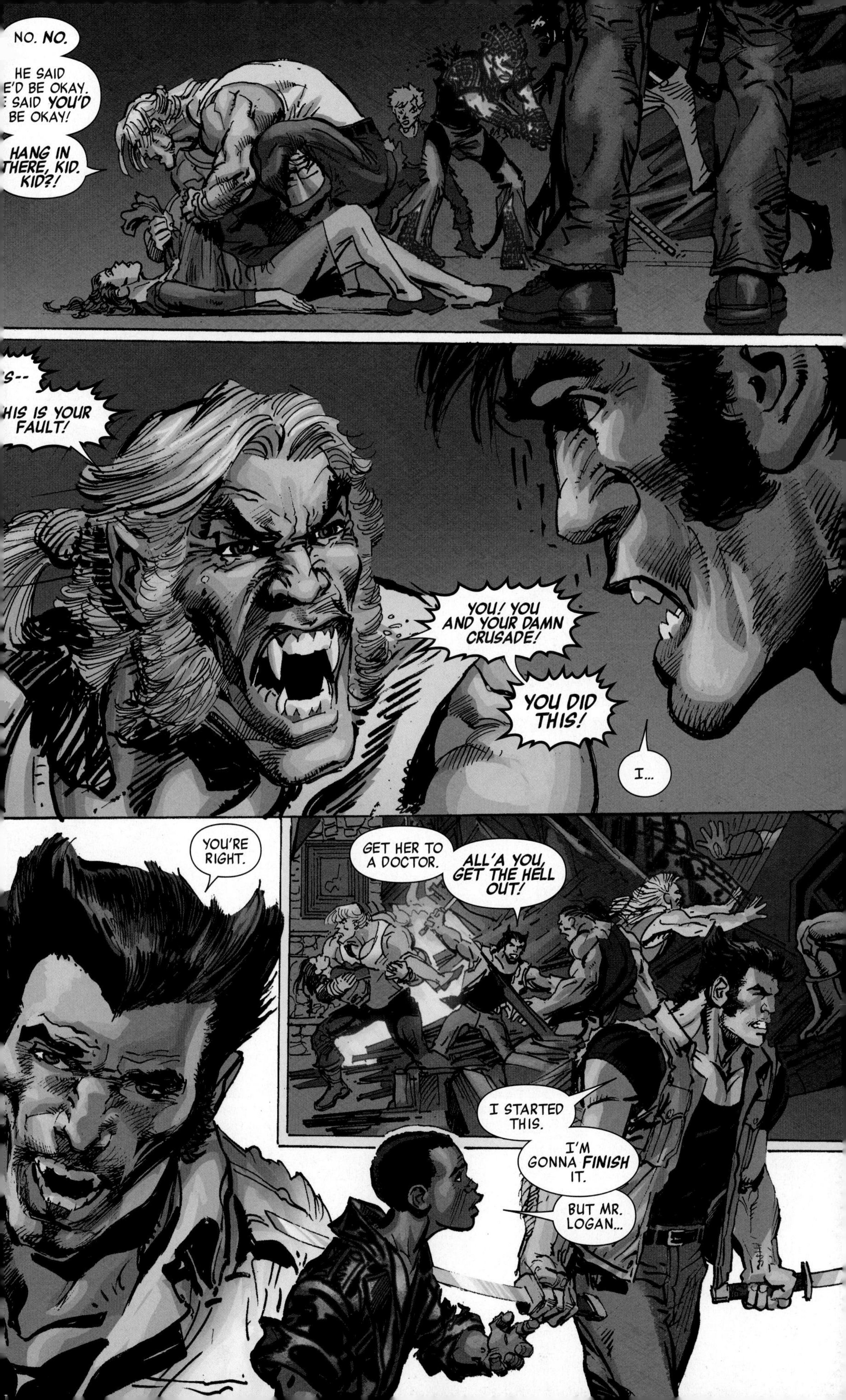
NO. NO.
HE SAID E'D BE OKAY. E SAID YOU'D BE OKAY!
HANG IN THERE, KID. KID?!
S--
HIS IS YOUR FAULT!
YOU! YOU AND YOUR DAMN CRUSADE!
YOU DID THIS!
I...
YOU'RE RIGHT.
GET HER TO A DOCTOR.
ALL'A YOU, GET THE HELL OUT!
I STARTED THIS.
I'M GONNA FINISH IT.
BUT MR. LOGAN...

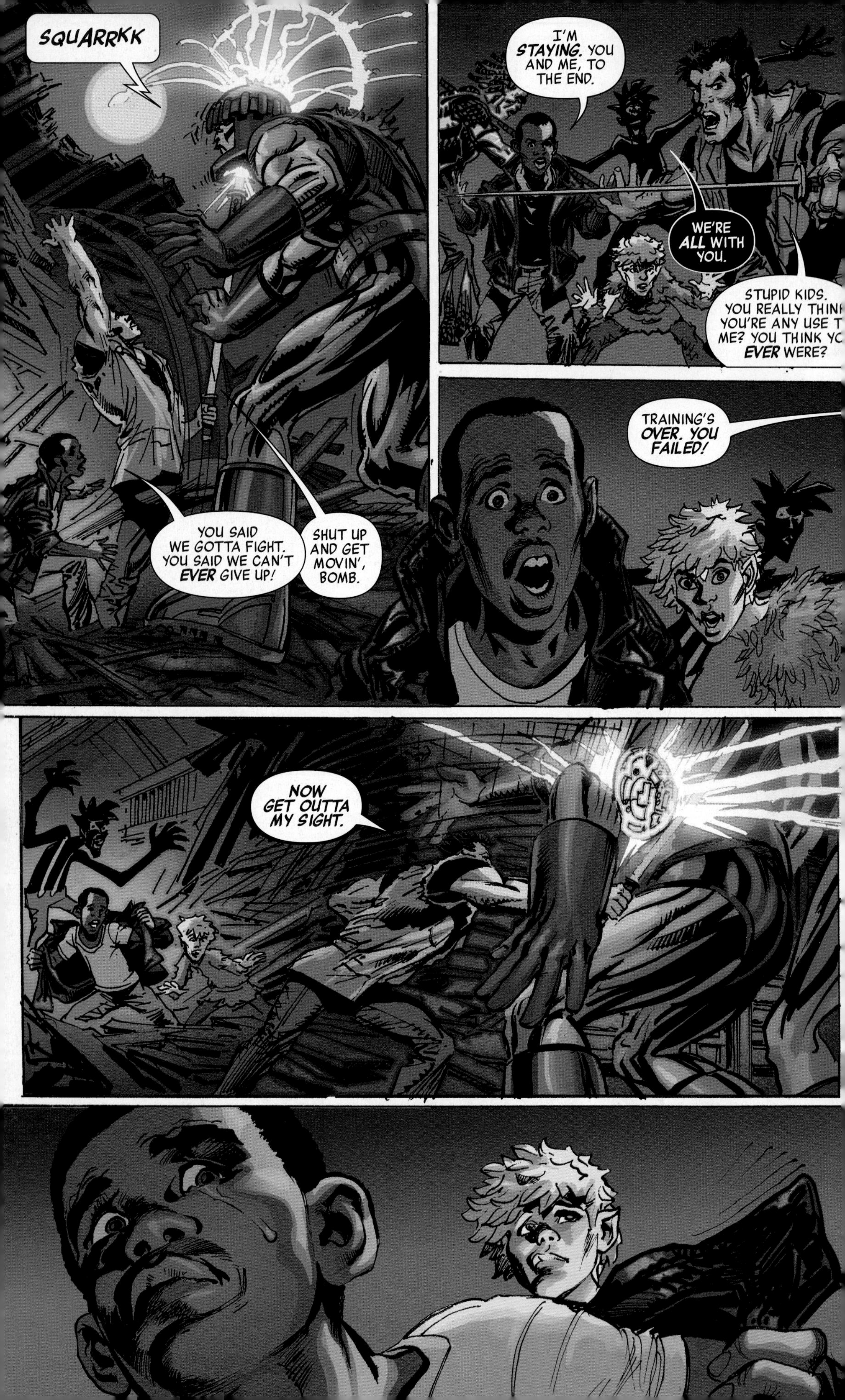
SQUARRKK
YOU SAID WE GOTTA FIGHT. YOU SAID WE CAN'T EVER GIVE UP!
SHUT UP AND GET MOVIN', BOMB.
I'M STAYING. YOU AND ME, TO THE END.
WE'RE ALL WITH YOU.
STUPID KIDS. YOU REALLY THINK YOU'RE ANY USE TO ME? YOU THINK YOU EVER WERE?
TRAINING'S OVER. YOU FAILED!
NOW GET OUTTA MY SIGHT.

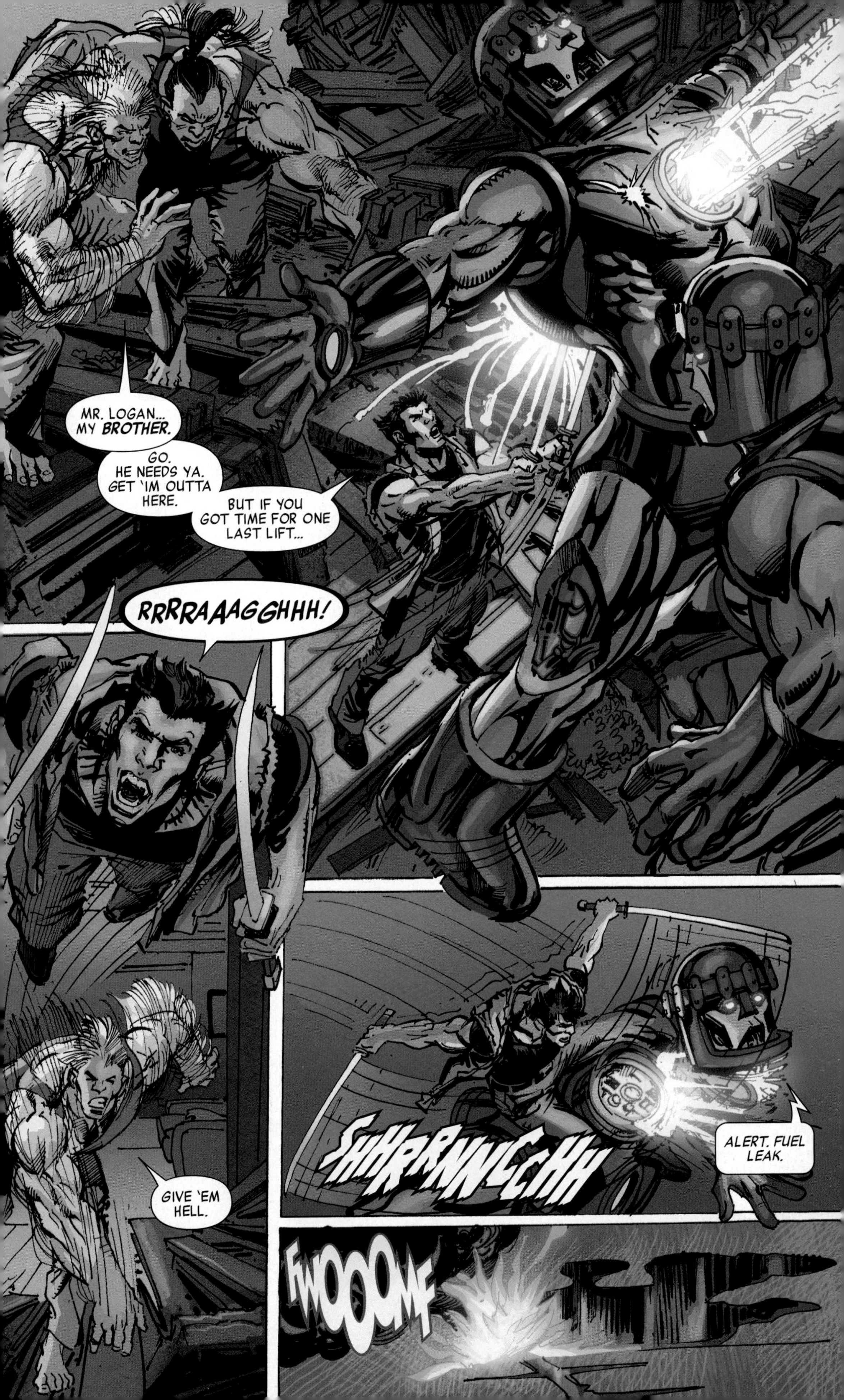
MR. LOGAN... MY BROTHER.
GO. HE NEEDS YA. GET 'IM OUTTA HERE.
BUT IF YOU GOT TIME FOR ONE LAST LIFT...
RRRRAAAGGHHH!
GIVE 'EM HELL.
SHHRRNNCHH
ALERT. FUEL LEAK.
FWOOOMF

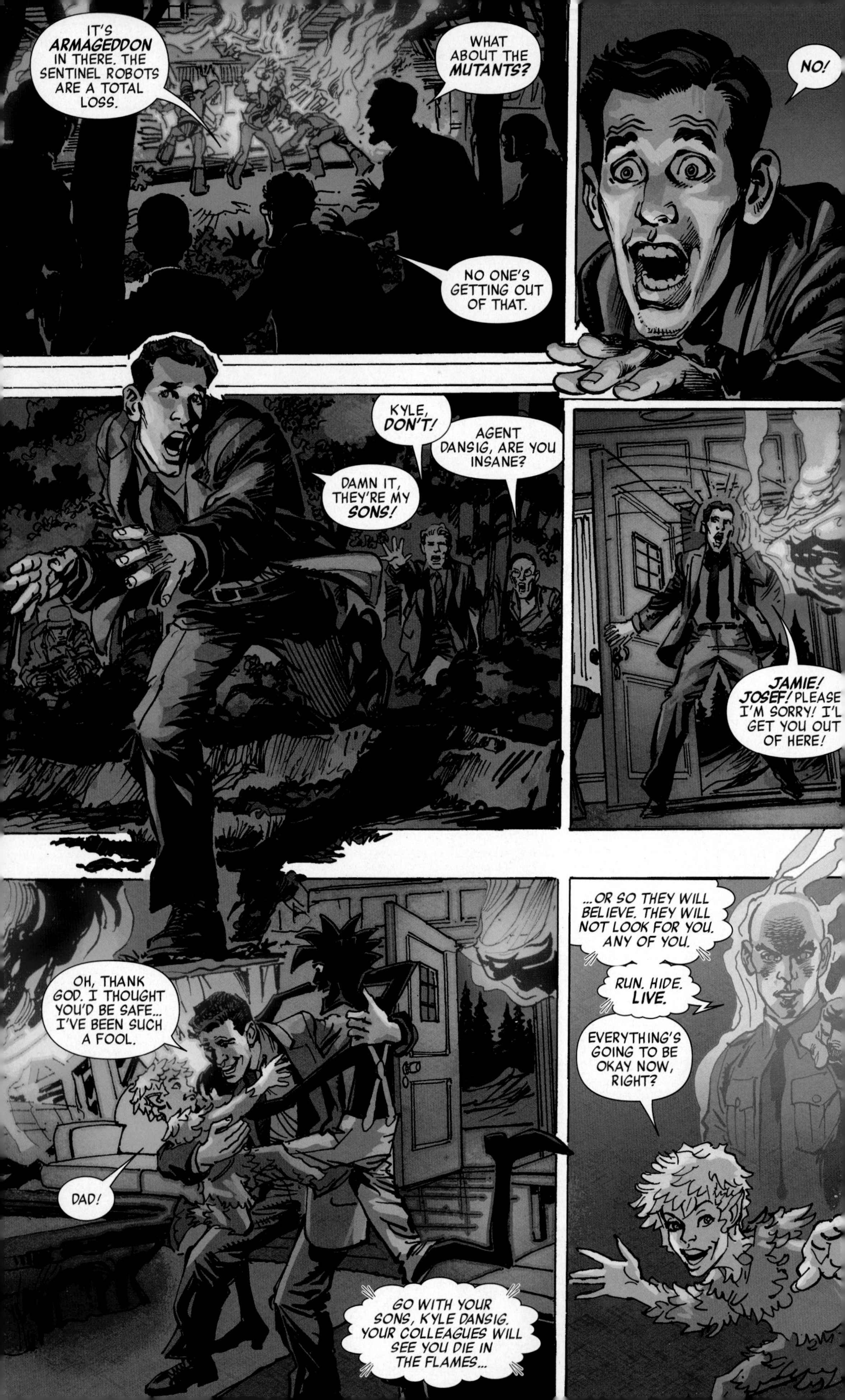
IT'S ARMAGEDDON IN THERE. THE SENTINEL ROBOTS ARE A TOTAL LOSS.
WHAT ABOUT THE MUTANTS?
NO ONE'S GETTING OUT OF THAT.
NO!
KYLE, DON'T!
AGENT DANSIG, ARE YOU INSANE?
DAMN IT, THEY'RE MY SONS!
JAMIE! JOSEF! PLEASE I'M SORRY! I'LL GET YOU OUT OF HERE!
OH, THANK GOD. I THOUGHT YOU'D BE SAFE... I'VE BEEN SUCH A FOOL.
DAD!
GO WITH YOUR SONS, KYLE DANSIG. YOUR COLLEAGUES WILL SEE YOU DIE IN THE FLAMES...
...OR SO THEY WILL BELIEVE. THEY WILL NOT LOOK FOR YOU. ANY OF YOU.
RUN. HIDE. LIVE.
EVERYTHING'S GOING TO BE OKAY NOW, RIGHT?

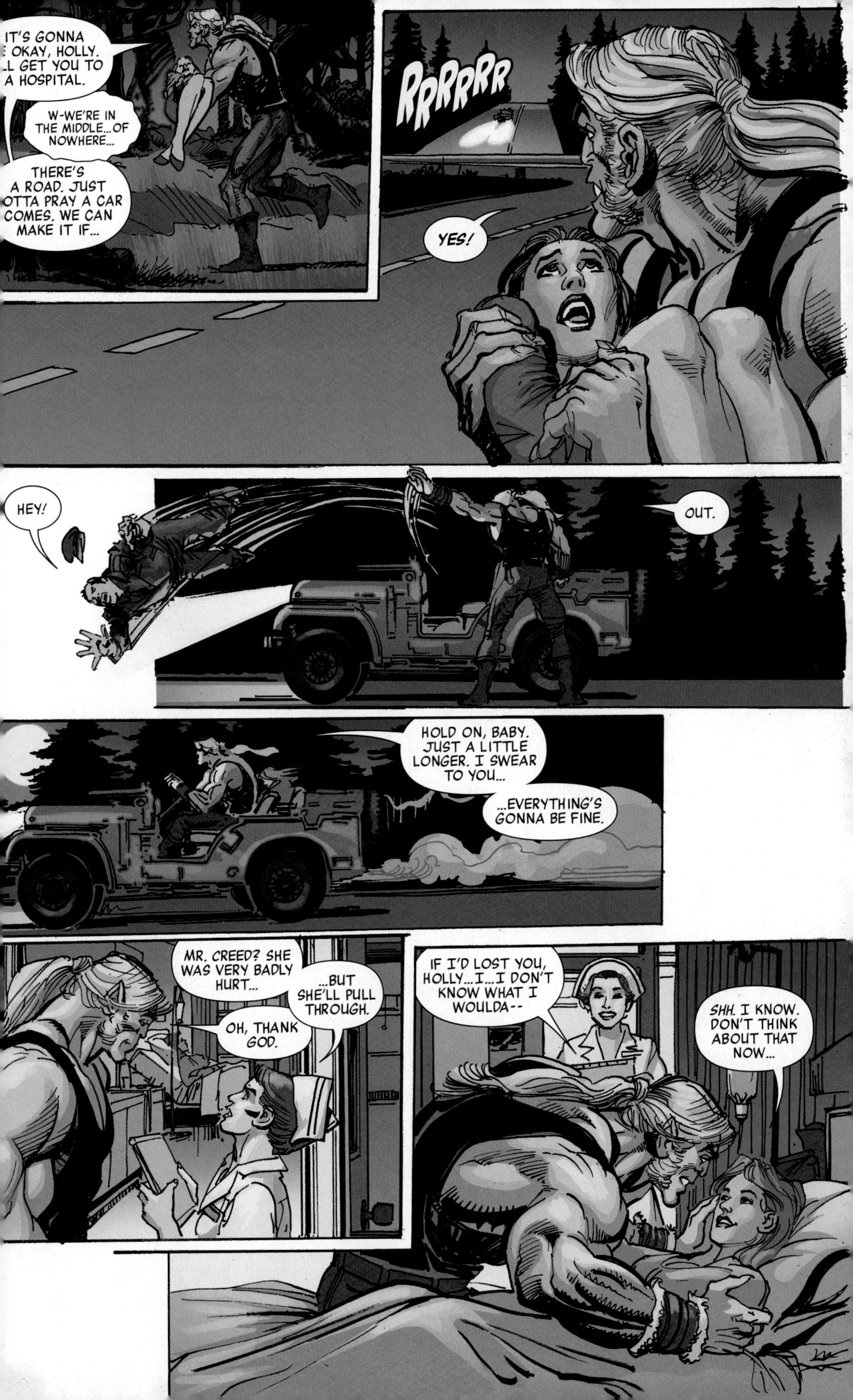
IT'S GONNA E OKAY, HOLLY. .L GET YOU TO A HOSPITAL.
W-WE'RE IN THE MIDDLE...OF NOWHERE...
THERE'S A ROAD. JUST OTTA PRAY A CAR COMES. WE CAN MAKE IT IF...
RRRRRR
YES!
HEY!
OUT.
HOLD ON, BABY. JUST A LITTLE LONGER. I SWEAR TO YOU...
...EVERYTHING'S GONNA BE FINE.
MR. CREED? SHE WAS VERY BADLY HURT...
...BUT SHE'LL PULL THROUGH.
OH, THANK GOD.
IF I'D LOST YOU, HOLLY...I...I DON'T KNOW WHAT I WOULDA--
SHH. I KNOW. DON'T THINK ABOUT THAT NOW...

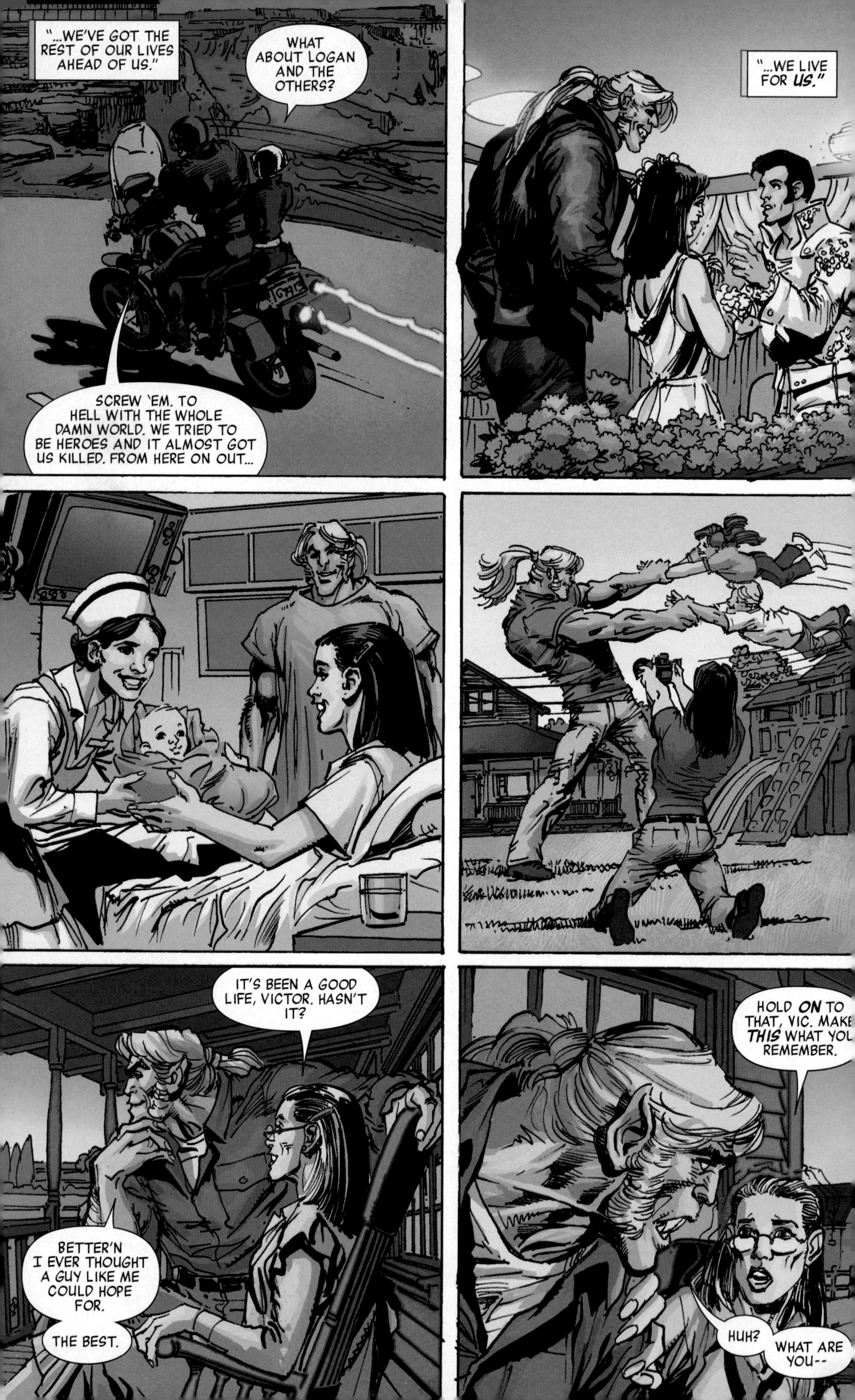
"...WE'VE GOT THE REST OF OUR LIVES AHEAD OF US."
WHAT ABOUT LOGAN AND THE OTHERS?
SCREW 'EM. TO HELL WITH THE WHOLE DAMN WORLD. WE TRIED TO BE HEROES AND IT ALMOST GOT US KILLED. FROM HERE ON OUT...
"...WE LIVE FOR *US.*"
IT'S BEEN A GOOD LIFE, VICTOR. HASN'T IT?
BETTER'N I EVER THOUGHT A GUY LIKE ME COULD HOPE FOR.
THE BEST.
HOLD *ON* TO THAT, VIC. MAKE *THIS* WHAT YOU REMEMBER.
HUH?
WHAT ARE YOU--

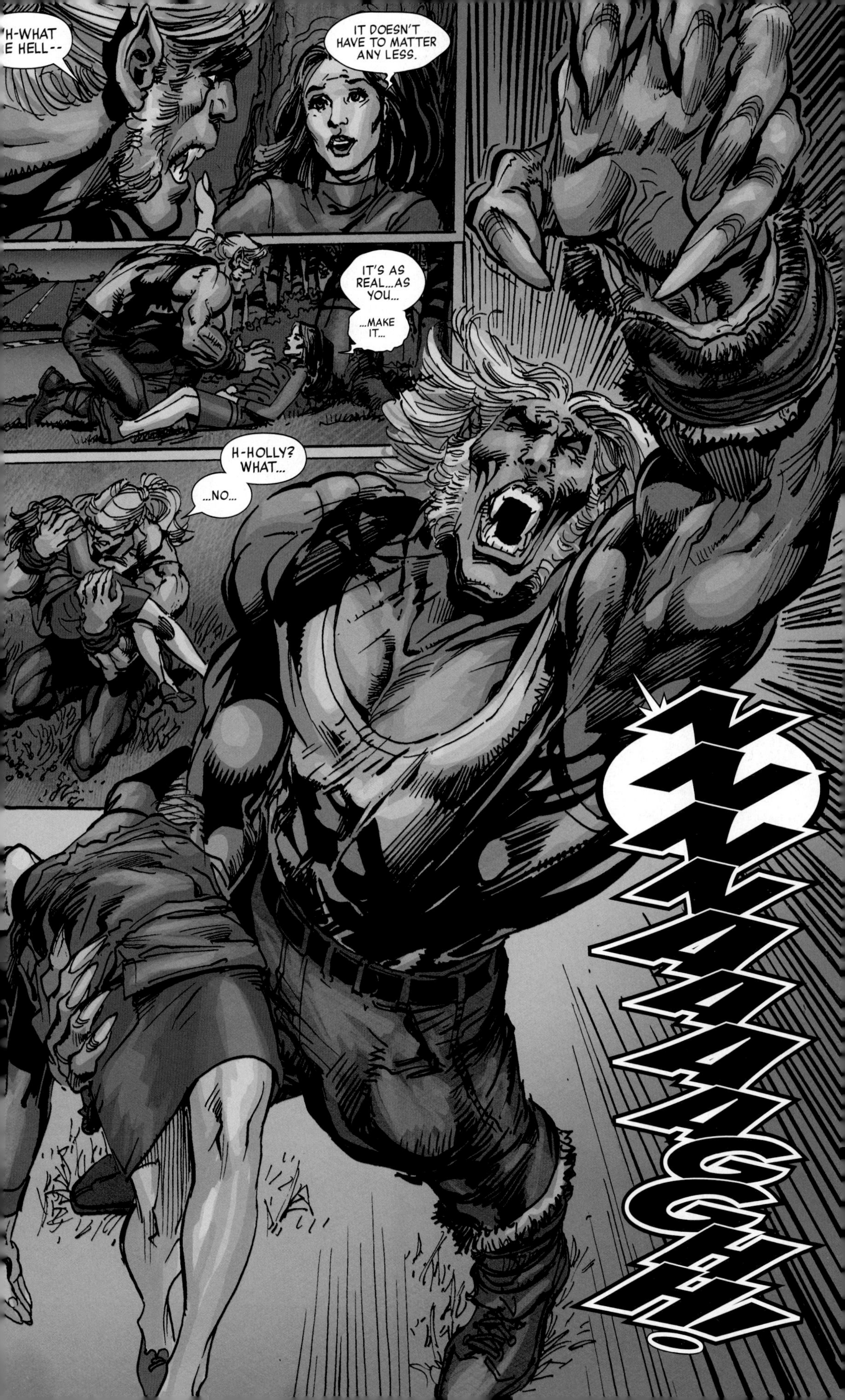
H-WHAT E HELL--
IT DOESN'T HAVE TO MATTER ANY LESS.
IT'S AS REAL...AS YOU...
...MAKE IT...
H-HOLLY? WHAT...
...NO...
NNNAAAAGGHH!

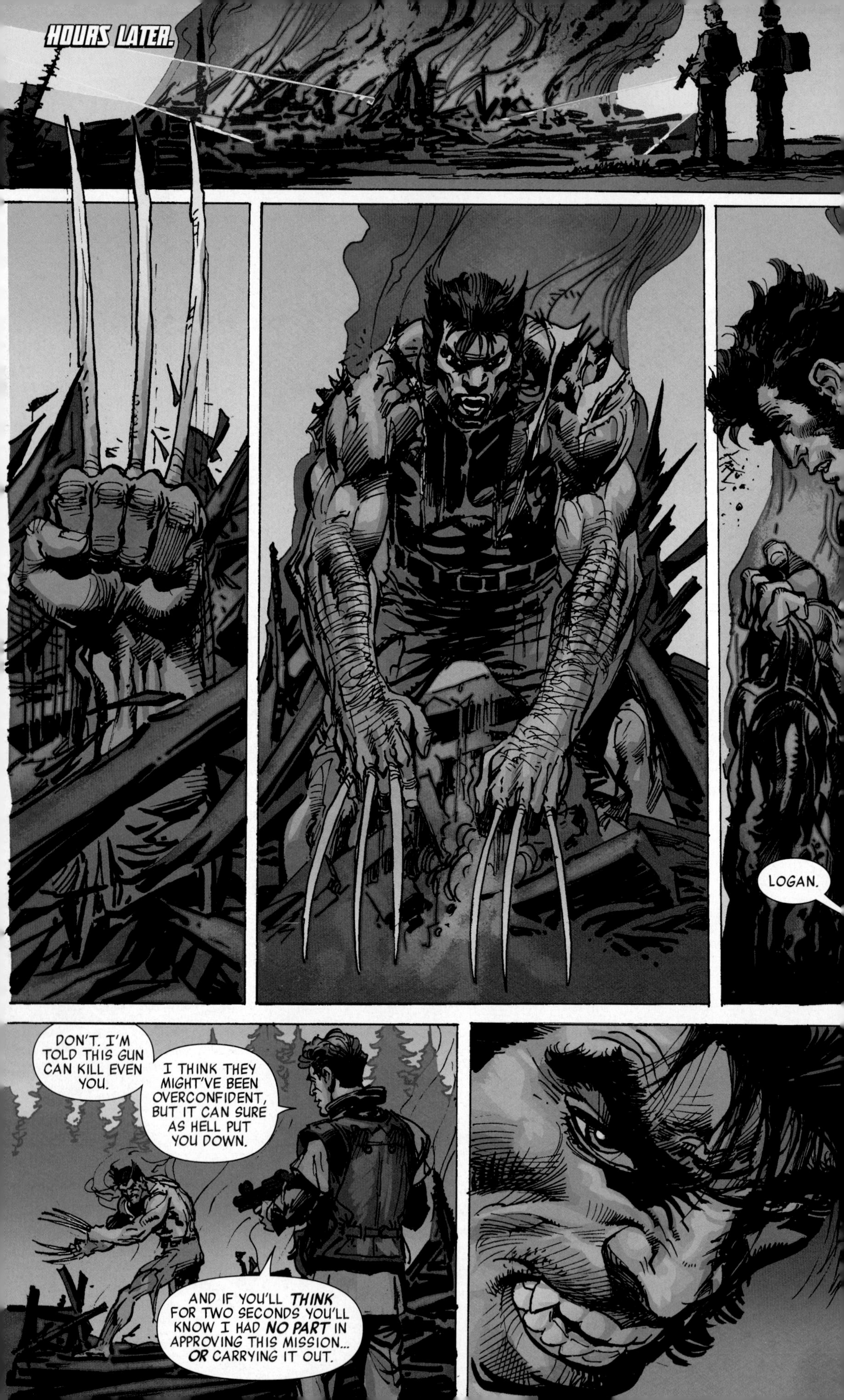
HOURS LATER.
LOGAN.
DON'T. I'M TOLD THIS GUN CAN KILL EVEN YOU.
I THINK THEY MIGHT'VE BEEN OVERCONFIDENT, BUT IT CAN SURE AS HELL PUT YOU DOWN.
AND IF YOU'LL THINK FOR TWO SECONDS YOU'LL KNOW I HAD NO PART IN APPROVING THIS MISSION... OR CARRYING IT OUT.

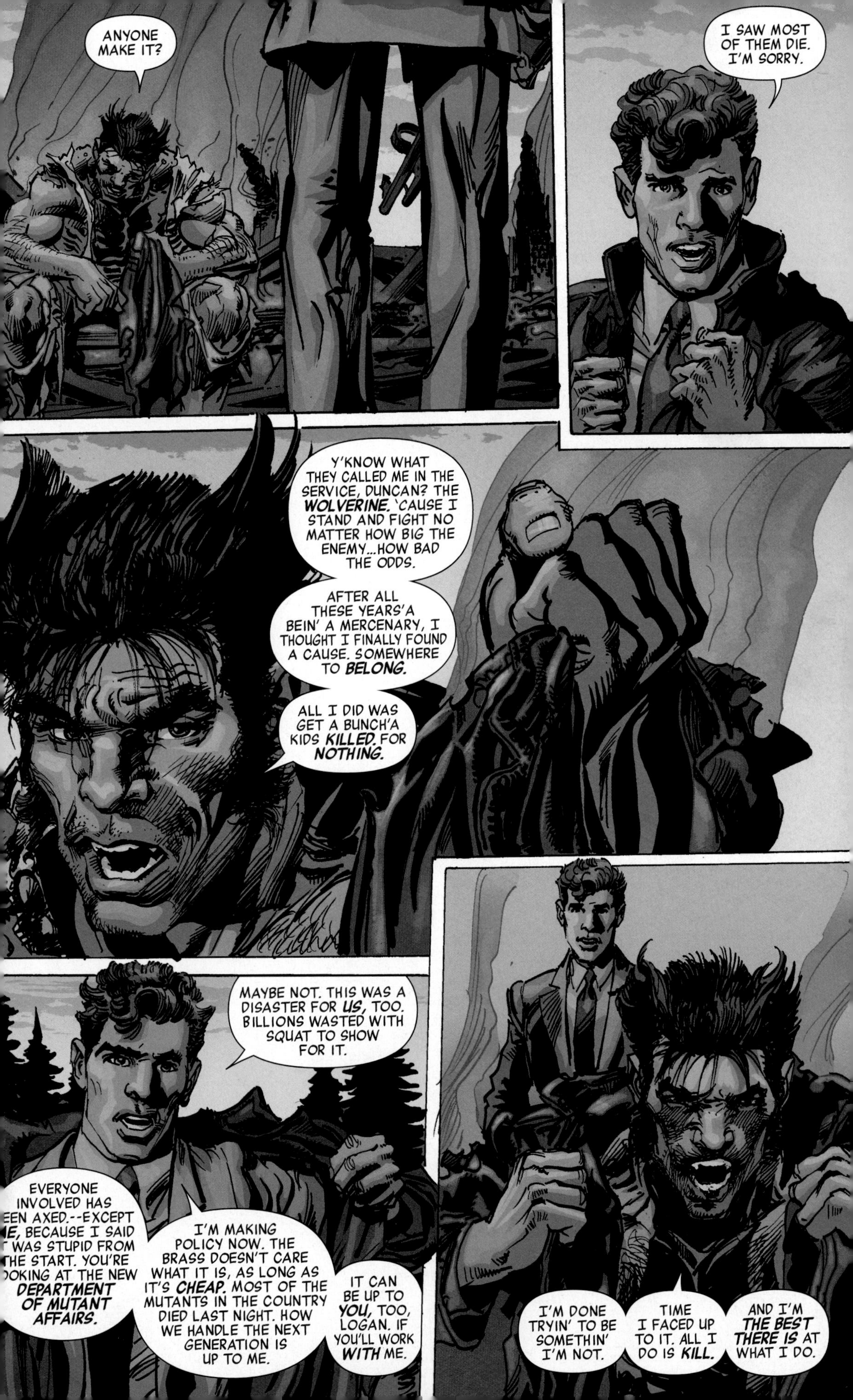

ANYONE MAKE IT?
I SAW MOST OF THEM DIE. I'M SORRY.
Y'KNOW WHAT THEY CALLED ME IN THE SERVICE, DUNCAN? THE WOLVERINE. 'CAUSE I STAND AND FIGHT NO MATTER HOW BIG THE ENEMY...HOW BAD THE ODDS.
AFTER ALL THESE YEARS'A BEIN' A MERCENARY, I THOUGHT I FINALLY FOUND A CAUSE. SOMEWHERE TO BELONG.
ALL I DID WAS GET A BUNCH'A KIDS KILLED. FOR NOTHING.
MAYBE NOT. THIS WAS A DISASTER FOR US, TOO. BILLIONS WASTED WITH SQUAT TO SHOW FOR IT.
EVERYONE INVOLVED HAS EEN AXED.--EXCEPT IE, BECAUSE I SAID T WAS STUPID FROM THE START. YOU'RE OOKING AT THE NEW DEPARTMENT OF MUTANT AFFAIRS.
I'M MAKING POLICY NOW. THE BRASS DOESN'T CARE WHAT IT IS, AS LONG AS IT'S CHEAP. MOST OF THE MUTANTS IN THE COUNTRY DIED LAST NIGHT. HOW WE HANDLE THE NEXT GENERATION IS UP TO ME.
IT CAN BE UP TO YOU, TOO, LOGAN. IF YOU'LL WORK WITH ME.
I'M DONE TRYIN' TO BE SOMETHIN' I'M NOT.
TIME I FACED UP TO IT. ALL I DO IS KILL.
AND I'M THE BEST THERE IS AT WHAT I DO.

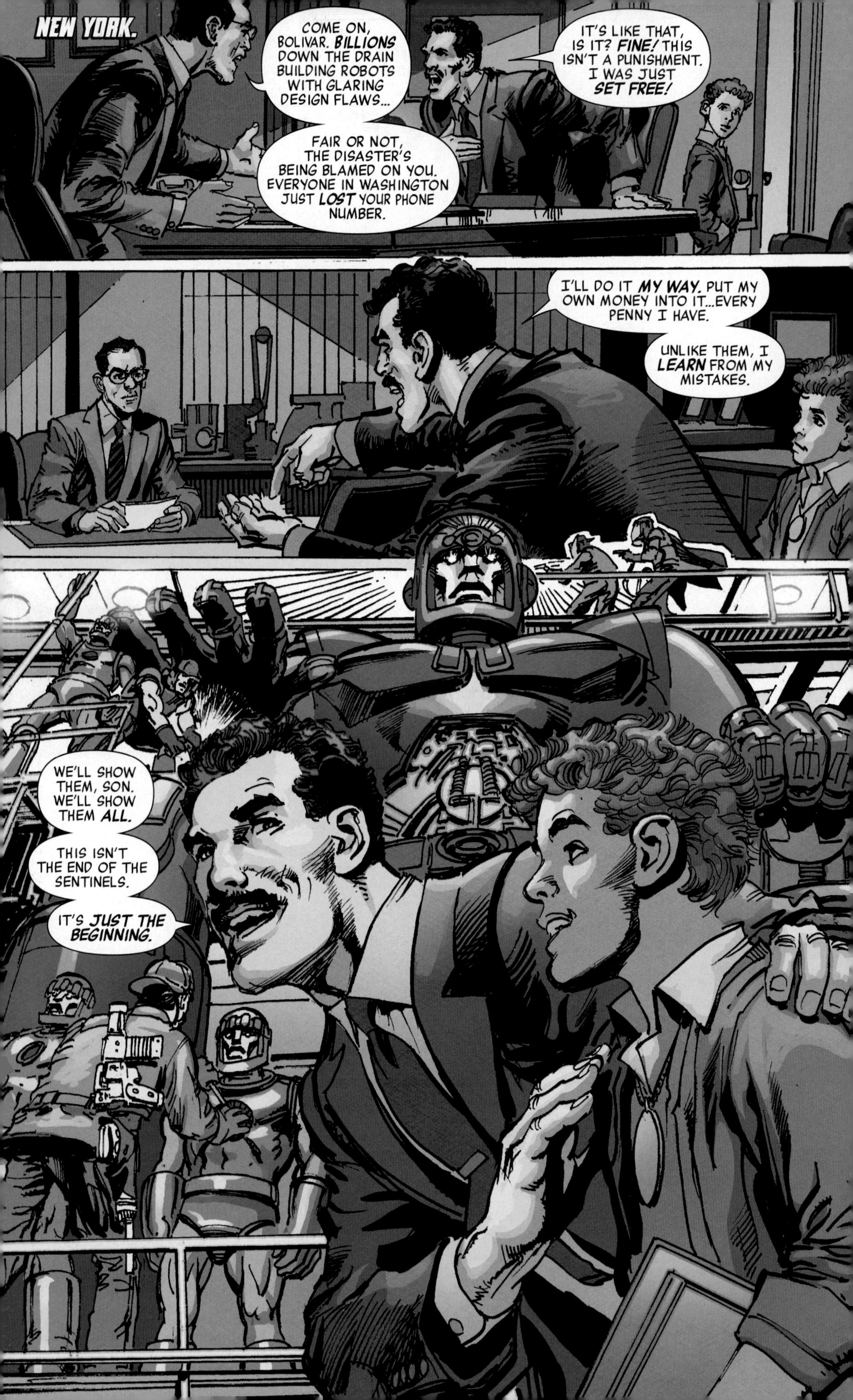
NEW YORK.
COME ON, BOLIVAR. BILLIONS DOWN THE DRAIN BUILDING ROBOTS WITH GLARING DESIGN FLAWS...
FAIR OR NOT, THE DISASTER'S BEING BLAMED ON YOU. EVERYONE IN WASHINGTON JUST LOST YOUR PHONE NUMBER.
IT'S LIKE THAT, IS IT? FINE! THIS ISN'T A PUNISHMENT. I WAS JUST SET FREE!
I'LL DO IT MY WAY. PUT MY OWN MONEY INTO IT...EVERY PENNY I HAVE.
UNLIKE THEM, I LEARN FROM MY MISTAKES.
WE'LL SHOW THEM, SON. WE'LL SHOW THEM ALL.
THIS ISN'T THE END OF THE SENTINELS.
IT'S JUST THE BEGINNING.

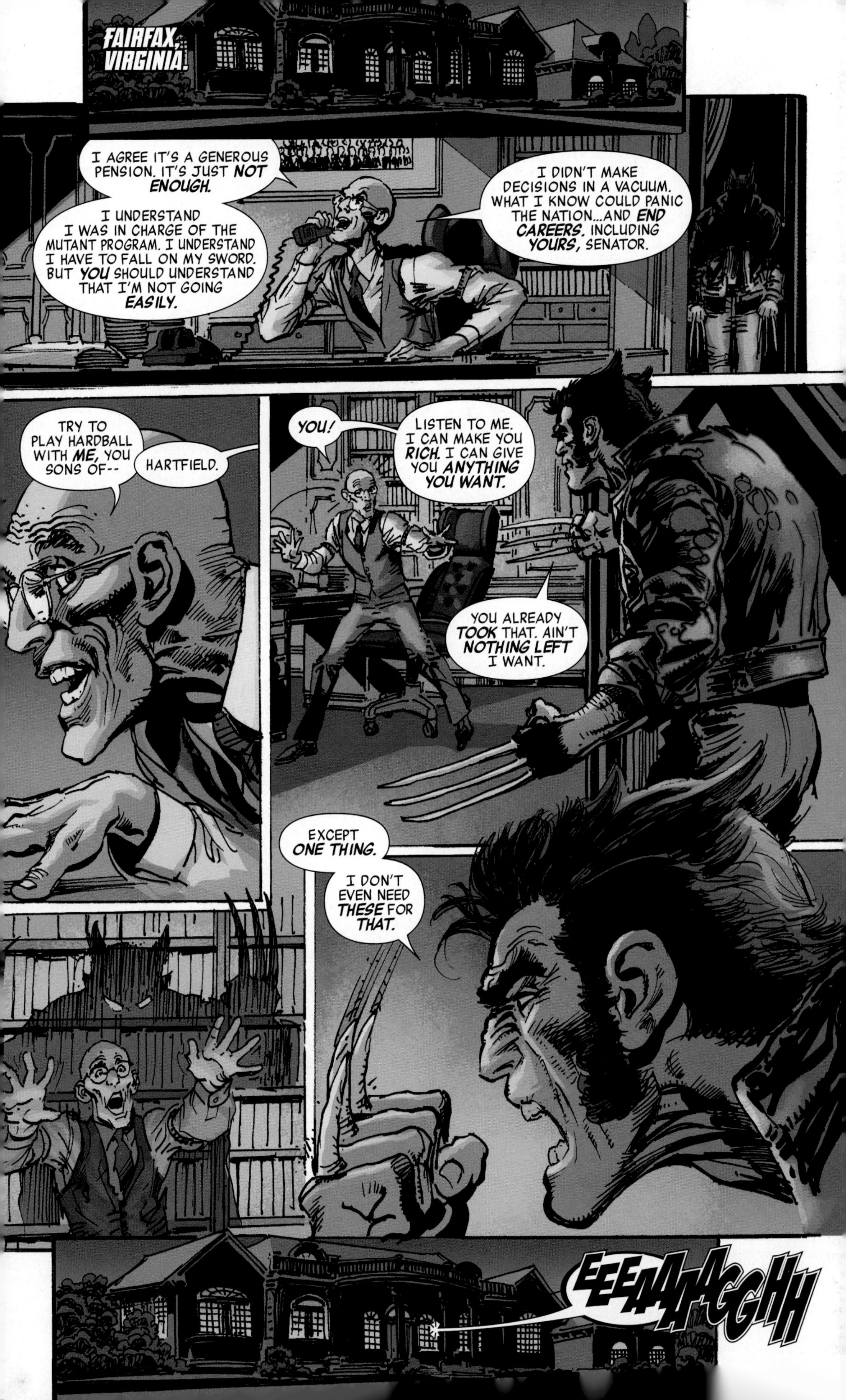
FAIRFAX, VIRGINIA.
I AGREE IT'S A GENEROUS PENSION. IT'S JUST NOT ENOUGH.
I UNDERSTAND I WAS IN CHARGE OF THE MUTANT PROGRAM. I UNDERSTAND I HAVE TO FALL ON MY SWORD. BUT YOU SHOULD UNDERSTAND THAT I'M NOT GOING EASILY.
I DIDN'T MAKE DECISIONS IN A VACUUM. WHAT I KNOW COULD PANIC THE NATION...AND END CAREERS. INCLUDING YOURS, SENATOR.
TRY TO PLAY HARDBALL WITH ME, YOU SONS OF--
HARTFIELD.
YOU!
LISTEN TO ME. I CAN MAKE YOU RICH. I CAN GIVE YOU ANYTHING YOU WANT.
YOU ALREADY TOOK THAT. AIN'T NOTHING LEFT I WANT.
EXCEPT ONE THING.
I DON'T EVEN NEED THESE FOR THAT.
EEEAAAAGGHH

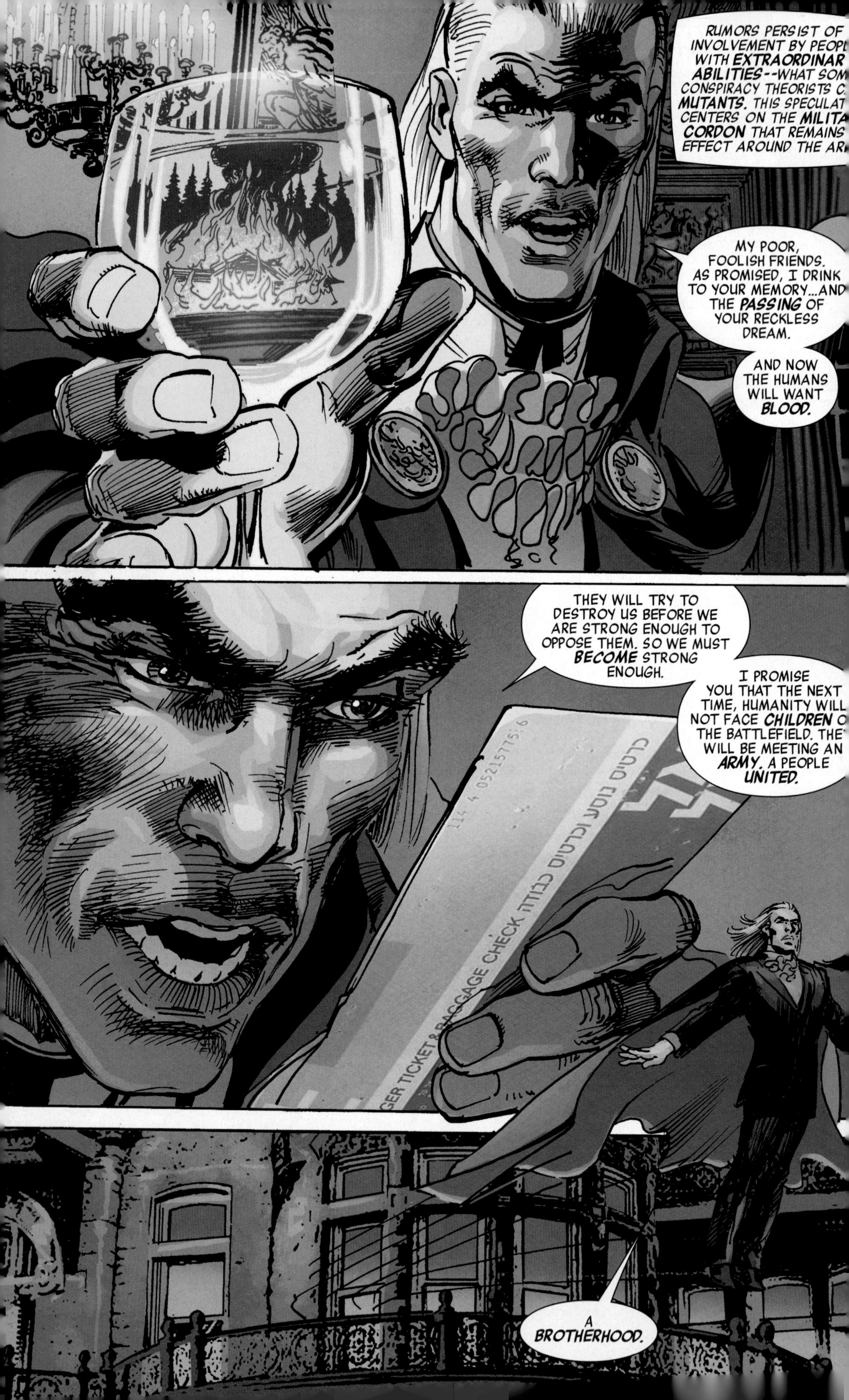

RUMORS PERSIST OF INVOLVEMENT BY PEOPL WITH **EXTRAORDINAR ABILITIES**--WHAT SOM CONSPIRACY THEORISTS C. **MUTANTS.** THIS SPECULAT CENTERS ON THE **MILITA CORDON** THAT REMAINS EFFECT AROUND THE AR
MY POOR, FOOLISH FRIENDS. AS PROMISED, I DRINK TO YOUR MEMORY...AND THE ***PASSING*** OF YOUR RECKLESS DREAM.
AND NOW THE HUMANS WILL WANT ***BLOOD.***
THEY WILL TRY TO DESTROY US BEFORE WE ARE STRONG ENOUGH TO OPPOSE THEM. SO WE MUST ***BECOME*** STRONG ENOUGH.
I PROMISE YOU THAT THE NEXT TIME, HUMANITY WILL NOT FACE ***CHILDREN*** O THE BATTLEFIELD. THE WILL BE MEETING AN ***ARMY.*** A PEOPLE ***UNITED.***
GER TICKET & BAGGAGE CHECK
A ***BROTHERHOOD.***

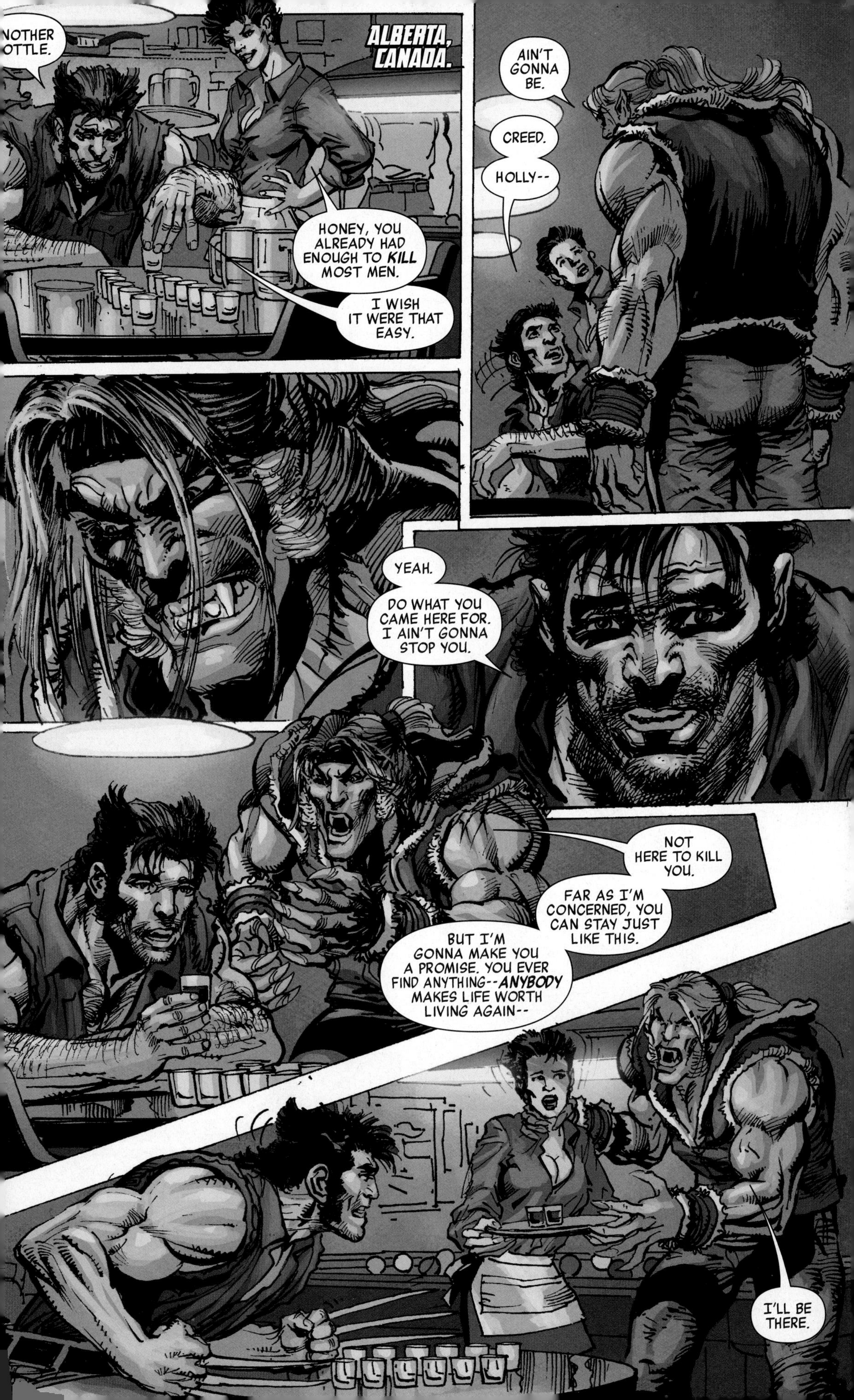
NOTHER
OTTLE.
ALBERTA, CANADA.
HONEY, YOU ALREADY HAD ENOUGH TO KILL MOST MEN.
I WISH IT WERE THAT EASY.
AIN'T GONNA BE.
CREED.
HOLLY--
YEAH.
DO WHAT YOU CAME HERE FOR. I AIN'T GONNA STOP YOU.
NOT HERE TO KILL YOU.
FAR AS I'M CONCERNED, YOU CAN STAY JUST LIKE THIS.
BUT I'M GONNA MAKE YOU A PROMISE. YOU EVER FIND ANYTHING--ANYBODY MAKES LIFE WORTH LIVING AGAIN--
I'LL BE THERE.

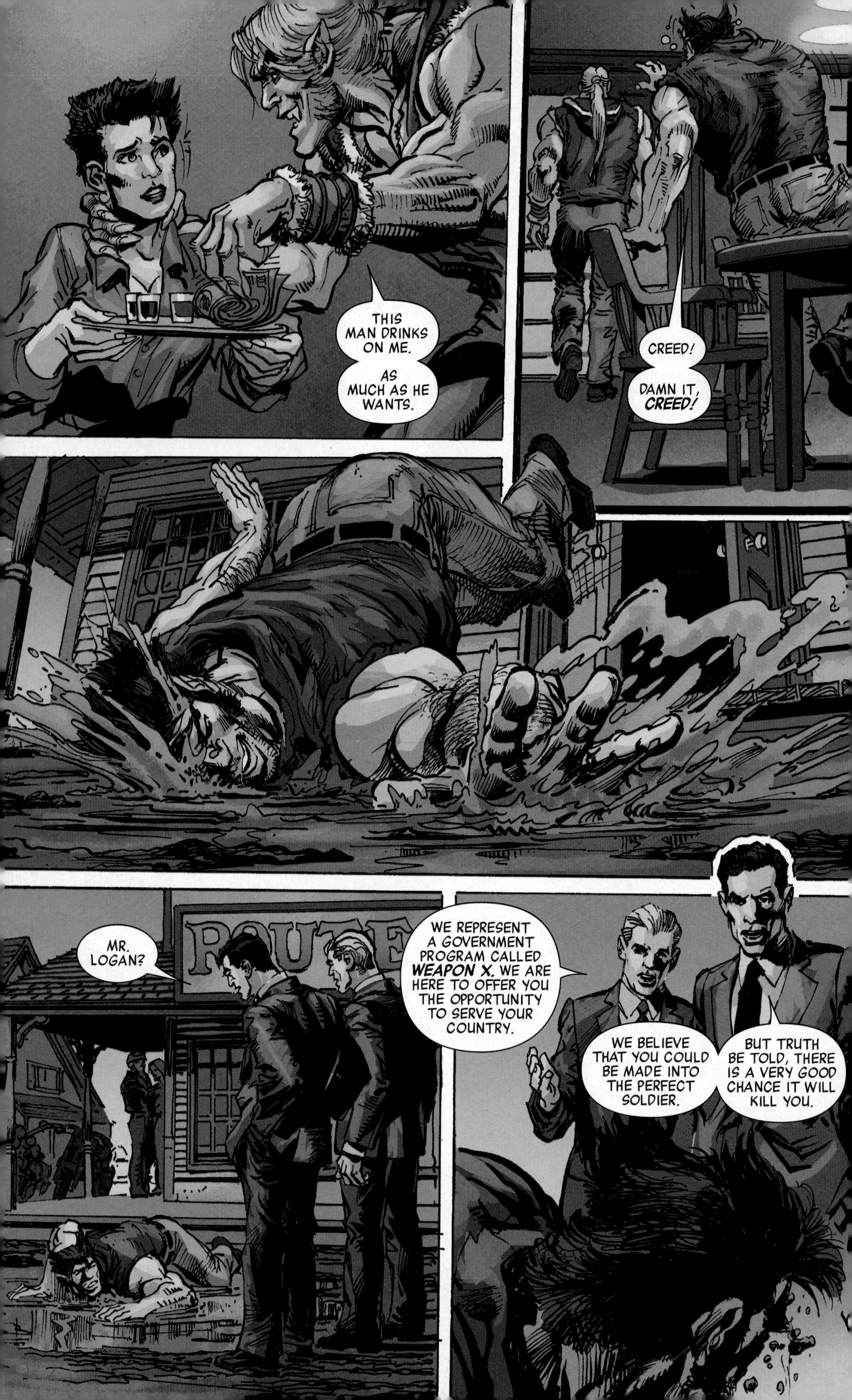
THIS MAN DRINKS ON ME.
AS MUCH AS HE WANTS.
CREED!
DAMN IT, ***CREED!***
MR. LOGAN?
ROUTE
WE REPRESENT A GOVERNMENT PROGRAM CALLED ***WEAPON X.*** WE ARE HERE TO OFFER YOU THE OPPORTUNITY TO SERVE YOUR COUNTRY.
WE BELIEVE THAT YOU COULD BE MADE INTO THE PERFECT SOLDIER.
BUT TRUTH BE TOLD, THERE IS A VERY GOOD CHANCE IT WILL KILL YOU.

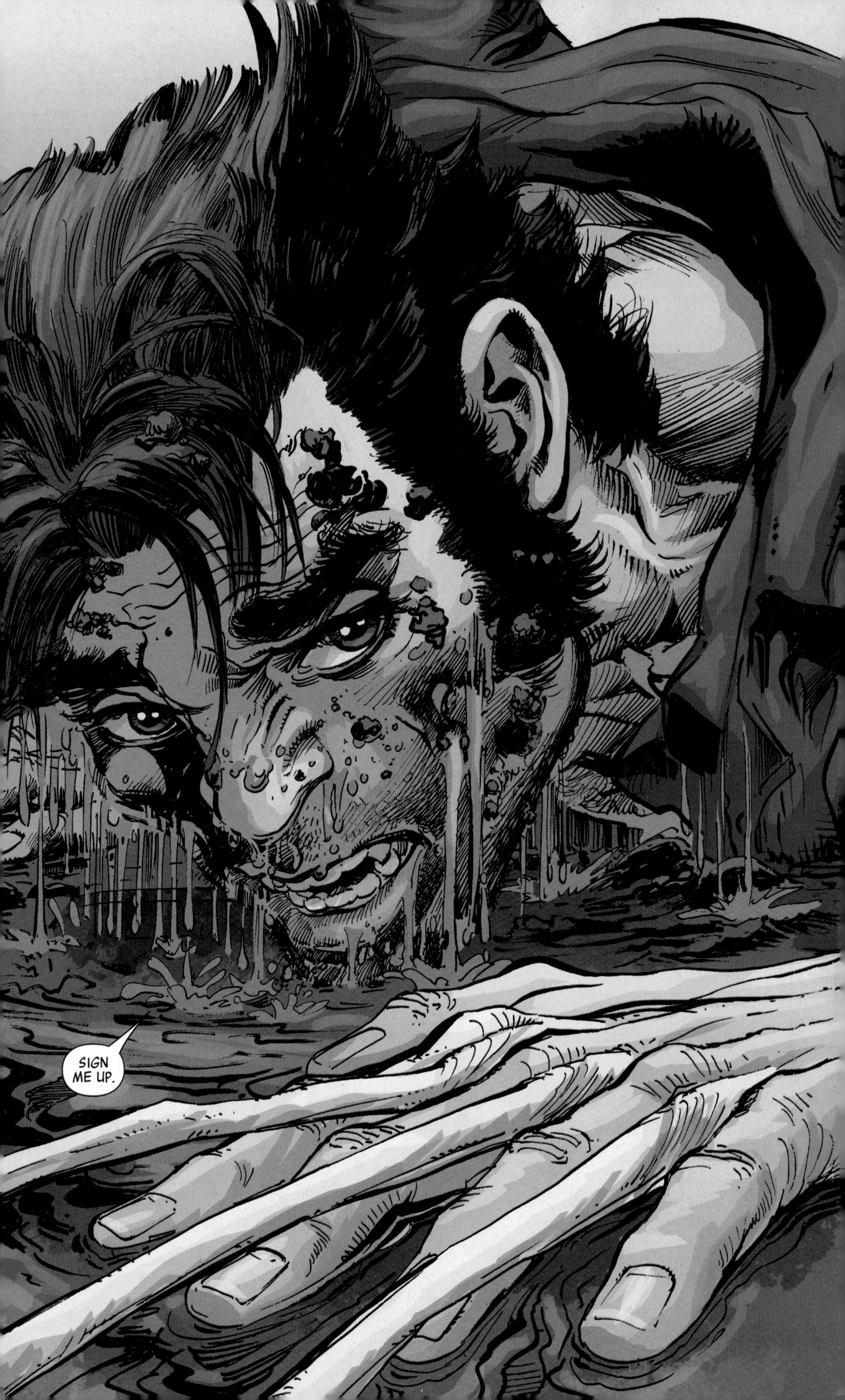
SIGN ME UP.

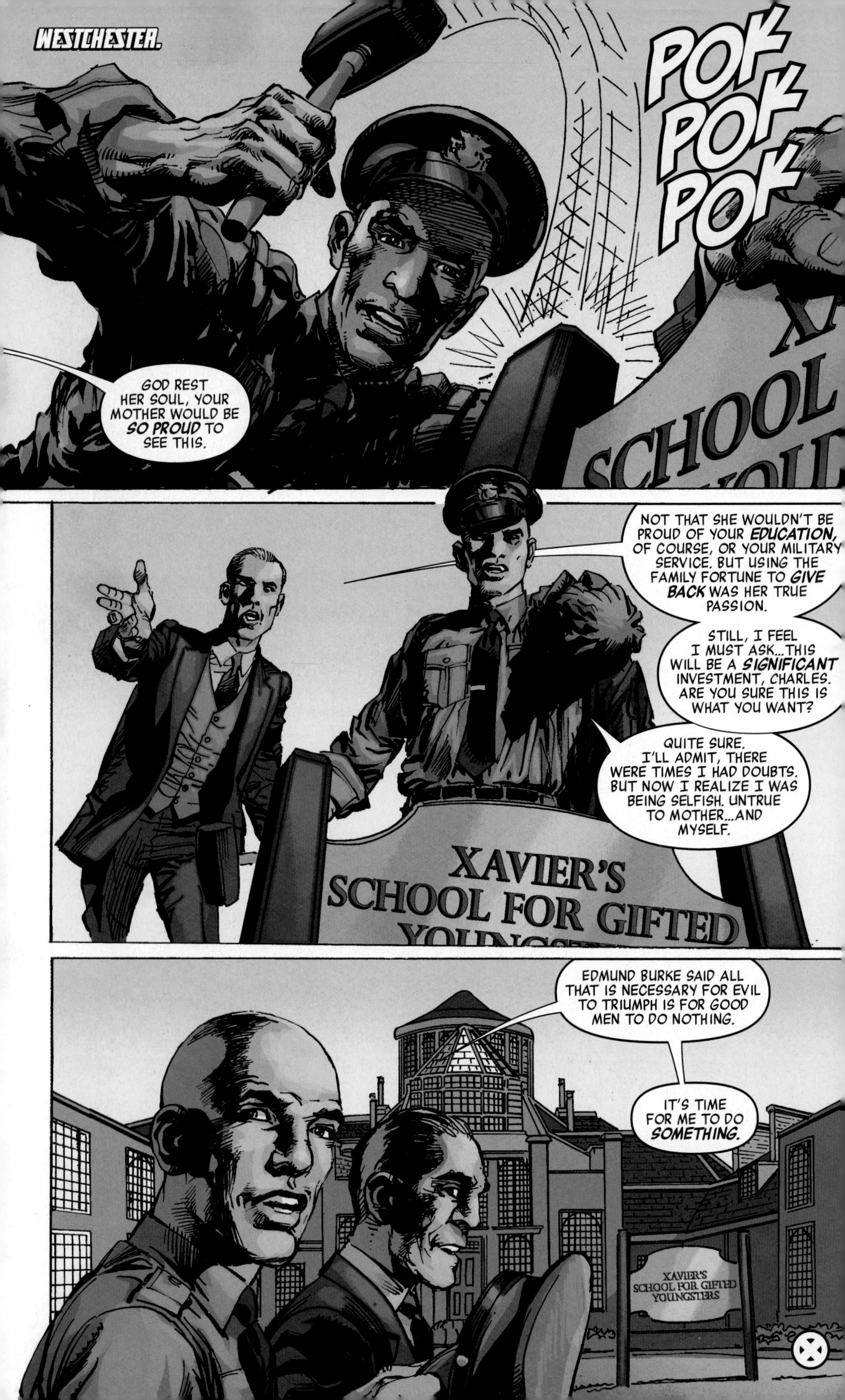
WESTCHESTER.
POK POK POK
GOD REST HER SOUL, YOUR MOTHER WOULD BE SO PROUD TO SEE THIS.
NOT THAT SHE WOULDN'T BE PROUD OF YOUR EDUCATION, OF COURSE, OR YOUR MILITARY SERVICE. BUT USING THE FAMILY FORTUNE TO GIVE BACK WAS HER TRUE PASSION.
STILL, I FEEL I MUST ASK...THIS WILL BE A SIGNIFICANT INVESTMENT, CHARLES. ARE YOU SURE THIS IS WHAT YOU WANT?
QUITE SURE. I'LL ADMIT, THERE WERE TIMES I HAD DOUBTS. BUT NOW I REALIZE I WAS BEING SELFISH. UNTRUE TO MOTHER...AND MYSELF.
XAVIER'S SCHOOL FOR GIFTED
EDMUND BURKE SAID ALL THAT IS NECESSARY FOR EVIL TO TRIUMPH IS FOR GOOD MEN TO DO NOTHING.
IT'S TIME FOR ME TO DO SOMETHING.
XAVIER'S SCHOOL FOR GIFTED YOUNGSTERS

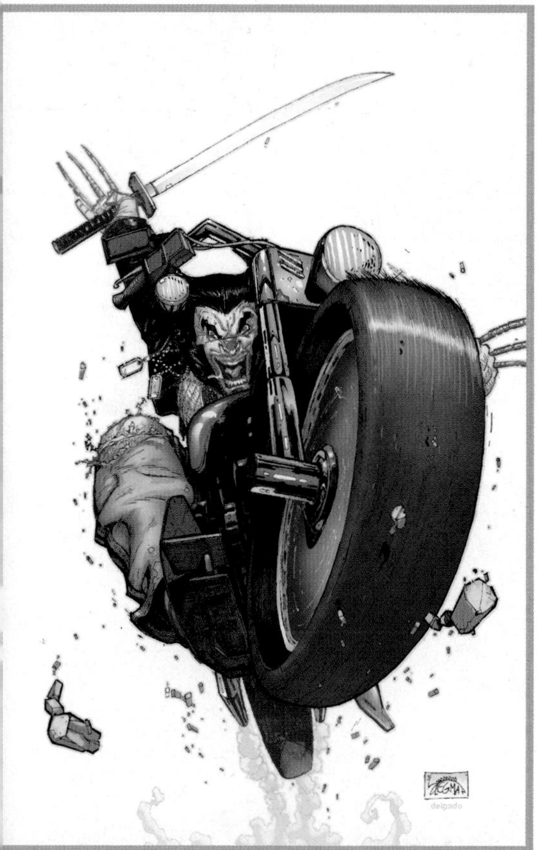

#1 VARIANT
BY RYAN STEGMAN & EDGAR DELGADO

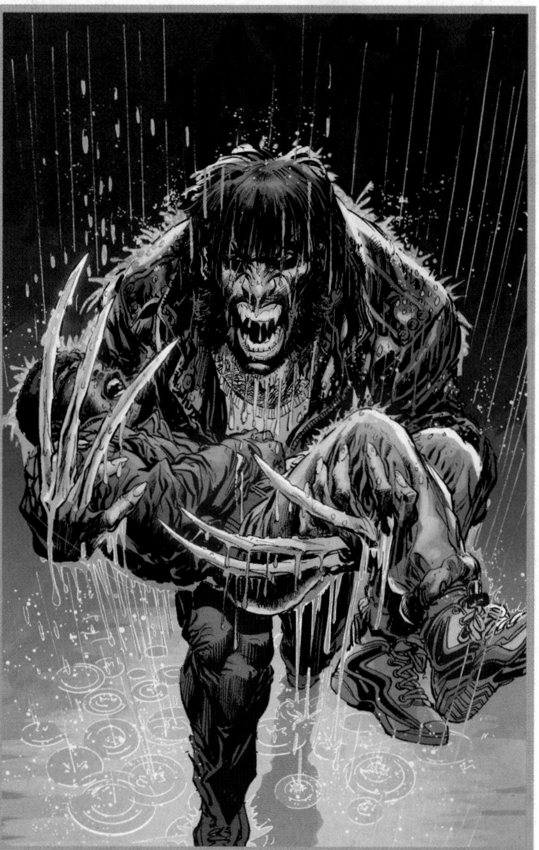

#1 VARIANT
BY NEAL ADAMS & MATTHEW WILSON

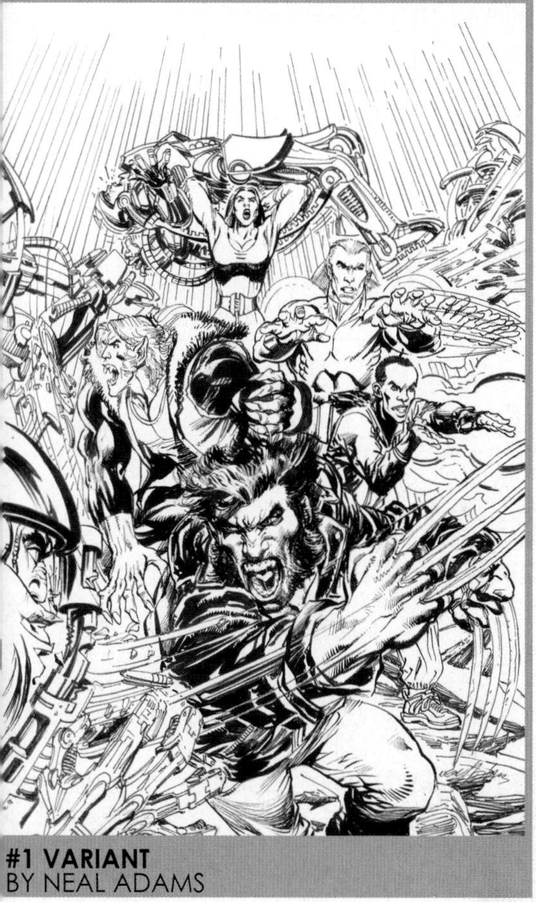

#1 VARIANT
BY NEAL ADAMS

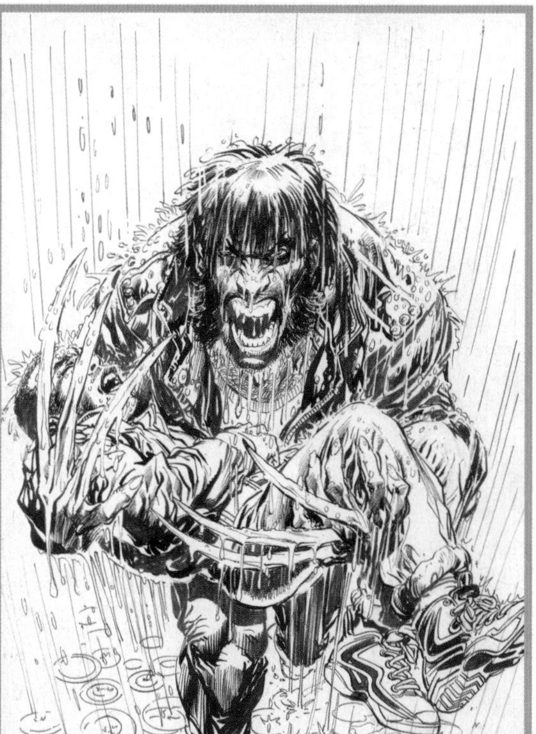

#1 2ND PRINTING VARIANT
BY NEAL ADAMS

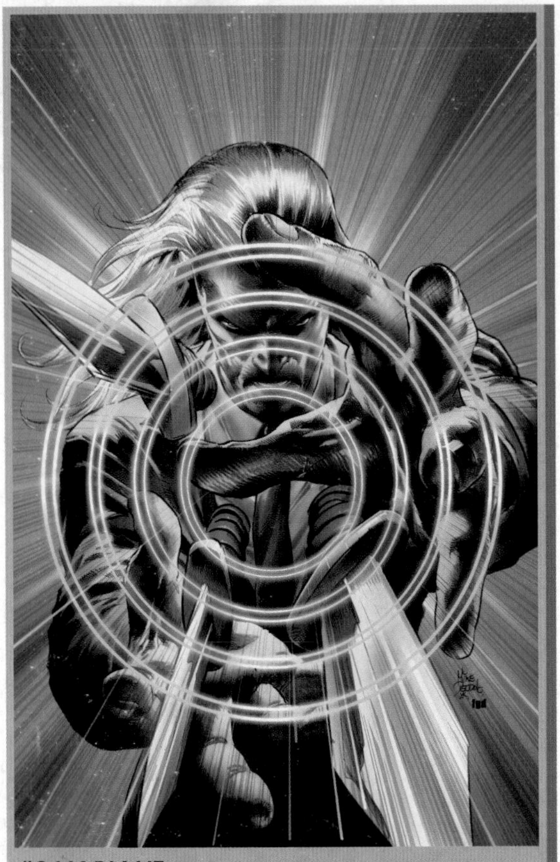

#2 VARIANT
BY MIKE DEODATO & FRANK D'ARMATA

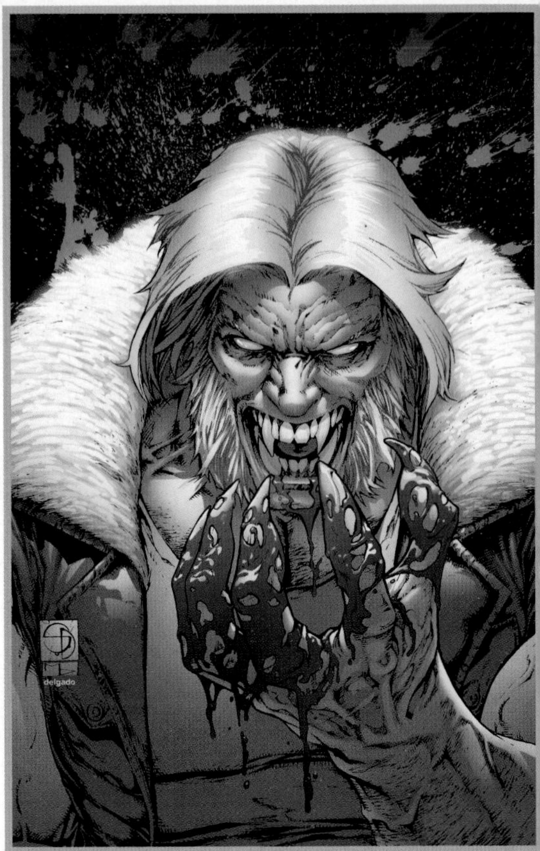
delgado

#3 VARIANT
BY SHANE DAVIS & EDGAR DELGADO

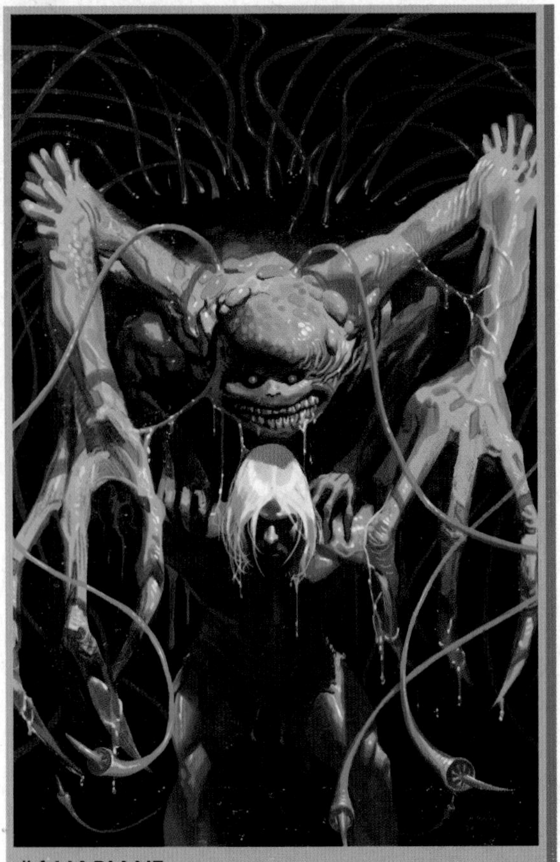

#4 VARIANT
BY DANIEL ACUÑA

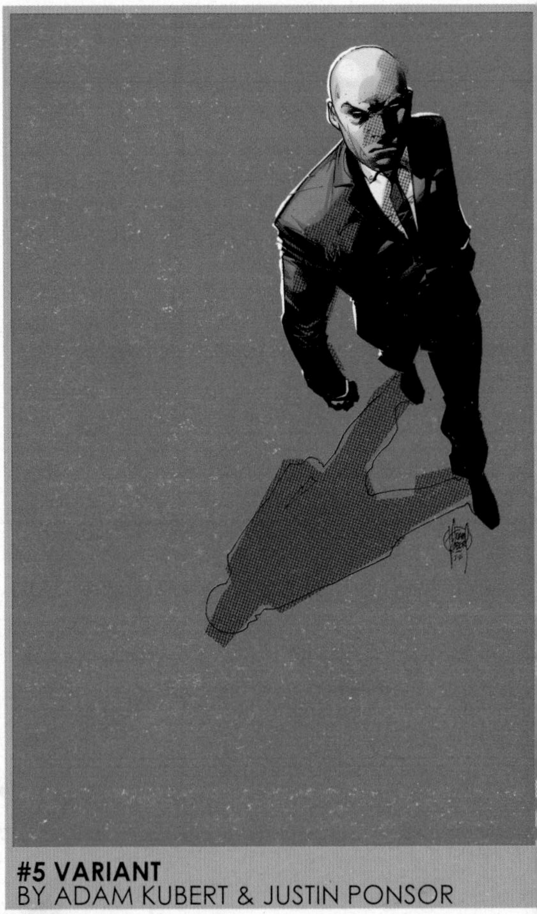

#5 VARIANT
BY ADAM KUBERT & JUSTIN PONSOR